MUSICAL COMEDY

in America

MUSICAL COMEDY

in America

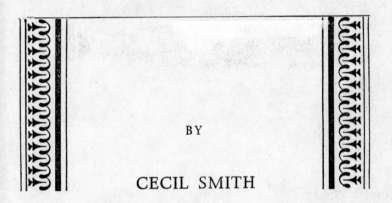

BY

CECIL SMITH

New York

THEATRE ARTS BOOKS: *Robert M. MacGregor*

Copyright 1950 *by* CECIL SMITH

Manufactured in the United States of America
by THE COLONIAL PRESS INC., CLINTON, MASS.
Design and typography
by Jos. Trautwein

TO my mother, affectionately

Author's Foreword

THE PURPOSE OF this book—the first to recount the history of the popular musical stage on Broadway and its intersecting streets—is to tell what the various entertainments were like, how they looked and sounded, who was in them, and why they made people laugh or cry. The values employed in the book are changeable and inconsistent. Sometimes an affable smile is bestowed upon a musical comedy, burlesque, or revue that was really very bad. Sometimes a harsh verdict is brought in against an entertainment that received widespread approval and praise. I can only plead that the book itself, in the writing of it, refused to come out any other way.

If the descriptions and assessments of the pieces and people it deals with are offhand rather than scholastic, or opinionated rather than measured and impersonal, this is because the medium itself does not suggest *Wissenschaft* and the devices of the doctor's dissertation. I have sought to treat the works on their own level and in their own terms, which are ordinarily very friendly and gay. A mere rambling narrative, however, would have left matters scattered and confused. I have endeavored to show the position of individual works and of the categories to which they belong within the historical continuity that led to musical comedy as we know it today. My personal critical judgments are tangential to this main enterprise, and may as well remain inexplicable to those whose minds and tastes are different from mine.

Many people with special reasons to remember them will undoubtedly lament my failure to mention certain specific pieces and people anywhere in the course of the book. I do not think any of the missing items, ancient or modern, were omitted unintentionally, though a multitude of different reasons led to their exclusion.

For all important purposes, the history of musical comedy in America starts with *The Black Crook*, as everyone has always said it did. In order not to begin the story *in vacuo*, I have sketched in a brief memento of some of the theatrical enterprises that preceded it. But this is no more than a prologue, and the main tale, as far as it can yet be told, stretches from *The Black Crook* at one end to *South Pacific* and other contemporary musical comedies at the other. Five years hence I hope it will be necessary to add another chapter.

I did not prepare this book all by myself. Many of its materials result from the successive researches of Raymond Ericson, James Hinton, Jr., Arnold Rood, and George Yacker, all of whom manifested a degree of accuracy and discrimination that is uncommon in the human race, let alone research assistants. Paul Myers, of the Theatre Collection of the New York Public Library, was at all times a paragon of helpfulness. Leslie H. Bradshaw, who knows more about the subject at first hand than most people, fixed an unflagging eye upon the manuscript, and pointed out some errors I was delighted to withdraw from public exhibition. Hermine Rich Isaacs, who was my colleague on the *Theatre Arts* magazine we both loved, read and improved the copy with tender inflexibility. Robert M. MacGregor, the publisher of the book, preserved an exemplary balance of patience and firmness during the irritating periods when I did other things instead of working on the manuscript, and supplied nothing but constructive suggestions from start to finish.

C. S.

Middlefield, Massachusetts
September, 1950

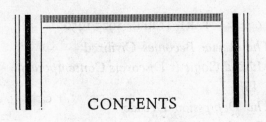

CONTENTS

PHOTOGRAPHS

Photograph numbers 1, 2, 3, 4, 5, 7, 8, 9, 10, 11, 12, 14, 16, 17, 20, 21, 23, 24, 25, 27, 31 and 33 courtesy Theatre Collection, N. Y. Public Library, 15, 18, 22 courtesy Museum of the City of New York, 26, 29, 32, 37, 38, 39, 40, 41, 45, 49, 51, 53, 54, 55, 56, 59, 60 (bottom), 62 and 63 courtesy Vandamm, 42, 44, 52, 60 (top), 61 courtesy Lucas-Moore, 48, 50 and 58 courtesy Fred Fehl, 13 and 36 courtesy Culver, 6 courtesy Harvard Theatre Collection, 19 courtesy White-Schomberg Collection, 30 courtesy Arsene Studio, 28 courtesy De Mirjian, 35 courtesy Richard Tucker, 47 courtesy Karger-Pix, 64 courtesy John Swope, 43 courtesy Ben Pinchot and 57 courtesy Eileen Darby-Graphic House.

PART ONE

1864-1907

Before The Black Crook

THE POPULAR musical stage in the United States reached major dimensions for the first time on the evening of September 12, 1866, when the curtain of Niblo's Garden, on the corner of Broadway and Prince Street in New York, rose on the opening performance of *The Black Crook*. Not that *The Black Crook* was, as has frequently been claimed, the "first musical comedy"; a far cry from George and Ira Gershwin or Richard Rodgers and Lorenz Hart, it was a splashy combination of French Romantic ballet and German Romantic melodrama, decidedly more retrospective than forward-looking in its style and materials. But on the evening of its première a genuinely metropolitan audience attended and applauded a costly musical spectacle produced at home, presented in the English language, and designed to appeal to sophisticated tastes. *The Black Crook*

3

was the first major triumph of Broadway over the monopoly of Europe on the one hand, and the Bowery on the other. It attracted the carriage-trade audience that customarily supported Italian opera, French opéra-bouffe, and the serious spoken drama. Yet it also lured from their usual haunts the devotees of fleshly diversion who had previously sought their theatrical pleasures in the lower-caste theatres of the Bowery.

Before the advent of *The Black Crook*, popular musical entertainment was varied and copious in the New York theatres, but the modest scale on which it was conceived precluded the possibility that any attraction would attain the "hit" status of *The Black Crook*, which rolled up a total of 474 performances in its initial engagement at Niblo's Garden. Extravaganza, pantomime, variety, and the minstrel show (in descending order of pretentiousness and production cost) were the ruling types of entertainment. Each of these—the minstrel show perhaps least—ultimately contributed its share to the developing form we now call musical comedy, and each provided anticipations of materials and devices still to be found in such mid-twentieth-century pieces as *Oklahoma!* and *South Pacific*.

The minstrel show, the homeliest form of mid-nineteenth-century musical diversion, is often assumed to be more or less ageless. It was not until 1841, in point of fact, that New York was offered for the first time an entertainment cast in what later came to be considered the classic form of minstrelsy. From this time onward, the minstrel show enjoyed a life-span of about twenty-five years before fading from the New York scene, outmoded by such white-face variety shows as those presented by Tony Pastor in his Music Hall after 1864, and by the elaborate productions that followed on the heels of *The Black Crook*. On the road, minstrelsy retained its audience until well into the twentieth century, particularly in towns too small to merit regular visits from more pretentious troupes, though even New York continued to receive occasional visits from such groups as Lew Dockstader's Minstrels. Only the celluloid product of Hollywood was finally powerful enough to rout the minstrel show from its last naïve strongholds.

The bigger companies, such as Bryant's Minstrels and the San Francisco Minstrels, provided their customers with a generous assortment of amusements. A classic, if perhaps unusually lavish, bill of Bryant's Minstrels in 1857—the high noon of minstrelsy in New York—divided the performance into three clearly defined parts. The first part employed the characteristic minstrel lineup, with its interlocutor and end men, its tissue of gags and topical quips. In the second portion, described as "terpsichorean divertissement," the members of the company offered an "Ethiopian Fling, à la Polka"; a "Conga Cola Dance"; a cinquetemps; and a local-color production number, "Essence of Old Virginny, Unequalled Plantation Dance." Vocal solos and duets, and, at one point, a "burlesque violin duet" by the Mullenhowen brothers (of which, unhappily, no description survives) were interlarded among the "terpsichorean" items.

The final section (or act, as we should call it now) was called "Plantation Holiday Sports." Starting placidly with a banjo song and a "Southern Scene," the entertainment proceeded in a crescendo of excitement through a comic skit called "Three Hunters, The Challenge Dance," a spectacle, "On the Levee" (glorified beyond the bounds of mere local color by the introduction of a trained elephant), and a "Burlesque Circus," to a final "Terrific Horse Combat," designed to leave the audience breathless at the final curtain. That showmanship took precedence over geographic and ethnologic literalism is indicated not only by the presence of the elephant on the levee but also by the fact that popular dances of the time—quadrilles, galops, and jigs—shared equally with Negro dances in the "Southern Scene."

Though variety—which we now call vaudeville—ultimately sounded the doom of minstrelsy, it was still under a cloud in 1857 when Bryant's Minstrels appealed to the family audience with the items detailed above. At that time, variety bills were almost always presented in saloons to which no reputable gentleman could take a lady—or even, if he was really careful, himself. The irresistible allurement of these resorts, which dotted the Bowery and the neighboring streets, was not the mediocre assortment of song-and-dance acts the managements saw fit to offer. It was, instead, the young, pretty, and open-minded "waiter-girls," available in an inexhaustible supply, and advertised in aphrodisiac fashion in the daily papers. Now and again the police descended upon the variety saloons, and the waiter-girls were temporarily withdrawn from circulation. These reforms never lasted long, however; if his saloon was closed by the law, a manager usually found it a simple matter to reopen in a nearby location.

During the heyday of the waiter-girls, a few managers tried, with varying degrees of success, to present variety shows bereft of this blandishment. The shrewdest of these operators was Tony Pastor, whose unwillingness to engage in the off-color aspect of the business was counterbalanced by an unusual gift for picking talent. He won an increasingly loyal patronage from those who approved his love of decency, and in 1864 opened his handsome new Music Hall, which remained for many years a popular rendezvous of the best family trade. The Music Hall soon became a celebrated showcase for promising talent. In the 1870s and 1880s, many graduates of Tony Pastor's—among whom the most famous was Lillian Russell—were numbered among the leading performers of the musical stage.

Against the counterclaims of variety and minstrelsy, of P. T. Barnum's circuses and Swedish prima donnas, of ballet and acrobatics, and of Italian grand opera and French opéra-bouffe, the art of pantomime—with characters dating back to Italian *commedia dell' arte* of the sixteenth century—maintained a steady following in the United States through the first three-quarters of the nineteenth century. In the pre-*Black Crook* period no pantomime ever occupied an entire evening by itself; it normally shared a bill with two short, non-musical pieces, either melodramas or farces. Only toward the end of its history, in the late 1860s and the 1870s, did pantomime expand into a full-length entertainment, encouraged by the example already set by the extravaganzas and burlesques of the time.

The basic procedure of every pantomime was essentially the same. The central participants were introduced at the outset, and very soon afterward—frequently at the instigation of a fairy's wand—were "transformed" into stock *commedia dell' arte* characters (Harlequin, Columbine, Clown, Pantaloon, Dandy), wearing the costumes and masks appropriate to their traditional functions. These conventionalized figures did not, however, constitute the entire cast of the play. Additional actors took part, as the plot might require, wearing realistic costumes and disdaining to employ the stylized manners of the pantomime performers. The representatives of the harlequinade acted entirely in dumb show, making their meaning clear by a simple and familiar language of gesture. The others were allowed to speak. Even the pantomime characters frequently regained their voices in order to sing.

The plots of the pantomimes were ordinarily drawn from Mother Goose rhymes and other widely familiar sources, or else they were evocations of the ever-popular and seemingly inexhaustible doings of the fairy world. Whatever the subject matter of their plots, the pantomimes were seldom very faithful to it, since the pieces were intended to serve primarily as vehicles for the exploitation of any special talents the players might be lucky enough to have—for comedy, song, character impersonation, or dance.

The more expensive pantomime productions also sought to impress their audiences by spectacular scenic effects, "tricks," and "deceptions," accomplished by means of the elaborate machinery that inspired awe in mid-century audiences. As early as 1847, for example, a "pantomimic fairy play," *The Golden Ax* (produced at the Boston Museum), rejoiced in a final climactic scene described as "Stars and Stripes, American Colors, *warranted not to run*, Bunker Hill and Buena Vista! Lots of Patriotism."

Though pantomime was as much a run-of-the-mill feature of the theatrical scene of the 1840s and 1850s as comic opera became in the 1880s and 1890s, it produced only one great practitioner in this country—George L. Fox. The career of Fox, which epitomizes the rise, triumph, and rapid decline of this specialized art, may be reserved for its proper place later on, in connection with *Humpty Dumpty*, the first musical attraction to surpass the run record of *The Black Crook*.

The term "extravaganza," applied in France (where the type originated) to the balletic evocations of fairyland also known as "*féeries*," was from the beginning much more loosely applied in this country. The word was first appropriated here by the Ronzani troupe, a ballet company of French and Italian performers who arrived in New York in 1857, and included in their first bill an "extravaganza," *Novelty, with the Laying of the Atlantic Cable.* The Ronzanis themselves made very little stir, and soon went back to Europe. But the term "extravaganza," as a description of an elaborate and frequently topical spectacle, became a long-lived member of American stage vocabulary, finally disappearing in the 1920s, after the revue, the elaborately staged musical comedy, and the motion pictures had divided its province among them.

Long before the arrival of the Ronzanis, mixed bills which might well have been called extravaganzas were already the stock-in-trade of the immensely popular Ravel Family. Specialists in French ballet, pantomime, and acrobatics, the Ravels catered to as many tastes as possible, and being top-level performers retained their hold over the New York public for more than twenty years, from the mid-1840s to the late 1860s. Toe-dancing, still a fairly new feature of ballet (it was introduced in France in the 1830s), appealed to those members of the Ravels' audience who prided themselves on their cultivation, while aerial and gymnastic acts satisfied those with heartier predilections.

The Ravels' bill on February 17, 1847—to take a random specimen—opened with a short farce without music, called *Thumping Legacy*. (The use of a short curtain-raiser was a habit that died slowly, persisting until after 1870.) This was followed by "the first act of the beautiful ballet of *La Sylphide*," featuring Mme. Léon Jomelli, the Ravels' perennial *prima ballerina*. The Sylphide and her companions were reasonably faithful to the layout of the ballet as Taglioni originally danced it; for their version, like Taglioni's, contained a *grand pas de deux*, a Scotch quickstep, a Grand Tableau, and "The Flight of the Sylphide." At the close of the ballet, several of the Ravels performed the tightrope act which was the troupe's most renowned accomplishment. After a comic pantomime entitled "The Milliners, or The Hungarian Rendez-vous" (if only the scenario still existed for curious eyes a century later!), Young Marchetti demon-

strated "feats of agility," and Mme. Jomelli threw herself
into "La Cachuca." The performance ended with a tableau
vivant, "Italian Brigands, or The Midnight Assault."

Although the musical bills of this time made frequent
appeals to both patriotism and provincialism, none had
attempted to deal with an indigenous American story until
John Brougham offered his *Pocahontas* in New York in
1855. Filling only half an evening, *Pocahontas*, which its
author (who played the role of John Smith) described as
a burlesque, endeavored to tell a historic American story
without falling back upon the devices of either pantomime
or ballet. It was a sober-sided imitation, in rather bleak
terms, of the contemporaneous French extravaganzas, without any of their spectacular features. *Pocahontas* created no
sensation in New York, nor did Brougham's sequel a year
later, *Hiawatha, or Ardent Spirits and Laughing Waters.*
Audiences on the road took more kindly to *Pocahontas*, and
Brougham was able to tour in it for a decade or so, meanwhile writing more plays, which had no discernible influence
on the development of the American theatre.

The most ambitious extravaganza before *The Black Crook*
was Thomas de Walden's *The Balloon Wedding*, given its
première in New York on January 15, 1866, in a refitted
minstrel hall known as Wood's Theatre. (Niblo's Garden,
soon to house *The Black Crook*, was the only theatre at
this time adequately equipped to take care of pretentious
musical productions.) Almost the sole source of pleasure
in *The Balloon Wedding* was the marvelous exhibition of
the Six Hanlon Brothers, a group of acrobats whose skill
dimmed the brilliance of the Ravels' tightrope exploits, as
they performed "summersets in the air from the shoulders
of one of the brothers to the shoulders of another, at eight
or ten feet away." The efforts of Frank Chanfrau, a popular

comedian who had appeared with the Ronzanis in 1857, to amuse the audience with his impersonation of an eccentric Frenchman were futile, for De Walden's script, according to *The Spirit of the Times*, was "so bad that not even the imbecile stock companies with which Mr. George Wood, from two theatres, nightly insults the intelligence of New York, could make it any worse."

Lacking an accomplished corps de ballet, *The Balloon Wedding* sought to replace beauty and charm with vacuous novelty. It provided, *The Spirit of the Times* reported, "any quantity of young ladies in the most eccentric ballet that was ever seen or *heard*, for this ballet *sing* as well as *dance*, and are perpetually saying or singing 'tra, la, la, la' on the slightest provocation. When anybody comes on the stage, they 'tra-la-la-la' him on—when he makes his exit, they 'tra-la-la-la' him off—they witness their lovers locked up, and remark 'tra-la-la-la'—they themselves are taken in arrest by blue-coated Policemen, and instead of entering a protest in the usual emphatic English, they merely remove their handkerchiefs from their mouths, and mention 'tra-la-la-la' —one faints away and falls down in to it—and others whisper 'tra-la-la-la' and she 'comes to'—and somebody slaps somebody's face to the pleasant chorus of 'tra,' etc.— somebody steps on somebody's toes, and the threats of vengeance are drowned in the howls of 'tra,' etc."

At the end of its first week, *The Balloon Wedding* was enriched by a scene showing a "mysterious fairy illuminated fountain," which the critic of the same periodical thought "by all odds the best lively stage effect I have seen." But this spectacular addition did not save the show, and the girls tra-la'd their way into oblivion at the end of a fortnight. We may write this costly failure off as a symptom of the growing pains of the American musical stage, and as a .

preamble to the discovery of the species later known as the chorus girl. Its demise was not mourned; for only eight months later *The Black Crook* came along to inaugurate a new era.

II

The Black Crook

THE MEMBERS of the audience at the première of *The Black Crook* arrived at Niblo's Garden in time for a 7:45 curtain. They remained enthralled until 1:15, when the final curtain came down after the stupendous transformation scene that was the crown of the production. In these five and a half historic hours, they saw the most expert and the best routined dancing, by a ballet of more than a hundred girls, yet offered on this side of the Atlantic. They marveled at stage spectacles more elaborate and magnificent than any American producer had ever before devised. And the baldheads and Fifth Avenue fops in the front rows saw legs— beautiful legs, over a hundred pairs of them. To be sure, earlier entertainments—particularly the French ballets, with their brief costumes—had confirmed the suspicion that the female leg existed. But there had never been anything quite as revelatory as *The Black Crook*. In addition to five and a half hours of white tarlatan, the new piece threw in for good measure in the second act a *pas de démons*, in which four girls—given the pretext of a diabolical incantation—advanced to the front of the stage, wearing tights, without a vestige of anything remotely resembling a skirt.

This unprecedented blend of art and bodily allurement, this first of the great Broadway hits, came into being through one of the most curious accidents of American stage history. In the summer of 1866, Henry C. Jarrett (an aspiring young theatre manager) and Harry Palmer (a Wall Street broker who was willing to be Jarrett's backer) brought over a French ballet troupe, with the intention of presenting a Parisian success, the Romantic ballet *La Biche aux Bois*, in the Academy of Music. Before their production was ready to open, the Academy of Music burned down. Jarrett and Palmer were left with an expensive ballet company on their hands, and no theatre in which to present it.

Meanwhile, William Wheatley, the manager-producer of Niblo's Garden, the most fashionable New York home of large and spectacular theatrical attractions, had signed a contract with Charles M. Barras, an unknown author, for the production of his melodrama *The Black Crook*. In their extremity, Jarrett and Palmer proposed to Wheatley that they combine forces by adding the French ballet as an adornment to *The Black Crook*, whose original script did not envisage the use of music or dancers. Already harassed by doubts as to the merits of a melodrama he had purchased hastily, Wheatley readily agreed to the idea. Barras objected, saying that the French dancers would "ruin his beautiful play." But since he was on the verge of starvation, he was willing to be silenced by a down payment of $1,500 and a royalty contract. His silence proved to be golden; in subsequent years his income from royalties on *The Black Crook* enabled him to buy an elaborate country home near Cos Cob, Connecticut, where he lived most comfortably until the day he walked onto a New Haven Railroad trestle as a train approached from the opposite direction.

As soon as Barras had accepted his $1,500, Wheatley went to work. At a reported cost of $25,400—a staggering figure in 1866—he completely made over the stage of Niblo's Garden. Every board moved in grooves, and could be taken up, pushed down, or slid away. Any part of the stage, in other words, could be removed altogether. Trap doors could be introduced anywhere. The cellar below the stage was made so deep that entire scenes could be sunk out of sight by the use of relatively simple machinery.

Properties, scenery, costumes, and machinery Wheatley purchased in London, for a total of $3,000. (The bill for transporting the entire shipment, weighing 110 tons, across the ocean, was $500!) The newspapers estimated the aggregate production cost at sums ranging from $35,000 to $55,000. Inasmuch as this was the P. T. Barnum era of grandiose overstatement, the $35,000 estimate is certainly closer to the fact, since even this was a far larger amount than had been spent on any previous theatrical production.

After the opening of *The Black Crook*, the newspaper reviewers were rhapsodic over its novel enchantments, though some ventured to express lukewarm views about Barras' play. Outside the press, opinions were sharply divergent. Many were overcome by the beauty of the spectacle; but those of a moralistic turn of mind were offended by its frank enticements. It is difficult to say which group performed a greater service to the box office.

One clergyman, suspecting that *The Black Crook* constituted a threat to the virtue of his congregation, went to see it for himself, and reported back in the following fashion (quoted in a letter from Charles Burnham to the New York *Sun*, September 23, 1932):

". . . the immodest dress of the girls; the short skirts, undergarments of thin material allowing the form of the figure to be discernible; the flesh-colored tights, imitating nature so well that the illusion is complete; with the exceedingly short drawers, almost tight-fitting, extending very little below the hips; arms and neck apparently bare, and bodice so cut as to show off every inch and outline of the body above the waist. The attitudes were exceedingly indelicate—*ladies* dancing so as to make their undergarments spring up, exposing the figure beneath from the waist to the toe, except for such coverings as we have described."

This description, if it was widely circulated, must have been a source of incalculable satisfaction to Wheatley and his partners. More helpful still was the vigorous opposition of the New York *Tribune*. That newspaper had recently engaged in an altercation with P. T. Barnum, who not only withdrew all his advertising from the *Tribune* but persuaded other managers, Wheatley among them, to follow his example. Perhaps in retribution, the *Tribune* sometimes printed harsh attacks upon the unadvertised plays. When the paper singled out *The Black Crook* for special disapproval, the production became a *cause célèbre*, and nobody could hold his own in conversation unless he had seen it.

Barras' play, so quickly lost in the shuffle of two hundred female legs, had been written in Cincinnati in 1857. The author at that time was hot with the inspiration enkindled by a performance of Weber's *Der Freischütz*, given by a touring English opera company. Seeking to supply the company with the libretto for a new opera, he appropriated from *Der Freischütz* as much as he possibly could, and incorporated it into the text called *The Black Crook*. The opera company did not buy it. Nine years later, however, Wheatley did, though his lack of judgment staggers the imagination.

In justice to Barras, it must be admitted that *Der Freischütz* was by no means the only source of his script. His borrowing was more extensive than this. Goethe's *Faust* prefigured the basic situation of the plot, and a literary detective would have no trouble in spotting *Undine*, *The Naiad Queen*, *The Swiss Cottage*, and other pieces familiar to readers, playgoers, and balletomanes of the period.

The *Freischütz* element was immediately apparent in the preliminary situation of the plot. Hertzog, the Black Crook, had made a compact with the Devil, agreeing to win over to the Devil's cause one human soul for each year of life vouchsafed to him. The account must be settled annually, just before midnight on New Year's Eve. Rudolph, the hero of the story, was a painter; Amina, the heroine, a rural beauty. A certain Count Wolfenstein used his feudal authority to take Amina capitive and lock Rudolph in a dungeon. Planning to make Rudolph his victim for the year, Hertzog—by virtue of magical powers given him by the Devil—freed Rudolph from prison and persuaded him to go in search of the treasure said to be in a cave of gold in the forest. On the way, Rudolph saved the life of a dove, who was pursued by a serpent. The dove turned out to be the fairy queen Stalacta, who promptly exposed Hertzog's trickery. Count Wolfenstein was appropriately killed; Rudolph married Amina; and the Black Crook, like Kaspar in *Der Freischütz*, was carried off to hell by the Devil.

However questionable its originality and dramaturgical skill, the book of *The Black Crook* allowed ample room for spectacle and balletic display. Nearly everyone felt that the first act contained too much alleged drama and too little else. With the "Grand Ballet of the Gems" at the opening of the second act, however, the excitement began. Later in the act, "hurricanes of gauze" blew through the Harz Mountains, and "cascading girls poured down the wild glens." At the end of the act, in an eerie locale obviously suggested by the Wolf's Glen in *Der Freischütz*, an elaborate ritual of incantation came to a climax in the startling *pas de démons*.

Most breathtaking of all was the transformation scene at the close of the play. "One by one, curtains of mist ascend and drift away," wrote a nameless reporter. "Silver couches, on which the fairies loll in negligent grace, ascend and descend amid a silver rain. From the clouds droop gilded chariots and the white forms of angels. It is a very beautiful pageant."

As the run of *The Black Crook* progressed, new features were added. Audiences in the summer of 1867 saw a "Baby Ballet," in which more than a hundred children, ranging in height from twenty-five to forty-five inches, executed military evolutions, led by the five-year-old nephew of a member of the Ravel family. In September, a dazzling new ballroom scene was introduced, with a grand carnival and masquerade.

The Black Crook is remembered today for its total effect, rather than for the individual performers who appeared in it. But in 1866, Marie Bonfanti, the fifteen-year-old ballerina who danced the role of Queen Stalacta, and her colleagues of similar age, Rita Sangalli and Betty Rigl, stimulated an adulation comparable to that of theatregoers nearly seventy years later for Colonel Wassily de Basil's three "baby ballerinas" of the Ballet Russe de Monte Carlo—Tamara Toumanova, Irina Baronova, and Tatiana Riabouchinska.

In its first engagement, *The Black Crook* achieved a run of 474 performances in sixteen months, and grossed more than a million dollars. For more than twenty-five years afterward, it was nearly always being presented somewhere—either in New York or on the road (where, as late as 1906, it could still be discovered, no doubt in shrunken form, in so remote a Western outpost as Provo, Utah). In the entire nineteenth century, only *Uncle Tom's Cabin*, *Rip Van Winkle* (neither of which was a musical attraction), and Edward E. Rice's burlesque *Evangeline* equaled or surpassed its widespread and long-continued popularity. *The Black Crook* was revived in New York eight times in the nineteenth century—in 1868, 1871, 1873, 1879, 1881, 1884, 1889, and 1892. Christopher Morley and Cleon Throckmorton brought it back to life in 1929 in Hoboken, New Jersey, with Agnes de Mille as Queen Stalacta.

The successive revivals increasingly replaced the formal French ballets with popular dancing and topical variety entertainment. In the 1892 production, vaudeville dancing completely obliterated the bits of ballet that had remained until then. But a quartet of French music-hall dancers—La Sirène, Serpentine, Eglantine, and Dynamite—created a furore with a so-called quadrille, in which they combined "serpentine" dancing with high kicking. A notable feature of their performance was the split, a contortion that had never before been demonstrated on the polite stage. Once again, the "chappies" and baldheads were delighted, and the moral custodians were displeased. Describing the specialty dancers as "four coarse and ugly French women of mature years," one critic maintained that "their exploits exceeded in shamelessness anything before brought over from the French capital for display in a respectable theatre."

If Wheatley, Jarrett, and Palmer had been able to foresee the flexibility with which *The Black Crook* could be modified to fit changing tastes and fashions, they might have reconsidered their decision to close it early in 1868. But like so many successful producers in later years, they were obsessed by the desire to present a sequel. Accordingly, on January 17, 1868, *The Black Crook* relinquished Niblo's Garden to *The White Fawn*.

Though its stupid book was attributed to James Mortimer, *The White Fawn* was basically an attempt to derive a second *Black Crook* from *La Biche aux Bois*, the Parisian ballet Jarrett and Palmer had expected to give at the Academy of Music in 1866 when they first imported their French ballet troupe. The plot revolved about a princess who was changed into a white fawn; everything was made right at the end in the Realms of the Dragon Fly.

The première was even more of a drain upon the patience of the audience than the opening of *The Black Crook*. It lasted six hours, and even then the final transformation scene, requiring eighty carpenters and twenty gasmen, was too balky to be attempted on the first night. There were the expected ballets and spectacles, the most admired of which was an enchanted-lake scene, featuring Signor Costa's "Firefly Ballet." But in spite of these allurements, and the producers' attempt to make it an even more unqualified apotheosis of the female leg than *The Black Crook*, *The White Fawn* suffered the fate of most sequels and perished, on July 11.

To call *The Black Crook* the first example of the theatrical genus we now call musical comedy is not only incorrect; it fails to suggest any useful assessment of the place of Jarrett and Palmer's extravaganza in the history of the popular musical theatre. It was, to be sure, the first American musical entertainment to achieve the long-run prosperity upon which producers subsequently learned to pin their hopes. But in its first form it contained almost none of the vernacular attributes of book, lyrics, music, and dancing which distinguish musical comedy, as a type, from ballet and spectacular extravaganza. True, it thrust two hundred legs upon the gaze of the beholder. But the unabashed leg is by no means an indispensable feature of musical comedy, since dozens of musical comedies have enjoyed great success without revealing more than an occasional ankle or part of a calf; and, on the other hand, the undraped leg is not, and never has been, the sole property of musical comedy—as witness the can-cans in Offenbach's opéra-bouffes, or the heroines in nautical or military tights in some of the most high-minded comic operas of the 1880s.

Moreover, it is too soon to be talking about musical comedy in 1866. Neither the term nor the concept it represents existed as yet. We first encounter the term, loosely used to describe a piece involving both music and comedy, in connection with the burlesque *Evangeline*, which was produced in 1874. Later on, it was used in offhand fashion in connection with musical farce-comedies, farces with occasional interpolated songs, and comic operas. Not until the middle 1890s did a relatively standardized form begin to emerge, to which the name of musical comedy was given for the sake of distinguishing it from the more traditional and less vernacular productions known as comic opera and operetta.

Even though it discovered a new audience and hinted at a new world of musical entertainment, *The Black Crook* was really the swan song of early nineteenth-century Romanticism. Half German melodrama and half French ballet-extravaganza-*féerie*, both its content and its manner of presentation continued the fashions and traditions of European stagecraft of the 1840s and 1850s. Its subject matter was out of style before it was produced. Its only aspects of modernity and only lessons for productions that followed resided in its expert command of the machinery of illusion and uncommonly successful address to its audience. The failure of

The White Fawn, which employed exactly the formulas of *The Black Crook* with the added advantage of previous experience, was to be expected, for the venerable and archaic materials in which Jarrett and Palmer traded deserved no further currency. Within the next few years Lydia Thompson, arriving from the London music halls, was able to offer a better leg show; the Kiralfy brothers devised even more breathtaking spectacles; and Edward E. Rice, with *Evangeline,* introduced homespun humor and plot elements that made *The Black Crook* and *La Biche aux Bois* seem very remote, very foreign, and very old-fashioned.

III

The Death of Pantomime

HUMPTY DUMPTY, which opened at the Olympic Theatre in New York on March 10, 1868, and ran for 483 performances—nine more than *The Black Crook*—in its initial engagement, signalized both the triumph and the farewell of traditional pantomime in the United States. Pantomime never became a deeply rooted theatrical institution in this country, as it did in England, where it is still in evidence, to the delight of British children during the Christmas holidays. In England an increased use of words soon brought pantomime near to the character of burlesque and extravaganza, the types that superseded it in the United States. After Edward E. Rice's trail-blazing production of *Evangeline* in 1874, American burlesque retained possession of practically all the features of pantomime except the dumb show and the stylized harlequinade. As a consequence, pantomine had no further raison d'être, except as a vehicle for the talents of those who performed in it.

George L. Fox, the producer and star of *Humpty Dumpty*, was the only pantomime performer with enough box-office power to keep the ancient art alive against the fresher and more informal appeal of burlesque. After his retirement, American pantomime died swiftly. In retrospect, indeed, the main history of American pantomime appears to have been contained in the history of Fox's career. One of the most gifted performers in the annals of our stage, Fox was frequently described in his own time as the greatest pantomime clown since Grimaldi. His fame was kept alive after his death by a wooden effigy in front of a drug store in New Haven; the statue might be there still if an ebullient group of Harvard undergraduates, elated by the victory of their crew over Yale's, had not taken it away one evening in 1911.

Born in Boston in 1825, Fox began his professional career as an actor in one of the early *Uncle Tom's Cabin* companies. In 1850, he turned to comedy, calling himself Lafayette Fox at that time, and taking part in various short burlesques, extravaganzas, and pantomimes—among them *The Frisky Cobbler* and *The Golden Ax*, in the latter of which he achieved a signal success in the character role of Farmer Gubbins.

Though he continued to act in various métiers, he soon decided that pantomime was his most promising field. Choosing to adopt the artistic style of the French performers rather than the crude, slapstick methods of the Italian school, Fox modeled his technique upon that of the Ravel family, whose potpourris of pantomime and other attractions were already in vogue in New York as Fox was beginning his pantomimic career.

As must be the case with every great clown, Fox concealed touching traits of human sympathy and understanding beneath his grotesque, painted exterior. The extraordinary control of his facial muscles made the technique of mugging famous; it would be interesting to know how much of the standard practices of today's and yesterday's comics might be traced back in a direct genealogical line to devices originated by Fox. For actually it was his mugging, far more than his command of the traditional gesture language and the roughhouse humor universally used by pantomime clowns, that accounted for his extraordinary popularity. "He was not content to please," one critic wrote, "merely by being knocked down numerous times and jumping over tables and through windows. His muteness and passivity were infinitely more ludicrous than the bustling antics of other clowns, as also was his affectation of ignorant simplicity and credulous innocence."

Fox grew rapidly in reputation and resources. In 1858, he became one of the managers of the Bowery Theatre, where he offered a long list of short pantomimes, in mixed bills with farces and melodramas. In 1862, his run of 150 consecutive performances in *Jack and the Beanstalk* established a New York record for a single performer.

Despite the warnings of friends who felt that he would be unable to compete with the established Ravel Family (who were not only masters of pantomime, but were also able to provide ballet and circus attractions), Fox ventured to move uptown from the Bowery to Broadway in 1866. These prophets of doom were mistaken, however, for after a few less epoch-making preliminary offerings, *Humpty Dumpty* brought Fox the supreme success of his career, outdrawing and outplaying anything the Ravels had ever presented, and shattering all run records before its time.

Humpty Dumpty was conceived as a show for the common people, even for low-brows; it was not intended to serve as a diversion for the baldheads, fops, and aesthetes who sang the praises of *The Black Crook*. Without displaying any legs, it could stand competition with the contemporaneous *White Fawn* and Lydia Thompson's newly arrived company of bleached British blondes, and outdo them in longevity and box-office intake; for it appealed to a homelier, and therefore a larger, audience. For the première of *Humpty Dumpty*, Fox brought uptown a great many Bowery vulgarities he soon sloughed off, as he began to understand the demands of even the low-brow uptown audience for proprieties and niceties that would have been wasted on Bowery patrons.

Humpty Dumpty was weakest in the elements in which *The White Fawn* was strongest. The ballets were feeble; Mlle. Rita Sangalli, a graduate of *The Black Crook*, "tried to be a grand ballet in herself," and did not repeat the impression she had made in the handsomer surroundings of the earlier piece. The spectacular effects in *Humpty Dumpty* and the inevitable final transformation scene, while conceived in broad and generous terms, were on the whole artistically unsatisfactory. When all was said and done, the pantomime was carried by the personality of Fox and by the simple, straightforward appeal of its naïve materials.

The title of *Humpty Dumpty* was as good as meaningless, for the pantomime had no real plot, and bore little discernible relationship to the Mother Goose rhyme. As with every other pantomime, the characters were introduced at the beginning, and marked time until the expected Fairy Queen came along to transform them. Goody Two-Shoes became Columbine; Old One-Two became Pantaloon; Tommy Tucker became Harlequin; Humpty Dumpty became Clown. For the rest of the evening, the dumb show of these pantomime folk was woven into an elaborate variety and spectacle show. A troupe of roller-skaters (the first important stage appearance of skaters) shared the footlights with circus acts, singers who presented songs of the concert-saloon and minstrel-hall variety, and a "Baby Ballet," headed by the five-year-old niece of Gabriel Ravel. (The Ravel Family seemed to have on hand an inexhaustible supply of tiny relatives, ready and willing to appear in the productions of their rivals.) There were spectacle scenes depicting the Valley of Fertility; a subterranean grotto; a market place in Naples ("La Tarantella by full corps"); the Olympic Theatre by night; a skating pond by moonlight ("Polish National Dance"); the Dell of Ferns; and the Retreat of the Silver Sprites. The Neapolitan market-place scene which came at the end of Act I culminated in a "Celebrated Trick Steamboat and Explosion." Great prominence was given in the program to the names of the two scene designers, Minard Lewis and J. A. Johnson; their names appeared after the titles of each scene, much as composers' names are printed opposite the titles of their works in contemporary musical programs. The music of *Humpty Dumpty* remained as negligible an element as it had been in *The Black Crook*, though in this instance a composer—A. Reiff, Jr.—was at least mentioned, though he apparently collected most, if not all, of his score from outside sources.

Subsequent revivals of *Humpty Dumpty* did not change the essential nature of the piece, though they sought to make it bigger and more expensive. The 1871 version was given in three acts instead of the original two, with the middle act devoted to a great array of variety and circus acts. Among the new additions were the "Tyrolean eccentricities" of the Martens Family; Signor Casselli in a balancing feat on wire; the Zig-Zags, grotesque comedians; Young Adonis, aged four and one-half, and Little Venus, aged two and one-half, riding bicycles; a "Cat Duett" by two of the Martens Family, which evoked sympathetic meows from the gallery, and a sensational Hungarian divertissement by the Kiralfy Brothers.

The 1871 revival of *Humpty Dumpty* was preceded by a short-lived sequel, *Hickory Dickory Dock*, mention of which is made only to add one more datum to the gloomy history of sequels. But the setback was a minor one for Fox, who was able to send *Humpty Dumpty* companies on the road without his personal services as Humpty, and to sell the English rights to the "merry Vokes Family."

In the course of a second return engagement at Booth's Theatre, New York, in 1873, Fox began to behave peculiarly. One day he abruptly started to chase his colleagues about the stage; he then leapt from the stage to a stage box and pummelled a decorous lady on the head with a loaf of property bread. As suddenly as he had left it, he returned to the stage, went back into his clown's character, and began mugging for dear life. This time he managed to carry the situation off, but the symptoms rapidly became worse. When he developed a fixation upon the notion of having a statue of himself erected in Union Square, his associates realized that the time had come when he must be taken to an institution. He survived only a few months longer.

Humpty Dumpty's momentum kept it going on the road for a few years, with Tony Denier, the Clown of the original road company, as its mainstay. The final revival in New York in 1880 was a confession of inadequacy, however. In order to bolster up a weak attraction, the management supplied the pantomime with two Harlequins, two Columbines, two Clowns, and two Pantaloons. There proved to be no safety in numbers, however, for the show was kept from a prompt closing chiefly by a novelty that was wholly irrelevant to its native character—the Spanish Students, who sang, danced, and played in an instrumental ensemble consisting of mandolins, guitars, and a solo violin. But there was no ducking the fact: Pantomime had died with George

L. Fox. By 1880 it was already a specter from the grave, and its best assets had been bequeathed to burlesque, extravaganza, and the modest farce-comedies of Nate Salsbury's Troubadours.

IV

The Bleached Blondes

IT SEEMS rather to be desired that the points of a fine woman should be somewhat better known and more thought of than they have been." This measured opinion was expressed by a noted editor of Shakespeare's plays, Richard Grant White, in comment upon Lydia Thompson and her company of British blondes, who arrived from London to make their first American appearance in the burlesque *Ixion, or The Man at the Wheel,* at Wood's Museum in New York on September 21, 1868. Possibly White might have tempered his speech if he had been able to look into the future, for it was Lydia Thompson who gave burlesque the initial momentum in its seventy-year journey toward Minsky's and legal obliteration.

Before Lydia burst upon the American consciousness, with her "troupe of British blondes that put a golden hirsute girdle around the earth," burlesque had been a naïve diversion. It consisted of brief travesties of current plays, novels, and fashions, confined to a secondary position in mixed bills chiefly devoted to one- or two-act farces, comedies, and melodramas.

In *Ixion*, originally devised a year or so earlier for her more sophisticated British admirers, Lydia found ways and means of expanding a burlesque of a familiar story into a diversified and racy entertainment that filled the better part of an evening. (*Ixion* was preceded by the farcical half-hour curtain raiser that was customary in those days, even in more serious branches of the theatre. In many of her subsequent bills, however, she followed the precedent of *The Black Crook* and devoted the evening to a single full-length piece.) The title of *Ixion*, suggesting cultivated subject matter of classical origin, imparted an air of spurious elegance to her first American offering. In the actual performance, however, the plot was the least of her worries. Neither Lydia nor her blondes (let it be recorded that two of the young ladies were brunettes, having refrained from the use of peroxide, which derived an early notoriety as a bleaching agent from the Thompson troupe) could act, nor did they pretend to. They did their duty by the incessant, unrelieved rhymed couplets that constituted the script, and they mouthed faithfully the laborious puns that passed for humor. No; it was neither the dramatic nor the literary qualities of *Ixion* that brought all of fun-loving New York to Wood's Museum. A few excerpts from the punning list of characters will serve as corroborative evidence:

"ixion (King of Thessaly)—but though a king with the prefix of an x, it does not alphabetically follow that he has a wise head on his shoulders.

"juno—fond of peacocks that sing pea-hens of joy while drawing her car.

"MARS—commander-in-chief, as Ma's usually are.

"THE NINE MUSES, including POLLY HYMNIA.

"Those Thessalians who would be these aliens if they weren't natives; dreadful Democrats, members of several secret societies who demand the right of free speaking in a state of free-dumb.

"Crowd of Red Republicans, unread Republicans, avengers, scavengers, Greeks, sneaks, and female furies."

It was the constant, unfettered romping of the girls, the frequent topical references to interests and foibles of the day, and, above all else, the extensive display of the female form that won the British blondes their loyal and considerable following. Lydia was the real discoverer of the tired business man. She elevated to the Broadway level the well-tried saloon technique of passing intimate remarks to the baldheads in the first row. Nor did she and the girls neglect to establish a rapport with the wealthy young fops in the stalls, who sat "ogling with an amorous idiocy" that even the fairy coryphées of *The Black Crook*, in their more remote loveliness, had not induced. Oblivious of the demands of art for art's sake, *Ixion* kept its spectators happy with a kaleidoscopic variety of opéra-bouffe songs, topical "hits" (as gags were called), can-cans, snippets of ballet, specialty dances, spectacles, and transformation scenes. If the ballerinas failed to dim memories of the corps de ballet in *The Black Crook*, and if the spectacles and transformation scenes were neither lavish nor particularly skillful in their mechanical handling, nobody cared much. There was too much else to see.

To display their legs, Lydia Thompson and her girls resorted to a subterfuge that was both less indirect than the *pas de démons* in *The Black Crook* and much more whole-hearted, since it lasted throughout the entire evening. Lydia merely put on male attire and played the title role of Ixion, and most of the other girls followed her example in their dress. Patently, no deception was intended, for the ideal mid-century feminine figure—with its transcendent bust and columnar calves and thighs—could scarcely conceal its gender. This device was by no means Lydia's invention, having long been a favored feature of burlesque when she first adopted it; but she gave it a new meaning, which was to influence stage fashions (in the more sedate comic opera as well as in burlesque) for forty years to come. This meaning became explicit when the girls sang a song with the refrain "How's that for high!" and all gave a high kick.

With the young women preëmpting the juvenile male parts, Lydia's company required little in the way of masculine support. But the seedy male comic, who in later burlesques was to adopt the red nose of the pantomime clown, had his place in *Ixion* in the form of a gawky rustic in blue overalls, whose presence in the celestial regions with such elevated characters as Juno and Jupiter would have been difficult to explain if Lydia had taken the plot more seriously.

At first Lydia was received with undivided approbation. E. F. House, the theatre critic of *The Spirit of the Times*, wrote in ecstasy that "jig-dancing is etherealized by her bewitching steps, and comic songs are sublimated by her modesty of manner and archness of expression." But a storm of public indignation soon began to gather, as the performance began to be the talk of the town. House himself, for reasons that are no longer discernible, jumped onto the moral bandwagon, and shortly afterward narrowly averted a physical attack by Lydia's manager, who called him a liar because he had impugned the propriety of the blonde charmer's deportment. House's paper did not abandon the battle, but continued, in its editorial columns, to take an agitated view of the British blondes' effect upon public morals:

"There are sad proofs enough that these gilded larvae breed to a vocation, and many a girl who months ago was modestly content with plain attire and an honest name now basks her nude limbs in the hot gaze of an abandoned crowd, or streams like a yellow meteor along the pave, luring weak followers to her new ambition."

It was in Chicago, however, that the most flamboyant episode of Lydia Thompson's career took place, on the occasion of her first visit to that plain-speaking city, early in 1870. Intent upon a crusade, Wilbur S. Story, the editor of the Chicago *Times*, caused his paper to roar incessantly against the "immorality" on display at Crosby's Opera House. Finally Lydia got tired of his daily abuse. As he left his office one afternoon, she waylaid him on the sidewalk of Wabash Avenue, and administered a horsewhipping. At the theatre that evening she retaliated further by appending outrageous verses employing his full name to one of her songs, "If I Ever Ceased to Love." Story brought Lydia to court, where she was judged guilty and fined $100—a trifling price indeed for the national publicity the escapade brought her.

Wood's Museum, in which Lydia began her New York career, was a second-class house. Having established her reputation, she soon moved—on February 1, 1869—to the more fashionable and more capacious Niblo's Garden, which had housed both *The Black Crook* and its sequel, *The White Fawn*. Here she presented a new burlesque entitled *The Forty Thieves*, whose "dialogue evidenced glancing acquaintance with the higher authorities—Mother Goose, Arabian Nights, Police Reports, Shakespeare, Dumas, and the La Crosse Democrat." This ran until May 28, when she embarked, "abundantly supplied with local allu-

sions for openings in the provinces," on the tour that ultimately took her to the home city of Wilbur S. Story. At
the close of her trial in Chicago, she returned to Niblo's
Garden, on April 4, 1870, in *Pippin, or The King of the
Gold Mines.* Her vogue proved to be relatively short-lived,
however, and she soon returned to England. In 1891, she
attempted an American comeback, but she looked pathetically middle-aged, and her outmoded style appealed only
to a few sentimentalists who had worshipped her in her
heyday.

V

Evangeline

and Edward E. Rice

UP TO NOW, the entrepreneurs of the American musical stage
had concerned themselves chiefly with the attempt to turn
European forms of entertainment into popular American
currency. John Brougham's *Pocahontas*, as we have seen,
was an endeavor to find an American parallel for the traditional French extravaganza, or *féerie*. *The Black Crook*
was the resplendent finale of a long period of interest in
French Romantic ballet and German Romantic melodrama.
Humpty Dumpty was the dying triumph of the ancient harlequinade. Lydia Thompson's burlesques clung to the classical references and stereotyped literary devices of old-fashioned English burlesque. Each of these entrants upon the

American scene had something new to offer, it is true (legs, more often than not), but essentially each was the ending and summing-up of an older convention rather than the initiation of a fresh line of development.

With his production of *Evangeline* in 1874, Edward E. Rice created the first American musical show of a character so homespun that it could in no way be described adequately by reference to foreign fashions and procedures. *Evangeline* created a world of entertainment in which Rice continued to enjoy the utmost success with the public for more than twenty years. The format of his "American burlesque" was permissive rather than restrictive; he invented an informal manner of presentation that allowed burlesque to grow along with the tastes and fashions of the time, to develop new performers, and to take on new colorations.

A Bostonian by birth, Rice settled down in his middle twenties, after a brief fling at acting in a stock company, to what looked like a steady, promising desk job in the office of the Cunard Line. One night he went with his friend, J. Cheever Goodwin, a young Harvard graduate employed as a reporter on the Boston *Traveler*, to see a performance by Lydia Thompson and her high-kicking blondes.

Finding the evening "highly depressing because of the peculiar density of its British humor," Rice and Goodwin maintained that they could write a much better burlesque themselves, and immediately set out to do it. They seized upon Longfellow's *Evangeline* as a suitably familiar subject for an American travesty. Goodwin wrote the book and lyrics, and Rice composed the music. A natural musician, but not an educated one, Rice played the piano by ear, and wrote his score in "a kind of phonography which no one but he could decipher." As a result of his efforts, *Evangeline* became the first full-scale American stage production with an entirely original musical score. And it is not a bad score, as the printed edition testifies. One looks in vain for any national or local qualities in the musical idiom, to be sure; but Rice knew how to give life to a march and lilt to a waltz, and how to reduce the tune of a comic or topical song to a proper subservience to the words.

Since Rice and Goodwin had more enthusiasm than money, they were in no position to produce their show lavishly. They were able to persuade the management of Niblo's Garden to take it as a stopgap attraction for the midsummer doldrums, in July, 1874. The production was economical—even cheap-looking—at every point. But it made an immediate hit, and when it was forced out of Niblo's Garden by other commitments for the house, Rice was able to obtain funds for a more sumptuous investiture for the Boston opening in the fall and an ultimate return to New York.

Since the initial booking at Niblo's Garden was a short one by foreordination, *Evangeline* could show no first-run record to rival those of *The Black Crook* and *Humpty Dumpty*. But by the time it had run its full course, *Evangeline* had remained alive for nearly thirty years, and was the only nineteenth-century musical production that rivaled, or perhaps surpassed, *The Black Crook* in perennial, nation-wide popularity. (It would be a hopeless task to try to gather definitive figures establishing the thirty-year grand totals of *Black Crook* and *Evangeline* performances; it is not likely that any twentieth-century musical attraction—even *Blossom Time*—has achieved a comparable record.)

Although *Evangeline* may properly be classified as a burlesque (in the pre-Minsky sense of a travesty on a familiar story, with the hero's part played by the leading lady in tights), Rice at first called it an "American opéra-bouffe," and later an "American extravaganza." His evasion of the accurate generic description was understandable, for he intended the piece as a diversion for the entire family, not merely for the roués, sophisticates, and black sheep who constituted an important portion of Lydia Thompson's audience. He dropped the term "opéra-bouffe" as soon as he realized that French comic opera, despite its support by many New Yorkers of means and advanced tastes, was discountenanced by thousands of simple, respectable people because of its devotion to double entendre and off-color situations. He sought, according to his own pronouncement when he became sole owner and producer of the show after its initial engagement at Niblo's Garden, "to foster a taste for musical comedy relieved of the characteristic and objectionable features of opéra-bouffe." (This, incidentally, appears to be the first incidence of the term "musical comedy" in connection with a popular piece on the American stage.)

Despite their contempt for Lydia Thompson's attainments, Rice and Goodwin (the latter of whom seems to have played second fiddle to his dynamic partner from the beginning) did not hesitate to appropriate any of her devices that looked serviceable to the new context. Since no better justification could be imagined in the 1870s for revealing the full constructional details of the female leg, they retained the artifice of putting the prima donna in tights and assigning the leading male role of Gabriel to her. They also managed to find reasons to clothe a good many of the other girls in similar fashion, and they introduced a corresponding transvestite character, a male comic who impersonated a maiden lady. George K. Fortesque, who created the role of "the ponderous Catherine," made this part his special property almost continuously from 1874 to 1901—with occasional excursions into other female impersonations, such as a burlesque, in the late 1880s, of Fanny Davenport's sensational performance in Sardou's *Fedora*, entitled *Well-Fed Dora*.

Two touches of particular originality were regularly praised wherever *Evangeline* was seen. One of these was a silent personage—whose debased descendant we have seen in our own day in the blasé individual who sat at the edge of the proscenium in *Hellzapoppin*—known as the Lone Fisherman. He had little connection with the plot, and maintained a serio-comic, pseudo-philosophic isolation from the people and events of the play. This mystifying mute figure won so firm a hold upon the fancy of the American public that James S. Maffitt, who created the part, was able —like Fortesque as Catherine—to round out an entire career playing very little else.

Another winning feature of *Evangeline* was likewise a conceit that still has the power to evoke laughter today. Inasmuch as Longfellow had awarded Evangeline a milk-white cow, Rice and Goodwin thought it a good idea to include the cow among the dramatis personae of their burlesque. Accordingly they dreamed up a trick heifer whose movements were negotiated by one man in the front legs and another in the hind legs. To the ungainly creature they allotted an eccentric dance, which proved to be not merely an instantaneous success but one of the unwithering attractions of the show throughout its whole life. With the passage of the years, indeed, the *Evangeline* heifer came to be one of the best-known celebrities of the musical stage. As late as 1896, the critic of the New York *Journal*, reporting upon one of the last metropolitan reappearances of the extravaganza, bracketed its girls and its heifer as comparable features, referring to its "perennial limbs and immutable cow." (The same weary first-nighter described the twenty-two-year-old piece as "that primal extravaganza belonging neither to life nor to drama.")

It is a bit tiresome to say it about each successive production, but truthfulness again requires the observation that the plot of *Evangeline* was the least of its attractions. Goodwin's book bore astoundingly little relation to Longfellow's poem, or, for that matter, to anything coherent at all. Africa and Arizona were locales of the action as well as Acadia, and nobody ever arrived in Louisiana. With padded legs, blacked eyelashes, and rouged cheeks, the girls engaged in "the pedal calisthenics which carried *Evangeline* like a centipede on its hundred legs," and carefully avoided giving offense to the family audience, which marveled at the sprouting of the whales, the vertiginous balloon trip to Arizona (shades of *The Balloon Wedding*), and, beyond all else, the sphinx-like demeanor of The Lone Fisherman, whom one reviewer so aptly called "an original and incomprehensible embodiment."

Dancing, as we expect to find it in a reputable musical production today, was decidedly a secondary interest in *Evangeline*. The piece was devoid of the familiar trappings of extravaganza—the Fairy Queen, the tarlatan costumes, the coryphées on their *pointes*. Except for the dance of the milk-white heifer, the primordial kickings and cavortings of the young ladies of the chorus, and a military drill by the entire cast to the music of the "Evangeline March" in the finale, evidences of choreographic planning were lacking entirely. Some of the principals, however, performed jigs and other popular routines in connection with their songs and ballads.

The structure of *Evangeline*, as opposed to its content, clearly betrayed dependence upon the usages of French opéra-bouffe and pre-Gilbert-and-Sullivan English comic opera, though the musical and literary craftsmanship was far more naïve than that of Audran or Offenbach and their librettists. The piece consisted of a series of songs and ballads, varied by an occasional duet or trio or chorus, with a connective tissue of rhyming, punning nonsensicalities.

Some impression of the quality of its literary humor is afforded by the description of the character of Evangeline as an early program gives it: "*Our heroine*, a creature of *impulse* and an *impetuous pet*, pursued through love's impatient prompting, by Gabriel, and with a view to edacious contingencies—by a whale."

Some of the more thoughtful observers of theatrical phenomena found the success of *Evangeline* as puzzling as later generations of critics found those of *Abie's Irish Rose* and *Tobacco Road*. The author of an unsigned review in the New York *Dramatic Mirror* in 1880 exclaimed, when it fell to his lot to deal with one of the frequent return engagements of *Evangeline*: "The vitality of the extravaganza is something wonderful, considering the length of time [six years] it has been before the public. Some of the old, pointless puns and gags have been eradicated, only to be replaced by new puns and gags just as witless and just as inane as their predecessors. . . . When it is all over, the question arises, What is there in *Evangeline* that should ever have gained for it the amount of public favor it has enjoyed?"

Nobody undertook to answer the *Dramatic Mirror's* query. But *Evangeline* continued to prosper, and Rice sent a multiplicity of companies out on the road, billed sometimes as Rice's Evangeline Combination and sometimes as Rice's Surprise Party. The puns finally disappeared from the printed programs, but they never vanished from the script; their deletion would have been as unthinkable as the banishment of the heifer or the Lone Fisherman.

The most famous revival of *Evangeline* occurred in 1885, when Rice was at the height of his affluence, thanks to the epoch-making success of his new *Adonis*. With revisions in the text (made by John J. McNally, since Goodwin and Rice had parted company soon after the first days of *Evan-*

geline) and some new music composed by Rice, the refurbished war-horse played 251 times in New York before setting forth on the road. Rice himself conducted the fiftieth performance; for the hundredth performance, Henry E. Dixey, who owed his stardom to Rice's management, came over from *Adonis* to join in the dance at the end of the first act. Seventeen-year-old Fay Templeton, who was to remain a favorite on the musical stage until her final appearance in Jerome Kern's *Roberta* in 1932, came up from touring the South to make her first Broadway appearance as Gabriel—in tights, and with a Lillian Russell hourglass figure. Her new song, "I Don't—Do You?", became the hit number of the show, for a time rivaling the popularity of Lillian Russell's contemporaneous specialty, "The Silver Line." A group of acrobats vied for favor with the heifer and the Lone Fisherman.

Evangeline was the one constant in Rice's life during all these years—his life insurance, so to speak; for whenever other enterprises failed he could safely fall back upon the assured earnings of his first-born. But he was tirelessly active in bringing out elaborate new productions and usually skillful in finding ways to capture the public fancy.

At one early point, however, he made a bad guess, because, like Brougham and Jarrett and Palmer and George L. Fox before him, he pinned his hopes upon a sequel. In 1880, Rice's Surprise Party (whatever Rice's surprise might be, one could apparently be sure it would involve Longfellow) offered "a new and original American operatic extravaganza, *Hiawatha*," with the gracious Alice Atherton as the Indian brave, about whom "all lisping ladies say 'He-aw-wath-a charming fellow.'" Chalk-faced, nervous little Willie Edouin, who became one of the most popular comics of the 1880s, was a member of the cast, and also young Henry E.

Dixey, who developed into a matinee idol in *Adonis* four years later, as well as a group of supernumeraries described as "adjunct-conspirators who *add junk*."

Again the entire score was composed by Rice, who dictated it to a secretary "with suggestions about its instrumental effects"—a procedure that has its counterpart in the methods of more than one contemporary musical-comedy composer. Goodwin having departed from Rice's fellowship to devote his talents to the authorship of a long series of dubious comic-opera librettos, Rice obtained the book of *Hiawatha* from Nathaniel Childs, who appears not to have had the magic touch. Neither a costly production by Arthur Voegtlin, who designed *The Black Crook*, nor a hit song called "Tea and Toast and Kisses" could save *Hiawatha*; it closed after two weeks.

Rice's next important production, *Pop*, revealed at the Bijou Opera House in New York in 1883, was described as "a new, highly sensational melodramatic operatic comedy mélange." A hybrid entertainment, it consisted of burlesque and extravaganza elements, organized within a framework borrowed from the small farce-comedies—such as Nate Salsbury's *The Brook* and William A. Mestayer's *The Tourists in the Pullman Palace Car*—which suddenly became popular in 1879.

The main source of humor in *Pop* was the portly George K. Fortesque (the Catherine of *Evangeline*) who appeared in this instance as Anthony Belsize from Alabama, "a Wealthy Southerner, who is never in a hurry, and who used to masquerade in female attire in his youth." The second act of the entertainment—by far the longest—took place in the saloon of the *S. S. Scythia*, en route from London to New York. The opening act merely showed preparations for the trip in London, and the closing act saw the members of the cast settled in New York.

The specialties in the second act were more diverse than those of *Evangeline*, for Rice drew upon the resources of the variety shows by including a group of Tyrolean warblers, various imitations, and vocal duets in music-hall style. The burlesque elements of *Pop* were confined chiefly to two episodes—a scene showing the awakening of the statue, from *Pygmalion and Galatea*, and a burlesque scene from *Romeo and Juliet*. In the third week, Rice added a new number to strengthen the last act—"The Dudes and the Dude Princes"—in which a number of the girls engaged in a march, dressed as dudes. This was an up-to-the-moment touch, for it was at precisely this time that the elegant dudes began their reign as the princes of New York's pavements, restaurants, and theatres. Their immediate predecessors, the mashers, were never—as far as the records indicate—similarly canonized in any theatrical entertainment.

Ten years after the first production of *Evangeline*, on September 4, 1884, Rice presented *Adonis* at the Bijou Opera House, initiating a record-breaking run of 603 consecutive performances. The New York opening was not the première of the piece, for it had been tried out at Hooley's Opera House in Chicago in July. For the first time, Rice was not listed as producer, but only as composer. William Gill was the producer, though there can be no doubt that Rice's money was generously involved. Gill was also co-author of the book with Henry E. Dixey, the male lead.

With *Adonis*, Rice allowed the hush-hush term "burlesque" to be used for the first time in the official description of one of his attractions. He called it a "burlesque-extravaganza"; and it was, in point of fact, vaguely a burlesque of the Pygmalion and Galatea theme, which had already haunted Rice's fancy in *Pop*, the previous year.

The hyphenated description, "burlesque-extravaganza," indicated that the earlier distinction between these two types of entertainment had now become blurred. Only the girls in tights, the puns, and the lip service to a familiar plot remained from the earlier conventions of burlesque; the hero was a handsome man rather than a woman in tights. The term "extravaganza" had by now been used to describe so many kinds of pieces endeavoring to be amusing through their diversity of materials and impressive by their spectacle that the word had come to mean almost anything, or perhaps nothing definitive at all. Rice apparently soon found the word a useless one, for except for *The Seven Ages*, in 1889, he abandoned it in the advertisements of the productions that came after *Adonis*, choosing to call them all burlesques, up to the last one of the kind, *Excelsior Jr.*, in 1895.

The long run of *Adonis* was partly explained by the inordinate popularity of the sleek Henry E. Dixey, who had made his start in *Hiawatha*. As Adonis, Dixey had ample opportunity to display his fine figure and his unusually shapely legs. He was also a nimble dancer, an adroit comedian, and a well-trained singer. In later years he remained one of the fixtures of the musical stage, seldom wanting for an assignment, though never again attaining the peak of popularity *Adonis* enabled him to reach.

Equally important to the success of *Adonis* was the way in which Rice—like Russel Crouse and Howard Lindsay many decades later in *State of the Union*—kept freshening the dialogue by bringing the topical references up to the moment. Since nobody could ever tell what new quips would add to the merriment, people went back again and again; the *Dramatic Mirror* observed that it was "an institution to be regularly patronized like the El railways or the Eden Musée."

While Rice continued to be an important producer for another quarter-century, his formative influence upon the American musical stage decreased as he tended to repeat earlier formulas. His own creative contribution also became less. For *The Corsair*, presented in 1887, he composed only part of the score, delegating the lion's share of the musical responsibility to the English composer John J. Braham. In his later productions, Rice undertook to contribute very little, writing no music and taking almost no hand in the preparation of the books. *The Seven Ages*, staged in 1889 as a starring vehicle for Dixey, employed a plot based upon the Seven Ages of Man detailed by Jaques in Shakespeare's *As You Like It*. The piece offered a touch of novelty in the behavior of its chorus girls, who abandoned their wonted aloofness to enter into chatty conversation with the audience. *1492 Up to Date*, presented in 1893, a year too late for the quadricentennial but in time to capitalize upon the nationwide interest in the World's Columbian Exposition at Chicago, was a "musical, historical, mellow drama" that threw together bits of opéra-comique, comic opera, stereopticon projections, extravaganza, farce-comedy, vaudeville, local comedy, burlesque, and even minstrelsy.

Obviously Rice had now departed a great distance from his starting-point; though *1492 Up to Date* was moderately successful, its effort to encompass the entire known range of light musical diversion amounted to the admission that the days of burlesque, as he had once conceived it, were now as good as finished. In *Little Christopher Columbus*, produced in 1894, Rice moved a long step further away from burlesque by engaging two especially well-equipped comic-opera composers, Ivan Caryll and Gustave Kerker, to write the score and Kerker himself to conduct it. It was an elaborate show with a costly and stunning production, but it was no longer a burlesque, and it presaged Rice's complete abandonment of burlesque in favor of musical comedy.

Excelsior Jr., introduced at Hammerstein's Olympia Theatre in 1895, constituted one last reversion to the now historic burlesque type. Once again one of Rice's pieces depended upon Longfellow for its inspiration; the book by W. A. Barnett was blithely advertised as "a perversion of Longfellow's *Excelsior*." But in brashly announcing that the burlesque was a "perversion," Rice revealed the sophistication that had come over his own thinking and over that of the theatre public as well. No longer could the homely hokum of *Evangeline* be offered in a new piece without self-conscious apology; whatever the durability of the heifer and the Lone Fisherman, they were now recognized to be period pieces. *Excelsior Jr.* survived for six months, less on its own merits than upon those of Fay Templeton, who was still a charmer, though she had put on enough weight to make her tights bulge embarrassingly; Theresa Vaughan, who repeated from 1492 *Up to Date* her artifice of singing local ballads with German words, strumming the guitar "somnolently"; and Arthur Dunn, who gave a raucous imitation of Paderewski, whose name was now beginning to be a household word.

Though Rice enjoyed a virtual monopoly of the field, two burlesques were introduced by a young actor-producer, Nat C. Goodwin. In *Little Jack Sheppard*, presented at the Bijou Opera House in 1886, on the heels of *Adonis'* closing, Goodwin acquainted the American audience with the skirt dancing of Loie Fuller. A sharper contrast to the prima donna in "trunks" could scarcely have been found. When Loie Fuller, with her voluminous yardage of swirling pleated skirts, demonstrated the pictorial possibilities of these neglected garments, the entire masculine sex found a new object of admiration, and the ladies in tights soon learned to fear and respect the competition of the growing tribe of skirt dancers.

Goodwin's second production, *Big Pony, or The Gentlemanly Savage*, was too weak a concoction to add new impetus to the skirt-dance enthusiasm, despite the continuing presence of Loie Fuller. It remained for a visiting English troupe—George Edwardes' Theatre Burlesque Company, who arrived at the Standard Theatre in New York on November 15, 1888, in *Monte Cristo Jr.*—to give impetus to the interest Goodwin had engendered. Though their visit was less successful financially than Lydia Thompson's tours two decades earlier, it exerted no less influence upon popular taste. The Edwardes company, whose London home was the Gaiety Theatre, offered a species of entertainment that differed radically both from Lydia Thompson's and from Rice's. The Gaiety burlesque abandoned the rhymed couplet and the pun, depending upon more spontaneous and swifter dialogue. Above all, it provided both the principal ladies and the members of the chorus with the long, swishy skirts that had been Loie Fuller's stellar prerogative in the Nat Goodwin burlesques. It is safe to assume that Loie Fuller had been impressed by the new uniform of the Gaiety Girls, and had hastened to capitalize upon it before the Edwardes company could get to this country.

The Gaiety company brought one more burlesque to New York—*Faust Up to Date*—under the new and important management of Abbey and Grau, in 1889. The piece did not prosper, for the critics felt that Edwardes had sent a company inferior to that of *Monte Cristo Jr.* The next time a Gaiety troupe crossed the Atlantic it brought not a burlesque but a musical comedy. And burlesque itself, having won a new lease on life through the rediscovery of the skirt, soon fell under the capable guidance of Weber and Fields.

VI

The Kiralfys

THE BROTHERS Imre, Bolossy, and Arnold Kiralfy, Hungarian dancers and pantomime performers, came to the United States in 1868. For a few years they lived by picking up any jobs they could find: Arnold danced in the 1868 revival of *The Black Crook*; Imre and Bolossy were the two Harlequins in the 1871 revival of *Humpty Dumpty*.

As they observed the tastes and reactions of the people of their new country they discovered a provocative fact: The American audience was completely overawed by the marvelous. Give any assembly of Americans a series of realistic, large-scale reproductions of famous or familiar spectacles, and it would remain rooted to the spot for an entire evening. One of the most prosperous entertainment enterprises of the 1870s was the Colosseum, erected at Broadway and Thirty-fifth Street, and modeled after the Colosseum in

London as a home for impressive cycloramas. Its first attraction, in 1874, entitled *London by Night,* exploited "wonderful effects of moving water, clouds, storms and numerous other wonderful mechanical deceptions, all devised by C. F. Brown, master machinist, imported from the Royal Colosseum in London."

Observing the effect upon the audience not only of the cyclorama but of the transformation scenes in *The Black Crook* and other musical attractions, the Kiralfy brothers determined to produce a spectacle of their own. Seeking a subject that would offer opportunities for many striking and realistic mechanical effects, they hit upon the popular Jules Verne romance *Around the World in Eighty Days.*

If they had been less sure of themselves, the Kiralfys might have abandoned their project before it reached the production phase, for two other versions of the same story were presented in New York before theirs was ready. One of these, without music or ballet, claimed attention with Ouina, a "trained war elephant." The other employed music and the other customary resources of the musical stage, but was small, economical, and unimpressive.

The tameness of these two earlier efforts in the same year apparently gave additional force to the Kiralfy production, which was revealed at the Academy of Music (rebuilt after the fire that led to the staging of *The Black Crook* at Niblo's Garden) on August 25, 1875. With shrewd theatrical imagination, the Kiralfys dwelt with special zeal upon the more exotic aspects of the story, and themselves appeared as natives of Borneo. Great admiration was bestowed by the public and the critics upon the scenes representing the places farthest from home—the Suez Canal, Calcutta, and the Taj Mahal. "Nothing so splendid as the scene at the Suttee and the ballet of the second act has ever been witnessed in this city," wrote one transported critic.

In their settings, which represented "the best French school of painting," the Kiralfys, or their unnamed designers, hit upon an important principle for the designing of spectacular scenes. They kept the backgrounds "in minor key and in pastel colors" to give an effect of atmosphere and space, and to throw the actors in the foreground into a vivid relief that would be lost if the backgrounds were too primary or too gaudy. Furthermore, they paid great attention to realistic detail. They were the first American producers, for instance, to make the cuts between the branches of trees naturalistic in shape and disposition, instead of using the monotonous, symmetrical holes which were customary in stage foliage at the time.

For a decade after their production of *Around the World in Eighty Days*, the Kiralfys remained unchallenged as promulgators of large pictorial pieces. Their supremacy rested upon their taste and discretion in the use of color and their unrivaled understanding of the potentialities of technical and mechanical effects. When the electric light was invented, they were quick to take advantage of its new possibilities. Their spectacle *Excelsior*, presented at Niblo's Garden in 1883 at an alleged cost of $75,000, boasted "novel electric effects by the Edison Electric Light Company, under the personal direction of Mr. Edison." The experimental nature of the lighting was indicated by the fact that Edison thought it important to be on hand to see that everything went well. Electricity by no means eliminated gas from the lighting of *Excelsior*. It was reserved for special effects; the program also advertised gas effects and electric-gas lighting. Nor, for that matter, was *Excelsior* the first production to make use of electricity, though it was the first and only one in which Edison himself participated. The Kiralfys themselves had already employed electric lights in the eerie incantation scene in their revival of *The Black Crook*.

It was not their technical ability alone that kept the Kiralfys at the top of the list of producers of spectacles. Having been trained as dancers, they were also aware of the requirements of spectacular theatre in this field. *Excelsior*, which proved to be their magnum opus, made use of the combined talents of the Parisian Eden Theatre Ballet Company, the Venetian Ballet Troupe, and "the most distinguished artists of the Scala Theatre of Milan."

In the course of the production, in which not a word was spoken, the entire rise and perfection of modern civilization was reviewed with relentless thoroughness. The cast of characters included such metaphorical figures as Light, Darkness, and Civilization, as well as representatives of practically every corner of the earth and every walk of life—Pepin, described as the inventor of the steamboat; Volta, the electrician; an Indian danseuse; an Arab merchant's daughter; a Chinaman; the chief of the Italian miners; a Mexican; a Grand Turk; a French engineer; a brigand in the desert; an Englishman; and a lady known as La Cosmopolete. The countless dancers and extras appeared as genii of civilization, of constancy, of invention, of harmony, of renown, of power, of glory, of science, of agriculture, of industry, of valor, of union; and as boatmen, peasants, musicians, postillions, telegraph boys, engineers, miners, workers in the earth, Europeans, Africans, Asiatics, Americans, sailors, and officers.

The vast mélange led up to a great apotheosis, "The Triumph of Light Over Darkness and the Peaceful Union of Nations." To arrive at this desirable final tableau, three acts and twelve preparatory "great tableaux" were required. Despite its cosmic sweep, the scenario did not fail to keep up to date; not only was the discovery of electric power celebrated by example, but the invention of the telegraph was noted in a ballet in which the girls were dressed as telegraph messengers.

The Kiralfys followed *Excelsior* with a number of other grandiose endeavors, none of which duplicated its success. Only *Lagarde,* among these, warrants passing mention, because of the tangential fact that Maurice Barrymore was a member of its cast; the piece itself was a tiresome blowing-up of an old melodrama, *The Duke's Moot,* by Le Bossu, and offered as its central attraction a ballet based on the Seven Ages of Man, a subject which seemed to haunt the theatrical mind in the 1880s.

In 1888, Imre and Bolossy Kiralfy had a falling-out, and the firm disbanded. Arnold Kiralfy went back to dancing, with diminishing success, and died in 1908. Bolossy continued for two more seasons as a New York producer, achieving his only success in 1888 with another Jules Verne piece, *Mathias Sandorf.* Imre left the theatre altogether, and turned to the production of outdoor spectacles. In 1888, he presented *The Fall of Rome* on Staten Island, with a cast of two thousand, tons of armor, a leviathan ballet, and quantities of chariot racing and Roman wrestling. He then moved to England, where he produced an even larger spectacle involving 2,500 participants. He died in Brighton, England, in 1919. Bolossy, who had retired from theatrical activity in 1889, lived on obscurely in this country until 1932, when he died at the age of eighty-four.

Though the period of their ascendancy was relatively short and the total number of their productions was not large, the Kiralfys left an indelible mark upon the New York stage. Their vast enterprises were never rivaled until the flamboyant years of the Hippodrome in the early twentieth century. The source of strength in their first productions—their technical acumen—became a weakness when they tried merely to make their spectacles constantly bigger and more eye-filling, without developing new ideas to replace the ballet-extravaganza materials on which they had learned to depend in the atavistic days of *The Black Crook* and *Humpty Dumpty*.

VII

Farce-Comedy

A LIVELY little group of five itinerant players known as Salsbury's Troubadours, newly arrived from Chicago, St. Louis, and other Western points, brought a trifle called *The Brook* to New York on May 12, 1879. To the patrons of the San Francisco Opera House, *The Brook* constituted nothing more than a pleasant way of passing a spring evening in the theatre occupied throughout the winter by the popular San Francisco Minstrels. To us, gifted with hindsight, *The Brook*—despite its tiny budget and its brief engagement of two weeks—was one of the most important productions of its time, outweighing from the historian's viewpoint such costly offerings as the Kiralfys' *Around the World in Eighty Days* or Fox's *Humpty Dumpty*.

The Brook was the germinal cell out of which musical comedy ultimately grew. It was the first full-length musical piece to adopt the distinguishing formula of musical comedy by putting its central trust in the topical materials of the variety show and arranging these materials upon the framework of a plot. For musical comedy may be distinguished from such other forms of entertainment as comic opera and burlesque by its direct and essentially unstylized appropriation of vernacular types of song, dance, and subject matter; and it may be distinguished from its chief source of inspiration, the variety show, by its employment of a plot and, at least in some slight degree, of consistent characterization.

If *The Brook* did not possess a musical score of its own, or make any pretense at choreography, or display the urbanities of staging that later generations learned to expect of a musical comedy, it did offer—within its modest resources of talent and investiture—an evening's diversion suffused with an informal, friendly charm that no spectacular machinery, pantomimic stylizations, or red-nosed, red-wigged comics and buxom women in tights could duplicate.

It is important, in view of the unyielding provinciality of New Yorkers, to observe that the most natural and spontaneous musical entertainment New York had yet encountered was a product not of the metropolis itself but of the hinterland. New York, in fact, was the last city to make the acquaintance of the musical farce-comedy (as the type soon came to be called), after Nate Salsbury, its first native exponent, had spent four years on the road perfecting it. Only when half of America had already found it palatable was the New York audience permitted to sample it.

Nate Salsbury began his theatrical career in the 1860s, being entrusted, in his first job, with a single line in Brougham's *Pocahontas*, a piece long forgotten in New York but still persistent on the road. After various stock-company experiences, he formed his own company, and on May 1, 1875, Salsbury's Troubadours made their first appearance in Chicago in a "comic absurdity," *Patchwork*. For the format and subject matter of this half-length piece Salsbury was almost shamelessly indebted to a similar troupe of five English performers, the Vokes Family, whose touring bill contained a divertissement entitled *Belles of the Kitchen*. Ringing minor changes upon the plot of *Belles of the Kitchen*, Salsbury's script for *Patchwork* involved an antic group of kitchen servants. At 7:30 in the morning, while the family was still "in the arms of Morpheus," the servants donned some costumes worn by the guests at a masquerade the night before, and demonstrated their talents in various song and dance specialties. The lark was interrupted by the arrival of members of the family, who caused the servants to disappear through stove-holes, windows, and chimneys as the final curtain descended.

The Brook, Salsbury's second composition, was scarcely longer than *Patchwork* when it was first presented in St. Louis in 1877. But as Salsbury's confidence in his product grew, its size expanded. At the New York première it was still preceded by a short, non-musical curtain-raiser, *Husband in Clover*, but the recitation of Tennyson's poem vouchsafed St. Louisans had now been abandoned. By the time the piece returned to New York in 1880 it occupied an entire evening.

The full title and subtitle of Salsbury's "laughable and musical extravaganza" (the rule still seemed to be: When in doubt call it an extravaganza) read:

THE BROOK

"For man may come and man may go, but I flow on forever"
Depicting the Pleasures of a Jolly Pic-Nic

The five Troubadours were cast as members of a theatrical company. In the first act they determined to take a boat trip down the river, for a "jolly pic-nic." The second act showed the picnic itself. The audience split its sides at an endless series of contretemps; fish-bait was mixed with the coffee; the jam was saturated with salt; vinegar was spilled on the sandwiches—and a basket thought to contain watermelons proved to be filled with theatrical costumes. This last mistake provided a pretext for the chief entertainment of the evening, for the performers made use of the costumes for impersonations, eccentric dances, and specialty songs. When their repertory was exhausted, they reëmbarked on the boat. The brief third act merely showed their return home, exhausted but happy.

Whatever its shortcomings in music, humor, and talent, *The Brook* established an important precedent by its assumption that naturalness could be thoroughly entertaining —that the audience, in this instance, could have a good time by sharing in the familiar pleasures of a picnic. As one critic wrote, "*The Brook* appeals to the natural impulses of everybody, and all nature is held up to the mirror." Salsbury himself explained that the farce-comedy "claimed to be a novelty, in the sense that it is different in its motive and execution from any musical production of its kind thus far presented for public consideration. The main object which we strive to attain is the natural reproduction of the jollity and funny mishaps that attend the usual pic-nic excursion."

Like Edward E. Rice with *Evangeline*, Salsbury established his reputation by offering entertainment the entire family could accept, though there was passing criticism of a song in the repertory of Nellie McHenry, the leading woman, entitled "Pretty, Though Fragrant, as a Picture." After delighting family audiences from coast to coast, Salsbury took *The Brook* to the British Isles—the first American musical production, in all probability, ever to appear there. It was approved by everybody except a Dublin reviewer who objected that it "does not gratify those who desire to see some division between the stage and the music halls." He also took exception—not unfairly, perhaps—to humor that defined a kiss as "a lip tickle (elliptical)" and permitted Salsbury at one point to say to Miss McHenry, "If you are going to smother me, do it s'mother way," and at another to observe, when she fainted in his arms, "How heavy a young woman is when she faints, especially after lunch!"

Salsbury kept the Troubadours on the move, partly with the perennial *Brook* and partly with new pieces of similar genre, until 1887. The last of his farce-comedies was *The Humming Bird*, given at the Star Theatre in New York on February 7 of that year. John Webster and Nellie McHenry still remained from the original company, and the troupe had been expanded from five to seven. From this time forward, Salsbury devoted himself to other interests. Signing as manager of Colonel William F. Cody, otherwise known as Buffalo Bill, he became the first producer of the celebrated Wild West Show, the predecessor of the present-day rodeo. Salsbury last functioned in New York as producer of a large spectacle, *Black America*, in Madison Square Garden in 1895.

The Troubadours' discovery of farce-comedy quickly set a fashion, for it was too successful and profitable not to invite imitation. To begin with, a farce-comedy could be mounted at extremely small cost, with an infinitesimal company and minimal settings, properties, and machinery. In the second place, it was easy to cast and direct, since it required no specialized techniques of pantomime or burlesque, no chorus, no French ballets, no transformation scenes. The form gave free opportunity to each performer to exploit whatever talent he might possess. As time went on, the freedom of farce-comedy from fixed traditions enabled a number of original and gifted comics to develop their individual styles of performance.

The second successful farce-comedy, and the only real competitive threat to Salsbury's Troubadours on the road, was *The Tourists in the Pullman Palace Car*, billed as "an entertainment of fun and incident," and presented in New York for the first time at Haverly's Theatre on November 8, 1879, with William A. Mestayer as producer and J. H. Haverly as manager. A more pulse-quickening tale than *The Brook, The Tourists in the Pullman Palace Car* strung its specialties upon a plot involving the trip of a group of tourists to California on an emigrant train, and the confusion arising out of a diamond robbery and complications of mistaken identity.

It possessed no musical score of its own, and its choice of music, like that of *The Brook*, was nothing if not eclectic. Among the items employed, according to the printed program, were Sullivan's "Serenade" from *Box and Cox* [sic]; "Nursery Rhymes (Original with the Tourists)"—"Poor Cock Robin," and "The North Wind Doth Blow"; "Luncheon Chorus," from *The Chimes of Normandy*; "The Kentucky Home"; "The Telegraph Boy" (words by W. A. Mestayer, music by David Braham); *German Emigrants—Der Wasserfall*; Scene from *Il Trovatore*; Harrigan and Hart's latest sketch, "The Skids Are Out Today" (music by David Braham); General Finale and "Forward to Do or Die" from *Fatinitza*; and End of Route.

The heyday of farce-comedy in New York lasted only about five years, although "combinations," as the farce-comedy troupes were called, continued to tour the rest of the country for twenty years longer. In the first rush of production, too many farce-comedies were produced to warrant a full listing here. A few, however, possessed features of distinctive interest. *Hobbies* (1879) brought Nat C. Goodwin to the musical stage for the first time, in imitations—not unlike those for which Nate Salsbury was famous—of such celebrated tragedians as Booth, Barrett, and Jefferson. Good win soon became a very popular performer, and, as we have already seen, produced two burlesques in the late 1880s, in which he shared billing with Loie Fuller. *Minnie Palmer's Boarding School*, exploiting the gifts of the comedienne Minnie Palmer, was, apart from *The Tourists*, the most prosperous imitator of *The Brook*.

A variant on the initial farce-comedy pattern was provided by *Dreams, or Fun in A Photograph Gallery*, offered in 1880 by a group called Willie Edouin's Sparks. This piece, thrown together after the failure of Rice's *Hiawatha*, used burlesque materials within a farce-comedy framework that was suited to Edouin, Alice Atherton, and James T. Powers, all of whom were left unemployed by the swift closing of Rice's sequel to *Evangeline*. *Dreams* justified its burlesque elements by having the dances in the photographer's shop take place in the dreams of an old man who had fallen asleep.

Within five years, the popularity of these small-scale farce-comedies faded. The last one to make even a moderate impact was *We, Us and Company at Mud Springs*, produced by Mestayer in 1884. The locale was a hotel built on a railroad turntable, an architectural device that enabled the proprietress to give each new patron the impression that he would have a sunny room. A mischievous youth turned the turntable one night when various lovers were abroad on nocturnal adventures—with farcical intrigues that were held to justify the usual songs, dances, knockabout antics, puns, and musical specialties.

Like many another novelty, early farce-comedy wore out its welcome speedily because its practitioners could not find ways of renewing the interest of their audiences once the initial freshness of the form had worn off. Lacking real validity of plot or characterization and the integrity of presentation that specially composed musical scores might have provided, the farce-comedies were easily nudged out of the Broadway scene by the comic operas which poured into the theatres after the triumphant success of *H. M. S. Pinafore* in 1879. Though its vogue began in the same year as that of the farce-comedy, comic opera prospered because it offered more substance and kept on discovering new facets and new subjects, while farce-comedy, becoming sterile and repetitious, retreated to the road. In the 1890s, farce-comedy enjoyed a whirlwind revival, but it was then conceived in more elaborate terms of production, and soon became indistinguishable from musical comedy, which supplanted it.

Akin to the early farce-comedies in their homely naturalness and disdain for artifice were the *Mulligan Guard* plays, written and presented in rapid rotation by Edward Harrigan and Tony Hart between 1877 and 1885. These farces, bearing such titles as *The Mulligan Guard's Chowder* and *The Mulligan Guard's Picnic*, represented the first attempt on the New York stage to achieve quasi-realistic local color by employing as characters familiar Bowery figures, whose manners and locutions were fairly accurately reproduced, though with broad satire and travesty. Harrigan's own stock part was that of an Irishman, and Hart played female roles.

The *Mulligan Guard* farces do not, strictly speaking, fall within the proper purview of this narrative. They were straight plays, dotted with interpolated songs, and, on rare occasions, dances; and they were followed by an olio of variety acts. But the songs were some of the wittiest and most professional of their day, for Harrigan and Hart maintained David Braham, a deft and well-trained musician, as their staff composer and musical director. Nearly every Harrigan and Hart show nurtured at least one song hit that was sung and whistled all over town and (as in the instance of *The Tourists in the Pullman Palace Car*) frequently borrowed for use in farce-comedies and other musical entertainments. Though the Harrigan and Hart farces employed none of the other appurtenances of the musical stage, they established a vogue for local and topical songs which helped prepare the way for the Broadway-conscious musical comedies of George M. Cohan after the turn of the century.

Perhaps the best of the entire Harrigan and Hart output was *Cordelia's Aspirations* (1883). One of the Mulligan series, despite the absence of the familiar name from its title, the farce dealt with Dan Mulligan's rise in society and consequent social blunders. In a fit of jealousy his wife drank from a bottle that was labelled "poison," but actually contained whiskey—with a resulting drunk scene that made Annie Yeamans famous as a comedienne. Among the songs —by David Braham, of course—were "Just Across from Jersey," "My Dad's Dinner Pail," and "Sam Johnson's Cakewalk." The last of these called upon a group of Negro dancers. Harrigan and Hart were the first major producers to employ Negro performers, almost two decades before *A Trip to Coontown* and *In Dahomey* called for recognition of the talent of Negro artists. In *Cordelia's Aspirations*, the Negro performers were brought into the play as a stranded *Uncle Tom* troupe returning from Germany.

After *Cordelia's Aspirations*, bad fortune began to overtake Harrigan and Hart. In 1884 the Theatre Comique, in which they had been appearing, burned down, destroying the scores and parts of nearly all of Braham's music for the many *Mulligan Guard* farces. The following year the partners had a falling out; and although each tried to continue on his own, the great days were over. But they had made their contribution: They had discovered New York, and whether in *Forty-Five Minutes from Broadway* or in *On the Town*, the American musical stage never afterward completely forgot its home town.

Somewhat more elaborate in their entertainment features, but in many ways similar in structure, were the comedies with music written and produced by Charles Hoyt. The first successful venture in Hoyt's career was a "farrago" called *A Bunch of Keys*, presented by Willie Edouin's Sparks at the San Francisco Opera House (from which farce-comedies and cognate attractions had nosed out the minstrel shows soon after the appearance of Salsbury's Troubadours) in 1883. The action took place in a hotel; and Willie Edouin's nervous cry of "Front!" became a byword all over town.

In a production directed by Edouin and including in the cast his partners of *Hiawatha* and *Dreams*, it was obvious that the mannerisms of burlesque would predominate. But in his subsequent farces Hoyt abandoned burlesque. He translated minstrel-show music and dancing into fresh terms, eliminating the blackface aspects, but basing the essential style of his divertissements upon typical minstrel stunts and techniques. He showed little interest in finding pretexts to weave the music and dancing into the structure of his plays, as was customarily done—at least superficially —in the contemporaneous comic operas. The program of *A Tin Soldier*, presented in 1886, even went so far as to call the songs "musical interruptions," and the list of musical numbers in the printed program included the "Faust Waltz," "composed expressly by Chas. Gounod for another purpose."

In *A Rag Baby* (1884), Hoyt for the first time assigned the stage direction to Julian Mitchell, who had begun his professional career as a bit player in *A Bunch of Keys*. Mitchell remained Hoyt's sole stage director from this time forward. Later he served briefly in a similar capacity for George M. Cohan, whose musical comedies were indebted even more, perhaps, to the example of Hoyt's highly localized and vernacular scripts and routines than to the more primitive conceptions of Harrigan and Hart. Toward the end of his career, Mitchell received the supreme accolade when Florenz Ziegfeld, Jr., engaged him to stage several editions of the *Ziegfeld Follies*.

Under Mitchell's guidance, one Hoyt comedy after another made its way into public favor, each distinguished by the author's special trademark, an initial indefinite article: *A Rag Baby, A Parlour Match* (which introduced the comic team of Evans and Hoey, and ran to less plot and more specialty dances and songs than most of the other pieces), *A Tin Soldier, A Hole in the Ground, A Midnight Bell* (in which Maude Adams made her debut, with no great fanfare), *A Brass Monkey* (the creature which suffers when the weather gets very cold), *A Contented Woman* (a satire on woman suffrage), *A Texas Steer, A Runaway Colt, A Black Sheep, A Dog in the Manger*.

Hoyt reached the zenith of his career with *A Trip to Chinatown*, which opened on November 9, 1890, and continued until it had exceeded by 47 performances the run record held for sixteen years by *Adonis*. *A Trip to Chinatown* chalked up a tally of 650 performances in its first engagement. A return booking in the spring of 1894 brought the total well above 700. In 1908, a sumptuous revival was staged by Ziegfeld.

In *A Trip to Chinatown*, Hoyt's technique of constructing an entertainment was indistinguishable from the helter-skelter method of the compilers of other farce-comedies. The plot dealt with the difficulties of two slumming couples in San Francisco who were trying to avoid each other but chose to visit the same restaurant. The story, however, was Hoyt's least concern. His responsibility to his characters ended when he had branded them with such names as Welland Strong, Ben Gay, Rashley Gay, Willie Grow, Norman Blood, Noah Heap, and Hoffman Price.

A *Trip to Chinatown* swept into national popularity to the tune of the still unforgotten song, first sung by Harry Conor:

> "The Bowery! the Bowery!
> They do such things, and they say such things
> On the Bowery; the Bowery!
> I'll never go there any more."

In the course of the run a second hit of almost equal proportions was added—"Reuben, Reuben, I've Been Thinking." The musical numbers were continually changed, and new specialty acts—such as that of Loie Fuller, making butterfly's wings of her skirts, with appropriate colored lights—were frequently added.

At least as late as 1896, A *Trip to Chinatown* was still being revised, as it filled a prosperous itinerary on the road. In that year an unidentified reviewer in the Boston *Transcript*, whose dim view of the music left him in an unmistakable minority, wrote: "Everyone knows A *Trip to Chinatown*. Pieces of this sort are generally furbished up at the beginning of each fresh season, to be sure. But the piece is still recognizable and as funny as ever. With the exception of an excellent burlesque on an operatic terzet, the songs seemed to us an unwelcome interruption of the bubbling fun and humor of the play. . . . To be sure, Mr. Hoyt's humor smacks far more of the barroom than of the drawing room . . . but . . . the use he makes of it has a conspicuous artistic side. But anything flatter than the songs is difficult to imagine." In justice to the author, it should be remarked that Hoyt, running true to form, endeavored to ward off criticism of the music by referring to A *Trip to Chinatown* as a "musical trifle."

With A *Trip to Chinatown*, farce-comedy approached its finish. Its possibilities were exhausted, for nothing more was likely to be achieved through the lackadaisical practices exemplified in the format of A *Trip to Chinatown*. Just around the corner were the new forms of musical comedy and revue, and already at hand was the Weber and Fields revivification of burlesque and extravaganza—fresh formulations that were to distinguish the new order from the old.

Subsequent farce-comedies accordingly came to seem like vestigial remains. Critics were invariably cynical about their merits, and the public, while it kept attending them for a while, turned more and more to fresher and better constructed types of entertainment. The reaction of the *Dramatic Mirror*'s anonymous reviewer to A *Straight Tip*, a farce-comedy with a book by John J. McNally and a compiled score from nameless sources, may be taken as typical of the growing disaffection toward such diversions:

"A *Straight Tip* made the public laugh, and it probably will put money in the pocket of its producer. There is no story to interest the spectator, but there is plenty of rough-and-tumble fun, catchy music, pretty girls, and . . . a number of old jokes which the farce comedian [James T. Powers] gets off in his best style." The high points of the show seem to have been the variety stunts of Powers, who offered a burlesque of the popular dancer, Carmencita—a butterfly dance—and performed one of his standard routines, a caricature of a woman doing her hair. Riotously funny Powers may have been, but those alone were hardly the materials to keep farce-comedy alive in the face of the competition soon provided by the Gaiety Girls and *The Passing Show*. Having made its twenty-five-year contribution, farce-comedy left New York for the road, and finally for oblivion.

VIII

COMIC OPERA:
The First Decade

THE ARRIVAL in America of the first Gilbert and Sullivan opera, *H. M. S. Pinafore*, in the 1878-1879 season, led to a veritable eruption of comic opera. Before Gilbert and Sullivan showed the English-speaking audience what it had been missing, comic opera had been largely the esoteric diversion of those who enjoyed hearing it performed in French or German. For fifteen years or more, French opéra-bouffe had been a source of special delight among connoisseurs, among whom it shared favor with Italian opera, and, in lesser degree, German light opera.

Maurice Grau, an indefatigable enthusiast for opéra-bouffe, gave New Yorkers in the late 1870s and early 1880s an opportunity to make an extensive acquaintance with this type of musical entertainment, in performances by visiting French companies, whose acting abilities and vocal endowments were considered the best the musical stage then offered. Lecocq's *Giroflé-Girofla* and *La Fille de Madame Angot* and works by Audran and Offenbach were regularly imported after they had been brought out in Paris, usually to the great satisfaction of Grau's discriminating but limited audience. The partisans of opéra-bouffe concurred in the opinion of the New York *Dramatic Mirror* that this Gallic form of musical pleasantry was superior to all others; the French composers alone, the *Mirror* argued, felt an adequate responsibility for keeping the plot and characterization of a good farce intact; and they were able to invest a piece with sparkling music and lively humors without sacrificing its dramatic features to the exigencies of musical art. Those who understood French of course took delight in the raciness of the dialogue, the double entendres, and the exposition of doubtful situations with a frankness that would have been inadmissible in an English-language libretto.

Thanks to the vitality of the works produced by French composers and librettists and to the high level of performance consistently maintained by Grau's imported companies, opéra-bouffe retained its popularity for more than twenty years. Even at the close of this period it did not die, for as the performance of foreign works in translation became more popular, many of the works of Lecocq, Audran, and Offenbach found their way into the repertories of English-speaking companies. Before 1879 and the Gilbert and Sullivan invasion, however, only *Giroflé-Girofla* and *Madame Angot's Daughter* had been given in English translation for those who were not attracted by Grau's French productions at Daly's Theatre.

German light opera was even less known to the English-language audience. The works of Marschner and Lortzing were given only for German-born and German-speaking audiences; and of the newer products of the Viennese operetta renaissance of the 1870s only von Suppé's *Fatinitza* had been brought forward in English.

The field was wide open, therefore, for *H. M. S. Pinafore* to reveal the joys of comic opera to a public whose sights were still leveled upon *Evangeline* and *Humpty Dumpty*. The spectacular success of *Pinafore* in England had led American managers to suspect that the nautical comedy would also win a cordial reception on this side of the Atlantic. Inasmuch as no reciprocal copyright arrangements existed with England at that time, *Pinafore* was the unquestioned property of anyone in America who chose to appropriate it. The race to get it on the stage involved the entire nation, as pirated productions were given in nearly every principal city from Boston to San Francisco, many months before Rupert D'Oyly Carte brought his company from England to acquaint us with the completely authentic version.

Boston stole a march on the rest of the country. The first American showing of *H. M. S. Pinafore* occurred at the Boston Museum (a theatre devoted to musical attractions, not the present fine arts museum) on November 25, 1878. Since the opera, like so many pieces of its time, was designed to be preceded by a one-act curtain-raiser, the evening began with Tom Taylor's non-musical farce, *Nine Points of the Law*. Three weeks later, however, Gilbert and Sullivan's *Trial by Jury* was substituted; this lampoon of Old Bailey has remained the regular companion of *Pinafore* up to our own day, and is so billed by the contemporary D'Oyly Carte company.

The success of *Pinafore* in Boston was enormous, surpassing the triumph of *Evangeline*, or of any other musical piece the city had ever seen. By August, 1879, no fewer than 241 representations had been given in Boston by a variety of companies, including one composed of child actors. (Juvenile *Pinafore* troupes were excessively popular for a season or two, and sprang up all over the country. There was also a Church Choir Pinafore Company.)

New York finally saw *Pinafore* in February, 1879, at the Standard Theatre, with Thomas Whiffen as the Right Honourable Sir Joseph Porter, K. C. B. The huge success of the production encouraged several other managers to get together competing companies, and all, in a measure, prospered.

Finally, more than a year after the first pirated performance in Boston, the D'Oyly Carte Opera Company deserted the Savoy Theatre in London long enough to undertake a month's engagement in New York, at the Fifth Avenue Theatre, beginning on December 1, 1879. Sir Arthur Sullivan conducted on the opening night, and W. S. Gilbert appeared on the stage as a sailor. Subsequent performances were conducted by Alfred Cellier, who himself was soon to become known as a capable composer of comic operas. By virtue of the distinction of its auspices, this authentic exhibition should have routed the pirated productions in disgrace. But it did not; the success of the D'Oyly Carte version was by no means as exceptional as we might assume it would have been, in view of the reputation the company has enjoyed for more than seventy years since that time. The audience and the critics found the performance satisfactory, but nobody found reason to praise it at the expense of the representation given ten months earlier at the same theatre.

In 1879, of course, there were no Savoyard purists capable of recognizing that the D'Oyly Carte company had exclusive access to the original orchestrations made by Sullivan, which are, as we now recognize, far finer examples of orchestral craftsmanship than the boiled-down or imitative scorings used by the rival companies and still used by touring Gilbert and Sullivan companies today. To be sure, odds and ends of the stage business invented for the English production gave new point and amusement to the book, but the force of these was lost in the general effect. A great personal success was achieved, however, by J. H. Ryley, as Sir Joseph Porter. He did not return to England with the company, but remained to continue his career in this country.

Gilbert and Sullivan and D'Oyly Carte were naturally deeply perturbed by the pirated performances of *Pinafore*, from which they received no royalties. When *The Pirates of Penzance* was ready for presentation, they determined that history should not repeat itself. Keeping their company in New York at the close of the month's engagement of *Pinafore*, they immediately—on New Year's Eve, 1879— gave the world première of the new piece at the Standard Theatre, relying on the British copyright law to protect their interests in London.

The Pirates of Penzance won acclaim from the critics, some of whom thought it superior to its predecessor. The public, however, did not quite recapture its earlier enthusiasm, and the run lasted only until March 6, 1880. Nor did any of the next four Gilbert and Sullivan operas, brought forward at an average rate of one a year—*Patience, Iolanthe, The Sorcerer,* and *Princess Ida* (written earlier than *The Sorcerer* but presented here later)—rekindle the *Pinafore* flame. All were well received and adequately supported, but the changeable public, having skimmed off the novelty of the Gilbert and Sullivan teamwork during the *Pinafore* craze, was eager to turn its attention in other directions.

Three elements accounted for the universal popularity of *Pinafore*—its wit, its workmanship, and its accessibility. The quips and rhymes and turns of phrase were really funny, surprisingly, outrageously funny; they are still funny today, and that is more than can be said of the jokes in *Evangeline* or *The Brook*. The high craft of both the librettist and the composer insured the full effectiveness of each individual conceit and thematic development; each lyric, passage of dialogue, song, and concerted number was a complete success in its particular way, and the audience was not expected to hunt out the good intentions behind professional inadequacy or incompetence. Words and music alike were written from the point of view of the audience; they were catchy and easy to learn, and fun to sing at home around a square piano in the evening. From *H. M. S. Pinafore* the American audience began to learn, whether it recognized the fact or not, the difference between hack work and first-class professional skill and integrity. Having sensed this difference, the public was now ready to listen to other works by first-class craftsmen, French and German as well as English, and to assume some responsibility for apprehending more complex musical and dramatic textures. Thus Gilbert and Sullivan won an audience not only for their own works in America, but for transatlantic light music generally.

With unprecedented vigor, the New York stage began in 1880 to devote itself to the presentation of almost every comic opera it could find. From the three principal sources —London, Paris, and Vienna—one comic opera after another was imported, fitted with an English translation (frequently of distressing crudity) and mounted as sumptuously as possible. The production of musical pieces quickly reached a volume that had never been known before. Indeed, the large-scale industry of musical production in New York dates from the discovery of English-language comic opera. Earlier, a season might bring forth a single *Black Crook* or *Around the World in Eighty Days*, but production was intermittent, and attractions appeared one at a time, usually at widely spaced intervals. But in 1880, in addition to the farce-comedies, burlesques and pantomimes we have already encountered, ten comic operas were produced; in 1883 the total rose to thirteen. A lean year then followed, with only six. But the triumph in 1885 of *The Mikado*, which restored Gilbert and Sullivan to the pinnacle of popularity, and the comparable success of *Erminie* restored the faith of managers and investors, and comic opera took a new and long lease on life.

The sudden rise of comic opera in the 1880s need cause no mystification. No other period in the nineteenth century witnessed so great a concentration of European talent in this field. Gilbert and Sullivan, in England, were turning out pieces at the rate of one a year. Offenbach and Audran, at the height of their glittering powers, were writing with ebullience and technical assurance. Viennese operetta had moved into its "classical" period, as the effervescence of French opéra-bouffe was added to the sentiment of the traditional Singspiel in the works of von Suppé, Millöcker, and the younger Johann Strauss. Never has the European musical stage been so amply supplied with composers of light music who possessed both artistic sensibility and sound musical and theatrical training. After the death of Offenbach, opéra-bouffe lost much of its sparkle. In the transition from Strauss to Lehár, Viennese operetta suffered a decline in intrinsic quality which was aggravated as Lehár later gave way to Stolz and the mechanical exploitation of *drei Viertel Takt*.

Many years were to pass before American-made comic opera and operetta could begin to hold its own with audiences accustomed to the competence and fecundity of Offenbach, Millöcker, and their contemporaries. Nevertheless, a few native products were fabricated and staged in the very first flush of the comic-opera craze. The initial experiment was *The First Life Guards at Brighton,* by J. S. Crossey, a Philadelphia composer of surpassingly slight talent. First presented in Crossey's home city in November, 1879, *The First Life Guards at Brighton* moved to Manhattan in January, 1880, where it was instantly reviled for its weak libretto and simple-minded music, and forced to close for want of patronage at the end of a fortnight.

The second comic opera of native composition, while far more professional in musical stature, was an equal failure with the public. Entitled *Deseret* (1880), it was composed by Dudley Buck of Brooklyn, the most noted Episcopal church composer in America at that time, to a libretto dealing with the Mormons. As churchgoers brought up on his *Festival Te Deum* will recognize, Buck was a well-educated, if appallingly academic, musician, head and shoulders above most of his colleagues in compositional technique. *Deseret* was an elaborate affair requiring a chorus of sixty, and manifesting the routine clichés of German conservatory style. Buck's temperament kept him from understanding the needs of the stage, and he was unable to keep his score from sounding churchy and deadpan. Recognizing the composer's prestige in ecclesiastical circles, one reviewer observed unkindly that "the length of *Deseret's* run will depend largely upon the liberality of these Brooklynites." Apparently church and stage did not mix, for the supply of friends of the composer and of W. A. Croffut, the librettist, ran out quickly, and *Deseret* left the boards twelve days after its opening.

Two other pitiful efforts made by American composers in the next two years may be brushed in passing, for the sake of filling in the record. *Elfins and Mermaids* (1881), with book and music by Charles Brown of Albany, N. Y., was terrible enough to be "unconsciously funny." *L'Afrique* (1882) was devised in amateur fashion by Wayman C.

McCreary of St. Louis, and performed by a cast as amateurish as the composer.

With *The Little Tycoon*, in 1886, American comic opera won its first modest toehold. Handsomely produced by Augustin Daly, its book and music were the work of an otherwise insignificant author, Willard Spencer. The sources of its success, unfortunately, lay largely outside Spencer's contributions to it, for it interested the audience more by its topical humor than by any intrinsic merits of plot or music. In a Philadelphia revival a year or two later, for instance, Digby Bell, who was not in the original New York cast, interpolated a topical song in ten stanzas, "What could the poor man do?", which was full of local allusions about the New Woman, "Billy" Penn, trolley cars, Napoleon, Trilby, and nearly every other subject people were talking about. The immediate influence of the Gilbert and Sullivan patter songs—particularly those in *The Mikado*—is obvious.

The Begum, described as a "Hindoo comic opera" and offered at the Fifth Avenue Theatre on November 21, 1887, marked the initial collaboration of Reginald de Koven and Harry B. Smith as composer and librettist. Despite the efforts of such adroit comedians as De Wolf Hopper, Digby Bell, and Jefferson de Angelis, it failed. The influence of *The Mikado* was again evident, this time in the oriental setting. But the book and lyrics did not fit the setting, and were described as "cheap wit of the variety or minstrel stage." De Koven's music scarcely attracted passing mention.

Far more shrewdly calculated than any earlier American comic opera was *The Lady or The Tiger?*, given at Wallack's Theatre on May 7, 1888, with a book derived by Sydney Rosenfeld from Frank R. Stockton's popular story, and with music by Julius J. Lyons, scored by Adolph Nowak, conductor of the piece. Hopper and De Angelis were again on hand, along with Maud Wilson. Conceiving the piece as a "spectacular lyric comedy," Rosenfeld concocted a libretto of more than the usual credibility. His promise to find a solution for the famous enigma at the end of the Stockton story was given tremendous publicity before the opening. Unhappily, the solution was something of a dud. When the door of the arena opened, a comic old lady (played by Mathilde Cottrelly) emerged. In other words, it was neither the Lady nor the Tiger; the Tiger had been poisoned by a court official who was himself in danger of the creature's jaws. The chief fault of the book lay in the fact that Rosenfeld spent two acts staving off all possible eventualities and enlarging a story that might have been told in about ten words. Hopper carried the main burden of the piece as well as he could, in his exuberant, noisy way. The music, however, lacked force, the orchestration was thin and primitive, and the entire score was wretchedly sung. But it lasted seven weeks—almost four times as long as any of the preceding American comic operas—and was even revived in 1892, with Della Fox, Hopper's leading lady in *Wang*, as the threatened heroine.

In view of the vise-like grip of "O Promise Me" upon the affections of the American people, *Robin Hood*, presented at the Standard Theatre on September 28, 1891, after an initial run in Boston, by the repertory company known as The Bostonians, would seem to merit respectful attention. But this opera, though it was the first genuine hit by an American composer and librettist and later proved to be the only durable work in Reginald de Koven's extensive list, bore little significant relationship to the past, present, or future of the popular musical stage. Its aspirations were basically operatic. Even when it was first produced, *Robin Hood* was thought to be "both in subject and spirit a light dramatic opera rather than a comic opera in the English sense of the term," though De Koven's share in it was considered "credit-able to his taste, if not to his originality." Except in the annals of the national box office, *Robin Hood* occupies no significant place in our story, for its stuffy manners led to nothing provocative in subsequent musical pieces—not even in those by De Koven and Smith.

Though *Fatinitza* had been given in English as early as 1874, the first Viennese work to profit from the new enthusi-asm for comic opera was not by von Suppé, or, for that matter, by either of the other top-ranking Viennese com-posers, Karl Millöcker and Johann Strauss, Jr. It was *The Royal Middy* (1880), an adaptation of *Der Seekadett*, by Richard Genée, now remembered primarily as a librettist for Strauss rather than as a composer in his own right. *The Royal Middy* was the first comic opera given under the man-agement of Augustin Daly, who quickly became one of the most active and reputable American producers of this form of entertainment.

Since it was inferior in musical quality, *The Royal Middy* demonstrated, by the warm response it received, a mounting interest on the part of the New York audience in the over-all effect of comic opera, rather than any musical discrimina-tion. The music was the weakest attribute not only of the piece itself, but also of the performance. Except for Cath-erine Lewis, none of the performers sang well. Ada Rehan, a newcomer who was soon to develop a large following, had little to do except look pretty. The production was lavishly staged and costumed, and was well provided with unusually attractive girls, who caused a stir when they appeared as a chorus of middies, wearing "trowsers." An inventive pro-duction number, presaging the Ninette de Valois ballet *Checkmate* many years later, represented a game of chess, with gaily dressed children as pawns, castles, knights, and bishops. Later in the year a second version of *Der Seekadett* was advanced in New York under the title, *The Sea Cadet*. Sydney Rosenfeld's slavish translation of the original German libretto served to prove that Fred Williams' free adaptation of *The Royal Middy* had greatly benefitted a stupid book. The only advantage of the second production was one the audience did not appreciate: as in the case of the D'Oyly Carte production of *H. M. S. Pinafore*, the composer's original orchestration was used.

Daly hoped to create a sensation with a second Genée comic opera, *Zanina*, which he presented at his theatre in 1881. Long before the opening, an energetic campaign of publicity whetted the public appetite for a glimpse of the nautch girls, six in number, who arrived in ample season, expressed their dismay at the American climate and the American diet to reporters who descended upon them in their hotel, and duly displayed their dances at the opening performance. From this remote vantage point, it is impossible to guess how authentic the art of the nautch girls may have been. In any case the entire audience, wholly conditioned to the extensions and elevations of French ballet, found the more restricted and floorbound movements of the little Indian dancers dull and uninviting. One critic wrote that their dance was "a monotonous, rhythmic movement of the hands and feet to the accompaniment of a drum and three-stringed sitarr. They are not pretty and their faces were disfigured by ugly ornaments. There was nothing improper, suggestive or licentious in the dance." Another reviewer commented that however much the snake dance may have charmed the snake, it did not charm the audience.

Ill luck hounded Daly's nautch girls. One of them fell ill shortly before the première of *Zanina*, and died a few days later. All the girls really suffered from the rigors of New York winter weather, and their complaints about their diet were based on grounds far more legitimate than a mere desire to supply newspaper copy. It was many a long year before any more Indian dancers were brought to this country; it was easier to provide counterfeit Oriental art, and the audience preferred it.

The Merry War (1883) was the first comic opera by Johann Strauss, Jr., to reach the English stage in this country. While the piece made a pleasing impression with its well-trained chorus of a hundred voices and its Japanese ballet (antedating The Mikado by two years), The Merry War did not create a major stir. The operettas of Strauss, indeed, stubbornly failed to achieve as much popularity as the products of von Suppé, Millöcker, Offenbach, Audran, and Gilbert and Sullivan. It is especially interesting to observe that no producer appeared to be interested in staging Die Fledermaus, which was to achieve a two-year run on Broadway more than half a century later, and which, from today's perspective, would seem to be the one work that might have catapulted Strauss to the fame we now feel he deserves.

The vogue of Vienna continued with Millöcker's The Black Hussar (1885), which achieved a run of 104 performances at Wallack's Theatre. An exceptional cast conspired with Millöcker's skillful score to make the piece a success. In it De Wolf Hopper, Digby Bell, and Mathilde Cottrelly sang a Gilbertian topical song, "Read the Answer in the Star," to which they constantly added new verses.

The greatest German comic-opera event of the 1880s, however, was the production of Genée's Nanon, which came to the Casino Theatre after runs of over 300 nights in both Berlin and Vienna (and, for that matter, a modestly successful engagement in German at the busy Thalia Theatre in New York). This time Genée, whose earlier music had been unimpressive, had provided a waltz serenade, "Anna, in Rapture I Come to Thee," which had become known all over central Europe, and instantaneously duplicated its European vogue in this country. The waltz appeared and reappeared again and again throughout the score of *Nanon*, and nobody ever got tired of it.

The production, one of the most forward-looking of its day, was conceived by Heinrich Conried, who later became manager of the Metropolitan Opera Association. In a sharp departure from the fashion of deploying the chorus in military drill formations (a technique habitually employed in the contemporaneous pieces of Edward Solomon), Conried sought to distribute the members of the chorus in a more naturalistic manner; he was one of the first to insist that chorus girls might be made to seem something more than brainless, identical mechanisms. Conried's imagination, along with the luxuriant investiture, caused *Nanon* to be described as a "sensual delight."

Sydney Rosenfeld, the translator of the book, had now popularized his style. The wooden treatment of *The Sea Cadet* was replaced by a sense of freedom that permitted him to introduce references to Henry Ward Beecher and Robert G. Ingersoll, even though the action of *Nanon* took place during the reign of Louis XIV of France.

Most of the French opéra-bouffes made known in English in the 1880s were bright but conventional formula pieces, attractive enough at the time, but without much interest to posterity. Audran's *The Snake Charmer* (1881) deserves mention because a young graduate of Tony Pastor's Music Hall named Lillian Russell made her first appearance on the comic-opera stage in this otherwise forgotten work.

It is one of the persistent ironies of the musical stage that the most popular attractions are often the products of composers and authors of inferior gifts. Opéra-bouffe provided a striking instance of this disparity between popular taste and the soberer judgment of posterity. While Offenbach's brilliant *La Vie Parisienne* drew only a lukewarm response in 1883, and *La Belle Hélène* was not given in this period at all, a piece called *Falka* rode to great success at the Casino Theatre in 1884. With music by an all-but-unknown composer, François Chassaigne, and an English book by a well-meaning hack named H. B. Farnie, *Falka* again demonstrated a truth already made plain by Genée's *Royal Middy* and *Nanon*—that the best productions, rather than the best compositions, are likely to become hits. *Falka* suffered from the perennial malady of comic opera books—a malady that continued, in later years, to afflict the books of musical comedies: All the good materials were used up before the beginning of the last act, which was weak and stale.

The tone of Farnie's adaptation was "of the street, rather than the drawing-room," and the fun, such as it was, lay in the contrived situations, the dialogue, and the well-executed farcical business—not, as in the best examples of Gilbert and Sullivan or Offenbach, in taut and witty plot construction or appositeness of the musical score to the dramatic situations and the idiosyncrasies of the characters. There was a tremendously intricate argument, confusingly full of military people. (A military plot, in the 1880s, provided an excuse for the ever-popular military drills by the chorus, and for masculine uniforms that left their legs in full view.) The stock characters were typical of the period, and suggested that comic opera, when conceived on the mundane level of *Falka*, was none too far removed from burlesque, despite its claim to a superior cultural intention. There were the fat, bald, red-nosed comic; the gypsy-dancer soubrette, with her tambourines; the dashing hero, with a handle-bar mustache; the buxom heroine, whose figure approached the hour-glass contour Lillian Russell was about to immortalize; the testy old man, easily duped; the ridiculous middle-aged fop; and the unlovely, strongminded maiden lady, of the Katisha type. The ladies of the chorus were mirrors of a fashion that was not approved by the *Dramatic Mirror*, which observed that they "would have looked very pretty if they had refrained from painting two inches thick with rouge, and from putting black under and on their eyelids, as if they were decorating a hearse." In the role of von Fulba, one of the memorable comics of the American stage, Francis Wilson, made his comic-opera debut, offering an impersonation that had "neatness, a peculiar dryness, and an unconscious and immense comic force."

Among the satellite English composers who owed their audience to the vogue for Gilbert and Sullivan, the most gifted was Edward Solomon, some of whose comic operas made enough of an impression to threaten the Savoy Theatre duo with important box-office competition. Solomon, who a few years later became the first of Lillian Russell's three husbands, introduced his talents to this country in 1881 with *Billee Taylor*, produced by the curious and short-lived partnership of Rupert D'Oyly Carte and Edward E. Rice.

With a story set in 1800, *Billee Taylor* provided an opportunity for the exploitation of archaic customs and fashions in dress that seemed as quaint to the 1881 audience as 1881 customs and dress seem to us today. The musical score, written with confident professional command, might be described as half way between *The Bohemian Girl* and *H. M. S. Pinafore* in style. The sentimental airs were afflicted with a mid-century, post-Mendelssohnian loginess (a little like the hymn-tunes of the period) which Sullivan was able to avoid. The nautical tunes (for *Billee Taylor* was naval rather than military) were considerably better, and had some of *Pinafore's* rakishness and bravado.

Upon *Billee Taylor* we must pin the responsibility—a grave one, when the stage routines of the 1880s are seen in retrospect—for popularizing those rigid and monotonous military drills which for a time eliminated nearly all dancing by the chorus girls from comic-opera performances. The chorus served as a mere utility, good for little except the construction of regular, foursquare group figures and rhythmic stepping. Certainly no noticeable effort was made to bring the girls into the development of the plot. Apparently this was entirely satisfying to the audience, however, for *Billee Taylor* ran for more than a hundred performances (an exceptional record for a standard-sized comic-opera production), reopened for a summer engagement at Niblo's Garden, and was revived in 1885 for Lillian Russell, who by that time had married its composer.

Solomon continued to produce comic operas as rapidly as his London contemporaries at the Savoy Theatre, though none of them were as good as those of Gilbert and Sullivan. After three mediocrities—*Claude Duval*, *The Vicar of Bray*, and *Virginia*—Solomon again struck pay dirt with *Polly, The Pet of the Regiment* (1885), produced by Rice without the assistance of D'Oyly Carte, who at that point was taken up with the imminent presentation of *The Mikado*.

Polly was the piece that turned Lillian Russell into a full-fledged star. In it she played a daughter-of-the-regiment role, and sang her way, as the press-agents would say, straight into the hearts of her audience. Polly Pluckrose, the lovely orphan child of a British grenadier who lost his life in the Ashantee War, was adopted by the 200th Hussars, and grew to radiant young womanhood under the protection of that gallant regiment. The plot was a remarkably hard-boiled variant on the conventional comic-opera triangle. Polly's two competing suitors were Private Mangle and Major General Bangs. With a worldliness as refreshing as it was rare on the comic-opera stage of the 1880s, Polly persisted in preferring the major general, who offered a more tangible recompense for her affections, until she discovered that Private Mangle was in reality a German prince. As soon as the truth came out, she promptly decided to marry the private.

Any integrity Miss Russell's characterization may have possessed was largely accidental. She designed her own costumes, or at least took credit for their design, and they were anything but simple and demure. And to make sure that she held her public in the hollow of her hand, she introduced into the second act the popular ballad, "The Silver Line," a sentimental ditty from the music halls, originally thrust into the context of Solomon's *The Vicar of Bray* by Marie Jensen in 1883, and forthwith appropriated by Miss Russell for use in both Gilbert and Sullivan's *Patience* and Offenbach's *The Princess of Trebizonde*.

To this day Lillian Russell remains one of the most deeply beloved and widely admired prima donnas of the American popular musical stage. Such latter-day celebrities as Marilyn Miller, Gertrude Lawrence, Ethel Merman, and Mary Martin have never received quite the same unbridled adulation; nor has any of them become the single, supreme, unchallenged symbol of all that was most desirable and most glamorous in her period.

"From early girlhood to the hour of her death," wrote Francis Wilson in 1922, "she moved in a court of beauty of which she was the undisputed queen." This beauty, which won her three husbands, the lifelong friendship of Diamond Jim Brady, and millions of advocates all over America, was combined with a temperament so generous that Lew Fields, after her death, called her "the dearest thing that ever was in show business."

Though she had little or no talent as an actress, she did not flaunt her beauty as a device to deflect attention from her dramatic shortcomings. She seemed almost unconscious of her physical endowments, apparently taking them for granted as gifts God intended her to preserve and cherish, but regarding them without vanity. Beyond argument, she was the best-dressed woman on the stage. She took her responsibility for the handsome and unblemished display of her expensive dresses so seriously that she bought substitute gowns of cheap fabric but identical color to wear at rehearsals, in order to preserve her wardrobe in complete freshness for the opening-night performance.

The daughter of an editor and a militant woman-suffragist, Lillian Russell was born in Cleveland in 1861. In spite of all feminist leanings, her mother recognized Lillian's exceptional beauty, and reared her with a full appreciation for her loveliness and a sense of her duty to protect it. With Lillian's naturally sweet face went an equally sweet voice, which her mother placed under the care of Leopold Damrosch, one of the leading musicians of New York, when the time came to begin serious vocal training.

Her sumptuous beauty alone might never have carried Lillian Russell to the summit of success if she had been a less capable singer. Already in 1880, when Tony Pastor introduced her to his Music Hall audience as an "English ballad-singer," her voice was admirably schooled. After her death, W. J. Henderson, the most exacting critic of vocalism in the history of the New York press, wrote in the *Sun*, "Her voice was a clear, full lyric soprano of beautiful quality, but entirely without warmth or variety of color." She developed steadily in vocal prowess, until in *Princess Nicotine*, in 1893, she ventured to sing eight high C's at each performance, seven times a week. After one performance Nellie Melba went backstage to chide her, saying, "No prima donna sings fifty-six high C's a week." If the cautious, calculating Melba disapproved of so rash a vocal expenditure, she nevertheless admired Lillian Russell greatly (perhaps because she herself was a similarly perfect, cool,

colorless singer) and remarked that she would have been
an ideal Marguerite in *Faust*.

In 1886, the year after *Polly*, Lillian Russell lifted to
prosperity another of her husband's works—*Pepita, or The
Girl with the Glass Eyes*. In addition to Miss Russell, the
cast included Chauncey Olcott, a fresh recruit from the
minstrel shows, who was to remain the most popular Irish
tenor of the American musical stage for nearly fifty years.
Pepita was the last piece in which Solomon and Miss
Russell were professionally associated. Shortly afterward,
their marriage was dissolved, and Solomon returned to England amid printed rumors that he had already possessed a
wife there at the time he married Miss Russell. Solomon's
name figured in American playbills once more before it
disappeared altogether. In 1889, *The Red Hussar* served as
a vehicle for the American debut of Marie Tempest, who
achieved more renown for herself than for the weak piece
in which she appeared.

Lillian Russell moved from *Pepita*, after it closed, into
another English comic opera, *Dorothy* (1887), which had a
highly successful run. An importation from the renowned
Gaiety Theatre in London, *Dorothy* was composed by Alfred Cellier, who conducted the D'Oyly Carte performances
of *H. M. S. Pinafore* and *The Pirates of Penzance* in New
York. The book was written by B. C. Stevenson. Cellier
shared in the polite tradition of Edward Solomon, and,
like him, imitated without essential originality the musical
style of Sullivan, displaying an educated, well-bred, solid
compositional technique. Stevenson's libretto was compli-
mented by high-thinking critics for its refusal to employ the
slangy diction characteristic of many American comic-opera
books and adaptations.

But both Solomon and Cellier, when all was said and
done, were scarcely more than pale counterfeits of the

master team of British comic opera. Any loss of prestige Gilbert and Sullivan may have suffered as a result of their two most recent efforts, *The Sorcerer* and *Princess Ida*, was recovered a hundred times over by the triumph of *The Mikado* in 1885. It would be difficult to say which of three pieces was the greatest hit of the 1880s—*Adonis, The Mikado*, or *Erminie*. But *The Mikado* is still full of vitality, half a century after the permanent disappearance of *Adonis*, and thirty years after the last big revival of *Erminie*.

D'Oyly Carte and the authors of *The Mikado* ought to have learned a lesson from their unhappy experiences with the pirating of *H. M. S. Pinafore*, but they did not. The first American performance of the Japanese opera was again an unauthorized one, in Chicago instead of Boston this time, on July 6, 1885. The producer was Sydney Rosenfeld, the translator of *The Sea Cadet, Nanon*, and other German-language comic operas. On July 20, Rosenfeld brought *The Mikado* to the Union Square Theatre in New York. It was allowed to play only one performance before it was closed by law. The legal difficulties were soon straightened out, however, and the production resumed its run on August 17, with Henry C. Miner as manager in place of Rosenfeld. It was an inept performance and was mildly received, though the work itself was favorably regarded, and Roland Reed won a personal success as Ko-Ko.

Two days after the reopening of the pirated Mikado—on August 19—D'Oyly Carte presented the official version, with John Stetson as his appointed American managerial representative. Sullivan did not arrive in time to conduct the authentic première, but came for a special gala performance on September 24. The production manifested the highest excellence in every regard. Accordingly, justice was finally done, for the D'Oyly Carte version ran for 250 performances at the Fifth Avenue Theatre, which had ample time to change its name to the Standard and back to the Fifth Avenue again before the engagement ended. All of the United States and Canada quickly went *Mikado*-mad. The rage for Japanese art, whose currency in England had prompted Gilbert's satire in the first place, swept the country. Nearly the entire text of *The Mikado* became household words; in due season the quips and lyrics were passed down from one generation to the next, and even today half the audience at a *Mikado* performance usually knows what the next line is going to be. Probably no other piece in the entire history of the American musical stage has settled so deep in the affections of thousands of perennial, unshakable devotees.

Judged on the merits of its book and music, the triumph of *Erminie*, the year after *The Mikado*, is inexplicable. Certainly the erudite H. T. Parker of the Boston *Transcript* found it so when it was revived in 1920. To him it seemed "a thin and pretty sentimental balladry, with high notes here and there, klinking little choruses, lightly running little ensembles." But there is no blinking the facts. Edward Jakobowski's "sentimental balladry" and "klinking little choruses" were listened to attentively by capacity audiences at the Casino Theatre for five months after the première on May 10, 1886. Contracts made before the opening then forced *Erminie* to go on tour; but within six weeks it was back to continue its run for ten additional months. Like the other major hits of the nineteenth century, it was revived repeatedly, usually with great success. By the end of the century it had established a total of 1,256 performances in New York alone.

Even Rudolph Aronson, the producer of *Erminie*, was taken completely by surprise. Shortly before the opening, he declined to buy the exclusive American rights for $500.

Subsequently, he claimed to have paid out $120,000 in royalties. We need not mourn his lack of foresight, however, for he reaped his full share of the benefits. On top of the Casino Theatre he built New York's first roof garden, and on pleasant nights during the run of *Erminie* presented an orchestra of thirty players "before crowds seated among blooming plants and green shrubs and flowing fountains."

Harry Paulton drew his libretto for *Erminie* from a nearly forgotten early nineteenth-century play, *Robert Macaire*. Originally devised in 1823 as a French melodrama, under the title *L'Auberge des Edrets*, the piece changed in its first Paris rehearsals from a blood-and-thunder tragedy to a comedy when its leading actor, Frédéric Lemaître, found himself unable to take it seriously. In its reoriented form, *Robert Macaire* traversed the theatre worlds of France, England, and America. Records of many performances in Greenwich Village and other downtown locations can be found in the early annals of the New York theatre. Years later, the story aroused the interest of Robert Louis Stevenson and William Ernest Henley, who wrote a joint version. Paulton's book for *Erminie*, however, did not undertake to borrow from Stevenson and Henley, but went directly to the historic farce. The plot, not worth recounting in detail, since it was not the source of *Erminie's* popular appeal, dealt with the adventures of two thieves, one dashing and brave, the other timorous and insecure.

The second act of *Erminie*, a ballroom scene done entirely in pink, was widely considered to be the most ravishing stage spectacle of the decade. The entire act was little more than a costumed ballad concert, ending with a dance. In rehearsal the scene was so spare that Aronson persuaded Jakobowski to interpolate a lullaby he had composed for an earlier, unsuccessful work. Sung at the première by Pauline

Hall, and on later occasions by Isabel Urquhart and by Lillian Russell, this lullaby became the most popular tune in the entire score.

Pleasing as it was, the pink ballroom scene would not have been enough to account for the first-rate success of a third-rate comic opera. It was the performance of Francis Wilson as Cadeaux, the timid little thief, with his tattered clothes and omnipresent valise, that raised *Erminie* to its otherwise undeserved pedestal in the hall of fame. As touching as George L. Fox, as inspired in the invention of comic devices as Bobby Clark, Wilson was one of the memorable comedians of the American stage. With the adroit aid of his partner, William S. Daboll, who played Ravennes (the character modeled after Robert Macaire), Wilson saw to it that *Erminie* never suffered a moment of letdown when he was on the stage.

A graduate of minstrelsy and stock-company acting, Wilson turned to the legitimate musical stage in 1880, appearing with Mitchell's Pleasure Party in a farce-comedy, *Our Goblins*, written by William Gill in the fashion established by Salsbury's Troubadours. Not long afterward, he acted in *H. M. S. Pinafore* on the West Coast, and in Strauss' *The Queen's Lace Handkerchief* in Philadelphia and New York. With *Erminie* the shape of his career was established once and for all. The Jakobowski operetta became the major fact of his life, and he appeared in countless revivals, forming his own *Erminie* company in 1894. His last appearance on the stage was with DeWolf Hopper in the 1920 *Erminie* revival.

On this last occasion H. T. Parker described the attributes of comic art that Wilson already manifested at the beginning of *Erminie's* career in 1886: "His bright eyes twinkled, out of a face that alarm and relief, self-satisfaction and self-depreciation, were constantly and comically traversing. He was a picture of comic dilapidation as he sprawled or slipped on the staircase, a picture of comic bewilderment." Lewis C. Strang, in a captivating volume of first-hand impressions, *Famous Stars of Light Opera*, names Cadeaux as by far the best of Wilson's parts, "consistent, well-elaborated, keenly theatrical, well-characterized, deceptively spontaneous, with nothing left to chance. He seems to have investigated the anatomy of merriment."

Instead of visualizing Robert Macaire's little friend in terms of Daumier's drawings, in which the artist drew upon the play for purposes of political satire, Wilson envisaged a Cadeaux who reminded old-timers of George L. Fox (who, as it happened, once played the role of Cadeaux, then known as Jacques Strop, in the original non-musical *Robert Macaire*). Apart from a surface resemblance, however, Wilson was not at all like Fox, who was essentially a jovial, rollicking, mugging clown, despite the element of pathos in his style. Wilson's comedy and farce were rooted in his sense of characterization. He achieved much of the force of his humor by the unerring consistency with which successive bits of business built up a rounded and believable character.

With *Erminie*, comic opera of the 1880s reached its climax. The next few years marked a period of general sterility, as though the musical theatre were taking a nap before launching into the new and exciting experiments of the middle 1890s. Three more Gilbert and Sullivan operas came along to relieve the monotony—*Ruddygore*, *The Yeomen of the Guard*, and *The Gondoliers*—but none proved to be another *Mikado*. The list of Viennese and German operettas was swelled by a variety of mediocrities.

One piece of some interest was *Castles in the Air*, the first comic opera by Gustave Kerker, a German émigré who established himself successfully in this country, and ultimately attained great fame from his music for *The Belle of*

New York. De Wolf Hopper, a rowdy comedian who maintained a long hold over a big popular audience, was starred for the first time in *Castles in the Air*, appearing opposite the vivid and petite Della Fox, who was shortly to share with Hopper the popular favor accorded the exotic *Wang*.

Just at the turn of the decade, *Poor Jonathan*, a Millöcker operetta presented in 1890, presaged the development in public taste the new decade was to witness. Though its music and many of its other features were shaped in the familiar mold of Viennese comic opera, *Poor Jonathan* was the first "dresscoat" piece—dealing with contemporary life and manners—to be staged at the Casino Theatre, the most fashionable home of traditional comic opera and operetta. Only the final scene, at West Point, allowed opportunity for the lavish colors and striking costumes which had always been considered a fundamental requisite of comic opera productions.

Poor Jonathan had a curious history. It was first produced in Germany, where its American locale at that time was thought to be the height of the exotic. Any resemblance it bore to life in the United States was purely accidental. The stage directions for the first act read: "Rubygold's plantation; happy darkies picking cotton along the Battery, New York." Since this scene could hardly be expected to elicit a favorable response from New York audiences, the setting was shifted, for local consumption, to West Point.

Lillian Russell was the leading lady in *Poor Jonathan*, a little out of her element in a piece which, unfortunately for her limited gifts, required a modicum of acting ability. Gustave Kerker was the musical director, and the stage director was Heinrich Conried.

The heaviest responsibilities of *Poor Jonathan* were carried by Jefferson de Angelis, who was by now fully established as one of the most popular comedians of the American musical stage. De Angelis had attained the status of a star by a long, hard route. Like most other comedians of his day, he received his basic training in variety, minstrel shows, and melodramas—largely in San Francisco. He appeared in the first San Francisco performance of *H. M. S. Pinafore*, though up to that time he had made his reputation as a Dutch comic, a species that was to become immortalized around the turn of the century by Weber and Fields, the Rogers Brothers, and Sam Bernard. In the course of a four-year tour (from 1880 to 1884) of Australia, China, India, and Africa, he developed his technique as a comic-opera comedian. Making his way finally to New York— where he had been only once before, briefly, as a youth —he found an opening with E. E. Rice's Surprise Party, in *A Bottle of Ink*. After a brief spell with W. A. Mestayer's combination, in *We, Us, and Company*, he was given his first big-time opportunity in Philadelphia, in *The Little Tycoon*. He next moved into the road company of *Ruddygore*, and from this point forward his career was assured. Though he had already appeared in New York in a variety of comic operas, *Poor Jonathan* was the first to bring him into major prominence. Three years later, in 1893, he took part in the first revue in the history of the New York stage, *The Passing Show*. In 1897 he produced one of his greatest successes, *The Wedding Day*, a comic opera in which he was co-starred with Lillian Russell and Della Fox. The later years of his career included an appearance as Ko-Ko in the memorable Shubert-Brady revival of *The Mikado* in 1910, with William Danforth as the Mikado, William Pruette as Pooh-Bah, Andrew Mack as Nanki-Poo, Fritzi Scheff as Yum-Yum, Christie MacDonald as Pitti-Sing, Christine Neilson as Peep-Bo (later played by Alice Brady), and

Josephine Jacoby as Katisha. His final appearances, in the late 1920s, were in two non-musical plays, *The Royal Family* and *Apron Strings*.

Without De Angelis' exceptional gift for characterization, which won praise even from the rock-ribbed Philip Hale of the Boston *Herald*, *Poor Jonathan* might easily have collapsed. Yet it was an important experiment in the direction of dramatic verisimilitude. Largely devoid of the elaborate dances, picturesque groupings, and effective military marches and formations that were the stock-in-trade of the comic operas at the Casino, *Poor Jonathan* rested its case on its plot and characterizations, and on its topical songs and concerted numbers. Breaking away from many of the expected conventions of comic opera, it paved the way for later musical comedies that adopted the informality of farce-comedy, yet strove to reach the better musical standard of comic opera.

Perhaps more important still, *Poor Jonathan* proved that the comic-opera stage, the sole field of operation of the most cultivated and craftsmanlike authors, composers, and performers of the light lyric theatre, could now make way for a piece that showed no concern for European royalty and nobility, foreign regiments and navies, or exotic, historical, and legendary scenes of far away and long ago. The validity of American life as theatrical subject matter was beginning to be apparent to the proponents of upper-level musical entertainment, as it had been from the first to the sponsors of burlesque and farce-comedy. When the top-grade authors and producers discovered America, the dawn of musical comedy was at hand.

IX

COMIC OPERA:
The Second Decade

THE MAJORITY like him very much; the minority detest him beyond endurance," wrote Lewis C. Strang of De Wolf Hopper in 1900. It must have been a large majority and a small minority, for Hopper had been one of the busiest comic-opera comedians of the 1890s, having reached stardom in the Gustave Kerker comic opera *Castles in the Air* in 1890. The fact that his success in New York was something less than triumphant partially justifies Strang's acid comment, for it was the road and not the metropolis that first gave Hopper his solid position in the American theatre.

His next piece, *Wang* (1891), was, however, quite as much of a hit in New York as on its elegant road tour in Wagner Palace Cars. (This trip is described in an illustrated

booklet entitled *De Wolf Hopper's Wagner Tour*, a title
that might lead the unwary to suppose that he went barn-
storming as Wotan and Hans Sachs.) *Wang* was followed
in quick succession by two more well-contrived vehicles,
Panjandrum and *Dr. Syntax*, which managed to keep Hopper before the public somewhere in the United States
nearly all the time.

Wang employed the petite Della Fox as its leading lady.
Whether in tights or in skirts, both of which the plot entitled her to wear, she was one of the most admired charmers
of the day. Time has dimmed her reputation, perhaps because her personal life was less colorful than that of Lillian
Russell; but she was no less effective a performer, quite able
to hold her own against Miss Russell's more buxom allurements and more operatic voice when they appeared together
in *The Wedding Day* in 1897. Though Lillian Russell was
the accepted queen of comic opera, Della Fox "had in her
day," according to Jefferson de Angelis' autobiography, "as
many women worshipers as Geraldine Farrar. It was nothing
uncommon to see fifty or a hundred women and girls wait-
ing at the stage door when she left the theatre." For the
"conscious buffoonery" and "classified mannerisms" of
Hopper her directness and simplicity served as an excellent
foil, and a good half of the success of *Wang* could be
credited to her.

A compound of familiar comic-opera materials with an
admixture of burlesque, *Wang* took place in Siam. "It might
equally well be laid in the interior of the dark continent,"
drily observed the *Dramatic Mirror*, which went on to say:
"The book is by far the better half of *Wang*. The score is
mediocre to a degree." For the book, the credit, if such it
was, went to the untiring J. Cheever Goodwin, who nearly
two decades earlier had collaborated with Edward E. Rice

in the early monument of burlesque, *Evangeline*. In the succeeding years, having broken off relations with Rice soon after the production of *Evangeline*, Goodwin had devoted himself to a long list of comic-opera librettos, all neatly cut and tailored for the class trade. Away from Rice he lost some of his feeling for the simple verities that gave *Evangeline* its peculiar validity, and he turned into little more than a high-grade hack. The book of *Wang* reached the summit of its wit when the regent of Siam remarked, "I don't reign, I sprinkle." Other word plays, we are told, "were equally good."

The composer to Goodwin's "syllabic gymnastics" was a fellow Bostonian, Woolson Morse. Except for *Cinderella at School*, produced in Springfield, Mass., in the late 1880s, and refurbished for New York purposes later on as *Dr. Syntax*, *Wang* was Morse's first important score. Trained in musical composition in Germany, he was one of the first wholly capable American comic-opera composers. Morse's talent so impressed W. S. Gilbert that he asked the American composer to become his collaborator after the split between Gilbert and Sullivan. Morse refused, however, and continued to compose pieces for New York production—many of them in conjunction with Goodwin—with the aid of the harmonium, at which he always wrote his music. The trouble with the score of *Wang* was not that it was incompetently written, but that it lacked freshness and originality in its musical ideas. Two or three pretty ballads and a topical song were all it offered to post-performance whistlers. Morse made little or no attempt to simulate Oriental color, except in the music for Wang's first entrance (on a full-scale imitation elephant) and for the wedding and coronation marches, of which it was said that for Morse "oriental equals loud cymbals plus cacophony." Another contemporary observer detected almost every kind of influence in the score, from Gilbert and Sullivan to the revivalist hymns of Moody and Sankey.

Wang was called an "operatic burletta" out of deference to the burlesque aspect that permitted Miss Fox to wear tights. But its conventions were those of comic opera, as was true of all Hopper's subsequent vehicles. His voice had been trained operatically, and his special talent was for a broad projection that required operatic singing and spectacular stage settings.

Almost exactly two years after the première of *Wang*, Goodwin and Morse provided Hopper and Miss Fox with their next piece, *Panjandrum*. It was described as an "olla podrida in two acts," as good a term as any for a work designed as a sequel to *Wang*. This time the Philippine Islands (a safe comic-opera locale, since nobody knew very much about the Philippines in 1893) provided the remote setting. The plot required Hopper to make his entrance with a toreador song, inasmuch as, "finding his sweetheart, Phiunta, has been attracted by the prowess of a matador, he resolves to regain her affection by himself fighting the bull." The resolution of the plot required a full evening: at the end of Act I, Hopper "returned to the stage tattered on the horns of a bull, after his expected victory."

A contemporary interview with Hopper's manager, Ben Stevens, gives some picture of theatrical finances in 1893. "Receipts for the first four weeks of *Panjandrum*," he reported, "have been $5,200 in excess of receipts of *Wang* during the first month at the same theatre. It may interest the theatrical profession to know how much *Panjandrum* cost. I will not give it in round numbers, but in exact figures —$23,870.86. I think you may say safely that that touches the topnotch of pecuniary investment in a light opera. I need simply say that *Wang* cost $12,600."

Edna Wallace Hopper, De Wolf Hopper's wife, was leading lady in *Dr. Syntax* (1894). The growing demand of audiences for comic operas with vaguely believable plots was reflected in the absence of an exotic locale, and in the comparatively tight construction of the libretto, which was based on Tom Robertson's play *Cinderella*. In a tradition kept alive today by the performances of Frederick Ashton and Robert Helpmann as the Ugly Sisters in the Sadler's Wells version of Prokofieff's ballet *Cinderella*, a school-mistress was impersonated in grotesque transvestite fashion, and engaged in a comic duet and dance with Hopper. The piece ended with a boat race between Harvard and Columbia, which "would have been even more exciting if Mr. Hopper had not explained in his speech before the curtain after the first act that Columbia would win in New York, but that Harvard would beat Columbia when he played Boston." Hopper was already displaying the penchant for curtain speeches that made it impossible, in later years, for his audiences to escape hearing him recite "Casey at the Bat."

Hopper next appeared in *El Capitan* (1896), a piece memorable chiefly because its music was written by John Philip Sousa. Six years earlier, Sousa, already director of the United States Marine Band in Washington, had ventured into the comic-opera field by making the orchestrations for *The Merry Monarch*, a vehicle for Francis Wilson, with music partly by Emmanuel Chabrier and partly by Woolson Morse. Though he had functioned as orchestrator on one or two subsequent occasions, *El Capitan* was his first complete score. Sousa made later efforts to win success in the comic-opera field, but his destiny lay with his marches.

Morse's willingness to take over Chabrier's opéra-comique, *Le Roi Malgré Lui*, and adapt it to American uses typified the belief in the supremacy of foreign comic opera which still prevailed in the early 1890s. Some years were still to pass before the output of competent native composers became large enough to render the contributions of Europe relatively unessential to Broadway's needs. The works brought to the United States in the 1890s reflected, however, a slump in the quality of the products of Parisian and Viennese composers. In Paris, Offenbach and Lecocq were dead, Audran was near the end of his career, and no younger composers had come along to replace them. The Viennese movement of the 1870s—the inspired combination of Offenbach's gaiety with the remnants of the indigenous Singspiel of Lortzing and Flotow—which had swept Johann Strauss, Jr., von Suppé, and Millöcker to the summit of popularity, had lost its energy. By 1900 all three of these composers were dead; and most of the pieces they wrote in the 1890s were inferior to their earlier ones. Not until *The Merry Widow* (1907) ushered in the neo-Viennese period of the Hungarians Franz Lehár and Emmerich Kalman did Central European comic opera—despite the contributions of the Moravian Leo Fall—really take a new lease on life in the United States.

One of the few French successes of this period was *Miss Hellyett* (1891), with music by Audran and a book by Maxime Boucheron, rewritten by David Belasco for the benefit of Mrs. Leslie Carter, who made her only appearance in a musical work in the leading role. Audran's *La Cigale* (1891), in which Lillian Russell sang, included new music by Ivan Caryll, soon to become in his own right one of the important composers for the American musical-comedy stage.

The supply of Viennese and German comic operas was larger, but hardly more distinguished. In the United States, for some incomprehensible reason, Johann Strauss, Jr., never attained during his lifetime the popularity he enjoyed in

Europe. When he came to America to conduct his dance orchestra in 1890 he enjoyed a considerable personal success, but *Die Fledermaus* did not fully capture the American imagination until more than forty years afterwards, and *The Gypsy Baron* never really has up to this very day. It is not surprising, therefore, to discover that the works of Strauss did not figure on the boards in the 1890s, despite his visit. Lovers of Germanic comic opera, whose taste seemed to be indestructible, were regaled instead by Zeller's *The Tyrolean* (1891), in which Marie Tempest was the star. It would long since have been forgotten if it had not shared a double bill with Mascagni's *Cavalleria Rusticana*, which was new to New York and created quite a stir. (This production of *Cavalleria Rusticana*, incidentally, is the earliest precedent in New York for the plan, now frequently proposed, of presenting grand operas for extended runs in legitimate houses.) Marie Dressler, whose subsequent career was associated with anything but German operetta, appeared in Charles Puerner's *The Robber of the Rhine* (1892). Hellmesberger's *Apollo, or The Oracle of Delphi*, in which Lillian Russell sang in 1891, was marked by a beautiful production, Grecian manners, little vitality, and an unending supply of waltzes. Slightly more distinctive was Adam Itzel, Jr.'s *The Tar and the Tartar* (1891), because Helen Bertram ventured to perform a barefoot dance. Stahl's *The Lion Tamer*, orchestrated by Sousa, owed its success to the low comedy of Francis Wilson, who played the title role. The one Viennese work of any special merit was Millöcker's *Poor Jonathan*.

American composers of serious stripe accelerated their efforts to compete with their foreign colleagues in the early 1890s, but most of their products were stillborn. Reginald de Koven attempted vainly to reinforce his *Robin Hood* success with *The Fencing Master* (1892), with Marie

Tempest in the cast. Edgar Stillman Kelley's *Puritania* dealt laboriously with Salem witchcraft, a vocation that was to return to the stage in grand-opera form in Charles Wakefield Cadman's *A Witch of Salem* (1926), produced by the Chicago Civic Opera Company, and Howard Hanson's *Merry Mount* (1934), produced by the Metropolitan. Salem witches do not seem to inspire American composers to their most inviting efforts, if the evidence of these three works may be regarded as indicative.

With so little to offer of either the homemade or the imported variety, comic opera slid out of favor considerably between 1890 and 1895. Its place in the affections of the public was largely usurped by extravaganzas and spectacle shows, which multiplied rapidly in that period of low production costs and ready spending-money. Such spectacles as those of the Kiralfy Brothers and Edward E. Rice had been a part of the American theatrical scene ever since *The Black Crook* set the original pattern of success. But they had been fairly widely spaced, on the assumption that not more than one or two at a time could succeed. Now, however, the rate of production was considerably accelerated, and for five years many of the interesting attractions of the New York musical stage were modernized variants of this elaborate form.

Chicago was a year late in opening its world's fair celebrating the four hundredth anniversary of Columbus' discovery of America, but the New York theatre was right on time. On May 15 of the appropriate year, 1492, an extravaganza with a book by R. A. Barnett and music by Carl Pflueger, opened, heralded by publicity calling it "a musical, historical melodrama." But its music was nothing to hum the next day; its historical data were open to suspicion, to say the least; and its melodrama, or drama of any kind, was minimal. Perhaps, on reconsidering, it is·wrong to dispose of its music so unfeelingly, for after the opening some additions to the score were made—pieces by Edward E. Rice, the producer of the show (and long ago the composer of *Evangeline*) and Anton Rubinstein. 1492 was no more than a big, undisciplined, spectacular variety show, with gaudy scenery and punning humor directly descended from that of *Evangeline*, but with none of the oldtime breathtaking Kiralfy tricks and transformations. Though it passed as an extravaganza, it was quite as much a burlesque, and in addition it was a mixture of French opéra-comique, standard comic opera, farce-comedy, vaudeville, local comedy, minstrelsy, and stereopticon views.

An especially successful extravaganza was *Aladdin, Jr.*, produced by David Henderson in 1895. The prolific J. Cheever Goodwin provided the book, which meant that puns were its main form of humor. The music, such as it was, came from W. F. Batchelor, W. F. Glover, and Jesse Williams. Hannah Boyd and J. J. Burke headed the cast, whose performances, like Goodwin's story, were largely subordinate to spectacular effects. One reviewer, awed by what he had seen, wrote, "Mr. Henderson is regarded as the most eminent contriver of this sort of entertainment in this country, and there are few who, having seen his former efforts and taken into account this, his latest, will dispute his position as head of the managers who work in this field." The story was that of Aladdin, moved to Peking and Egypt and told serio-comically, with magnificent scenes representing "the grand square in Peking, the exterior and interior of the mystic gardens of the imperial palace, and a place on the banks of the Nile."

"In the third act," reported the voluble *Dramatic Mirror*, "is seen the cascade of the Golden Glen and the resort of the Silver Storks, where is descried the amber ballet, one of the finest features of the show. In the last act, a barbaric pageant is unfolded. The final scene is one of transformation called 'The Birth of the Butterfly.' " As for the plot, "symmetries of happening [what reviewer would not love to have coined that expensive phrase?] are lost sight of among entertaining details that please one or another sense of the person who finds pleasure in such displays."

Even the newspaper writers of the day used theatrical terms ambiguously. Although one critic announced in 1890 that "burlesque as a satirical medium is dead," producers continued in many cases to call their pieces burlesques, and to incorporate "satirical"—or as we should say today, parodistic—elements. Perhaps the chief feature of burlesque—one it shared with extravaganza and with certain comic operas—was the use of women who were really not performers at all, but merely exhibitors. To any of us who might be spirited back to see a comic opera of the 1880s, this might seem a distinction without a difference; but there actually was a difference in social caste and stage routines between the burlesque chorus girls in their exaggeratedly revealing tights and the more decorous comic-opera girls, even when the latter wore abbreviated military costumes for their eternal drills and marches. Not that the burlesque girls were indecent; the road to Minsky's was still a long one. But the dress and convolutions of the girls in genuine comic opera were handled with what, for want of a more precise description, might be called better taste.

And so some pieces were described as burlesques and others, not greatly unlike them, as extravaganzas and comic operas. Moreover, the more elaborate farce-comedies of the early 1890s were often hard to tell from comic operas on the one hand and from burlesques on the other. To make matters worse, the term "musical comedy" began to appear in print with some regularity. If the reader is confused about these descriptive terms, so is the author; and so were the producers and critics of the day. It required the fresh viewpoint of Weber and Fields in the later 1890s to give burlesque a new specification and a new lease on life.

The last successful extravaganza of the 1890s was *The Man in the Moon*, presented in 1899 by George W. Lederer, who had now joined the front rank of musical producers. The music involved three well-known composers—Ludwig Englander, Reginald de Koven, and Gustave Kerker; the book was by Louis Harrison and Stanislaus Stange. The cast included Sam Bernard, who was later to crown his career as a Dutch comic with the *Potash and Perlmutter* farces, Marie Dressler, and Christie MacDonald, later one of the best-loved of all leading women. The extent of popular interest in *The Man in the Moon* was indicated by the production of a burlesque version of it, *The Maid in the Moon*, which soon opened on the Casino Roof, and by the fact that it prompted a sequel, *The Man in the Moon, Jr.*, for which De Koven provided the entire score (and which, like all sequels, failed to repeat the success of the original).

The mixed genre of comic opera-burlesque-extravaganza was somewhat painfully exemplified by *Tabasco* (1894), which deserves to be put on record because it was the only light-minded essay of George Whitfield Chadwick, the Boston composer who was, along with Edward MacDowell, the Aaron Copland or the Virgil Thomson of his day—one of the most respected and most frequently performed American musicians of two generations ago. After *Tabasco*, Chadwick must have dreaded comic opera as a burned child dreads the fire. The *Dramatic Mirror*, apparently overlooking the composer's high station, considered *Tabasco* "hardly worthy of serious mention. Of late, almost anything that contains musical jingles, slangy witticisms and a variegated assortment of coryphées and multi-colored costumes is styled a comic opera on the American stage. But it is time to call a halt, and give the style of entertainment to which

Tabasco belongs its proper classification. *Tabasco* is nothing more nor less than a musical hodge-podge of this, that, and the other."

The previous year, Hammerstein's version of *The Talisman*, a minor example of French opéra-comique, had introduced the elements of extravaganza more acceptably; but its lesson was wasted. In a period of skirt dances, barefoot dances of spring, and hefty high-kicking chorus girls, Hammerstein's attempt to revive French ballet as the *pièce de résistance* of *The Talisman* was ill-timed, even though his dancers substituted high kicks for some of their arabesques. The ballet of the Zephyrs and Bacchantes celebrating the rotation of the four seasons would have guaranteed the success of a production in the 1870s. But ballet was dead as dead could be in the 1890s, and only the innovations of the Ballets Russes twenty years later, interpreted for America by Gertrude Hoffman, reinstated ballet dancing—temporarily—in the esteem of American audiences. Fashions in dancing have always run in cycles in the American theatre. Successive exotic importations of the balletic variety have had to take their turn with all the vernacular dances that have worked their way up from variety and vaudeville, and with the more pretentious native styles, such as, in later years, the idealized ballroom dancing of the Castles, the modish pseudo-modernity of the Albertina Rasch girls, and the genuine modernism of Charles Weidman and Martha Graham. Even now, ballet is not a secure partner in musical comedy, and some recent productions have boasted proudly that they had none of it.

Out of the peculiarly meaningless welter of pieces spawned in what we nostalgically call the Gay Nineties, two other comic operas merit notice, for purely tangential reasons. *The Rainmaker of Syria* (1893), a German importation with music by Leo Fall, which remained open for only a few days, is the earliest production in connection with which there appears the term "angels," as a description of its misguided backers. A *Daughter of the Revolution* (1895), by J. Cheever Goodwin and Ludwig Englander, represented a new low in historical drama, for it made the mistake of taking its subject seriously, and actually contained a scene showing Washington crossing the Delaware. It is easy to see why George P. Scannell, writing in 1894, had already decided that comic opera had declined in favor of more exhibitionistic musical shows.

The one really unique and unclassifiable item of the mid-1890s was an unbelievable entertainment called *Hamlet II*. Given in the guise of burlesque, the play combined Shakespeare's poetry with "the language of the Rialto with a speed and dexterity as amusing as it is clever." The hero, Laertes, Rosencrantz, Guildenstern, and Osric were all girls in tights, and Hamlet danced a skirt dance.

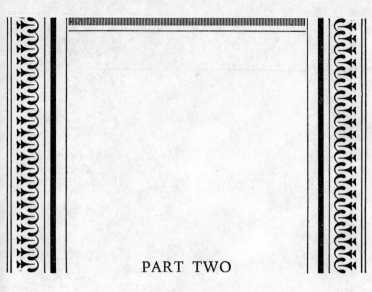

PART TWO

1908-1925

THE GAIETY GIRLS, THE PASSING SHOW,
AND WEBER AND FIELDS

THE TURN OF THE CENTURY

THE MERRY WIDOW AND THE ZIEGFELD FOLLIES

BEFORE AND DURING THE FIRST WORLD WAR

A NEW ERA

NEW ART AND OLD FORMULAS

THE POST-WAR REVUE

MUSICAL COMEDY FROM 1919 TO 1925

X

The Gaiety Girls, The Passing Show, and Weber and Fields

CREATING a tidal wave of enthusiasm comparable only to that rolled up a generation earlier by Lydia Thompson and her bleached blondes, the Gaiety Girls disembarked in New York in the late summer of 1894. George Edwardes, the manager of the Gaiety Theatre in London, presented his English charges at Daly's Theatre on September 18, 1894, in a so-styled comic opera, A Gaiety Girl. But it was not A Gaiety Girl which "became the talk of the town" and kept the piece running until it had to leave because of the players' commitments back home in England. It was the Gaiety Girls themselves, who now occupy a special page in the theatrical memory book along with their American successors, the Florodora Girls and the Follies Girls. An audience jaded by the standardized come-ons of padded burlesque queens and empty-headed comic-opera chorus girls performing empty-headed drills fell wholeheartedly in love with the vivacity, the superior attractiveness of face and figure, and the good breeding and grooming of the pert visitors. Unlike the sirens of Lydia Thompson's troupe, the Gaiety Girls moved the entire genus chorine one step up the ladder toward the position of respectability and social acceptance musical-comedy girls enjoy today.

George Edwardes was one of the great showmen of his time. The London theatre to whose name he brought immortality was built in 1868. Under the first manager, John Hollingshead, the Gaiety was at first devoted to a variety of attractions. The opening bill offered a one-act operetta, a comedy-drama, and a short extravaganza with a book by W. S. Gilbert, who had not yet entered into partnership with Arthur Sullivan. In the first five seasons alone, Hollingshead presented a miscellaneous assortment of some 150 pieces (which meant about fifty complete bills)—comedies, dramas, burlesques, and comic operas. In 1876, stimulated by the example of Lydia Thompson, who had popularized the full-length burlesque in England, Hollingshead turned his theatre over to that form of entertainment exclusively, beginning with *Little Don Caesar*. He improved on the quality of Miss Thompson's productions, and engaged performers whose abilities were sufficient to build and hold a loyal following.

In G. G., a book of memoirs, George Grossmith—a later manager of the Gaiety—recalls these halcyon years in connection with his decision to try a revival of old-fashioned burlesque there in 1921:

"Why not again put the Gaiety to the use for which it was

built? Burlesque. . . . [Grossmith's nostalgia carried him away from the facts; the Gaiety was not actually built for burlesque, but took it on as an acquired characteristic.]

"Relight the 'Sacred Lamp'! The idea kept me awake for nights. . . . Burlesque . . . I doubt if the description were applied to a new production today whether ninety-nine per-cent of playgoers would know what sort of entertainment they were invited to see. In America the term had become attached to a cheap and coarse type of continuous vaude-ville. The old burlesque of the Gaiety, Strand, and the Avenue and a few other theatres was the predecessor of musical comedy and revue—much like the English panto-mime minus the harlequinade and fairy element. In my boyhood its reigning stars were Edward Terry, Nellie Far-ren, Kate Vaughan, Fred Leslie, Florence St. John, Arthur Roberts, Charles Danby, Millie Hylton and many others. Fred Leslie was in those days what Jack Hulbert is today. Nellie Farren, though entirely different in method and per-sonality, was the prototype of Gracie Fields. The play con-sisted of a musical and rhyming travesty on some well-known romance, play, opera or legend, often with a punning title such as *Faust and Loose*, *Knife and Falka*, or else *Little Jack Sheppard*, *Carmen Up-to-Date*, followed by *Cinderella Up-Too-Late*.

"The hero was always played by a girl, and the chorus, like the hero, were mostly clad in tights. The comedians wore costumes and wigs and almost inevitably red noses."

For the record, Grossmith's "new old burlesque," called *Faust-on-Toast*, was a flat failure in London, even with Jack Buchanan in the cast. The rhymes and puns irritated the audience, and the girls looked "hideous" in their tights and high boots.

The Gaiety Theatre was always up-to-date, whether with its *Carmen* or with its swiftness to install arc lights (in 1878) and incandescent bulbs (in 1879), improvements with which it set an example for all other London theatres. When Fred Leslie died and Nellie Farren fell ill and there were no reigning favorites to replace them, George Edwardes, now the manager, determined to strike out on a new course. He eliminated the red-nosed comics and the girls in tights, but retained the informality of burlesque presentation. He festooned a comic-opera plot with embellishments and variety acts, in the fashion of the American farce-comedies. With shrewd directorial skill, he brought order out of chaos, gave his mélange a production that was "spirited, tasteful, and almost recklessly elaborate," and in 1893 offered to the public what he called a "musical comedy," *A Gaiety Girl*. The application of the term "musical comedy" to a modernized, dressed-up, popularized variant of comic opera was not, however, Edwardes' invention. A piece of similar plan but more moderate scope, *In Town*, had been given at the Prince of Wales Theatre a year earlier.

If any single moment can be elected as the moment of the birth of modern musical comedy, this was it. American farce-comedy, from its humble beginnings with Salsbury's Troubadours, had grown up and, so to speak, taken a trip to England, where it entered into a liaison with British comic opera and burlesque. *A Gaiety Girl* was the result of that union; she was part English and part American in parentage. When she came to this country in 1894, the American audience recognized her, despite the heavily British strain in her make-up, and took her to its heart.

In 1903 the old Gaiety closed, and a new Gaiety was opened in London with *The Orchid*, in which, as always, the chorus quickly became famous for its beauty. But by then, we no longer needed to import all the principal Gaiety productions, though *The Orchid* was given in America in 1907. Our own musical comedy was firmly and permanently established. We were beginning to have our own librettists, our own composers (most of them, to be sure, still European-born), our own interests; and American musical comedy had started off blithely down the highway that led to *Show Boat* and *Of Thee I Sing*, *Pal Joey* and *Oklahoma!*

When *A Gaiety Girl* reached New York, the critic of the acerb *Dramatic Mirror* was not gifted with prescience as to the historic role the piece was to play in the development of the American musical theatre. For him, it was "really an indefinable musical and dramatic mélange," containing "sentimental ballads, comic songs, skirt-dancing, Gaiety Girls, society girls, life guards, burlesque, and a quota of melodrama." Not much, in all truth, could be said for the plot, though it was adequately functional. Blanche Massey appeared as the particular Gaiety Girl of the title. She was accused of stealing a diamond comb, but was ultimately able to clear her character and marry a handsome young life guard. The rage for skirt-dancing, initiated by Loie Fuller several years earlier, remained unabated, and Cissy Fitzgerald won acclaim for a dance tantalizingly described as "somewhat sensational."

Both the veteran Edward E. Rice and the somewhat younger Augustin Daly were quick to profit from the example of *A Gaiety Girl*, and to bring forward productions marked by the same light, sophisticated tone and style. In 1896, Daly staged a musical comedy entitled *The Geisha*, which, despite its Oriental title, was topical in content. In the latter part of its run it employed the services of Isadora Duncan, who had not yet discovered ancient Greece and Beethoven's Seventh Symphony. The music was by Lionel Monckton and Sydney Jones.

Rice followed with *The Girl from Paris*, for which he imported a company of British players. As a variant on the skirt-dance theme, now becoming a bit frayed around the edges, he presented Mabel Clark in a novelty, a "toe dance in long skirts." *The Girl from Paris* served to initiate the American reputation of Ivan Caryll, who became one of the popular composers of musical comedy in this country for upwards of three decades.

Daly tried to duplicate the success of *The Girl from Paris* in 1897 with *The Circus Girl*, another London production from the Gaiety, with a score by Caryll and the equally gifted Monckton. Daly made a move in the right direction by using an American cast instead of importing British performers, but the essentially English genre of the piece rather thwarted the American players. The prize comic scene was not written by the librettist, James T. Tanner, but was interpolated by James T. Powers, who convulsed the audience with his sketch of a man trying to see around, above, or under the enormous women's hats that were in fashion.

Another Daly production brought over from the Gaiety was *A Runaway Girl* (1898), also by Caryll and Monckton. Though the materials were slender, the expertness of Daly's staging made it a go. Even more than Rice—who had carried on with such British pieces as *The French Maid* and *Monte Carlo*—Daly was able to capture the light touch, the brisk direction, and the eye for a pretty chorus line that were the Gaiety's chief enduring gifts to the American musical-comedy stage. Rice was never really sure of himself in the new genre, and kept revising his productions after they had opened, in the hope of sharpening them up and extending their runs. Daly possessed the outlook of a modern producer, and made sure that all was well before the curtain went up on opening night.

Actually, burlesque was more Rice's métier than the new musical comedy. None of his efforts in the new field matched the success of his final burlesque, *Little Christopher Columbus*, which he offered to the public in 1894, less

than a month after the arrival of the Gaiety Girls. Even this
attraction indicated Rice's new preoccupation with things
British, however, for unlike his earlier burlesques, *Little
Christopher Columbus* was not of his own devising. It
was a London product, with a score by Caryll, to which Rice
added, for New York consumption, some items by Gustave
Kerker. The *Dramatic Mirror* gave a thumbnail sketch of
Rice's mode of production:

"It is characteristic of Mr. Rice's methods throughout.
There are gorgeous costumes and sumptuous scenery. There
are pretty girls and shapely limbs in the chorus. There is an
abundance of action and tableaux, and everybody bursts out
in song and in dance on the slightest provocation." Not
much, in fact, of the original London format seems to have
remained in *Little Christopher Columbus* after Rice had
indulged his predilection for revising and tinkering.

With comic operas, extravaganzas, and burlesques all
bursting at the seams from their eagerness to cram in the
variety entertainment that the public liked, it was inevitable
that some producer should hit on a formula that would entitle him to bring variety to Broadway without the traditional encumbrance of a plot. Neither in the 1890s nor
since has the theatregoing public been willing to concede
(except in a few rare cases like the wartime *Priorities of
1942*) that outright vaudeville or music-hall bills warrant
first-class theatrical status or first-line prices. A replica of one
of Tony Pastor's variety shows, however engaging it might
have been in its proper setting, did not belong in a legitimate
house. Variety was variety and theatre was theatre. Yet the
musical-comedy public, with sublime illogic, demanded a
dressed-up, thinly disguised variant of the very entertainment it would not accept as top-grade without the dress-
ing-up and the disguise.

The magic name of Paris came to the rescue. A vogue

had set in there for topical entertainments called "revues," containing satires upon the fashionable life of the city, with specialty acts and choruses of pretty girls interlarded. Would the same device work in New York, as a framework for a diversified show without a plot? That remained to be seen: The Paris audience was more sure of itself, more formed in its tastes, closer and tighter and more specialized in its gossip. The entire audience could be expected to react more or less alike—to laugh at the same things, and to be scandalized by the same things. The New York audience was less attuned to subtleties, and infinitely less uniform in its tastes and attitudes. Moreover, the principal Broadway attractions had already begun to depend heavily on the trade of out-of-town visitors. Could a tourist from Syracuse or Cincinnati be expected to enjoy sketches and jokes lampooning a city he did not live in, whose ways were strange to him? The fate of a French-style review (the English spelling was used at first) obviously lay in the hands of the gods; but it was a gamble worth taking.

And so, on May 12, 1894, the Moorish interior of the Casino Theatre—diagonally across Broadway from the southeast corner of the Metropolitan Opera House—sheltered an elegant and knowing audience which had come to see The Passing Show, the first American example of the kind of show that later came to be known as a revue. Good talent went into the production, which had a score by the capable Ludwig Englander, now on the swift upgrade as a theatre composer, a book by the experienced Sydney Rosenfeld, and a cast including Adele Ritchie, Johnny Henshaw, and Paul Arthur. It was a long, loose, poorly organized affair, but it succeeded with its audience on the timeworn, and sometimes risky, principle of providing a little of everything, so that nobody could fail to like something in it. There were imitations of well-known actors, ribs of contem-

orary plays, and jibes at a nameless prima donna, "whose
repertoire will be *Faust, Faust*, and after which *Faust*."
This was the period in which Gounod's opera was so popular that the Metropolitan was known as the "Faustspiel-
haus.") Lucy Daly and "a dozen colored youths" submitted
a plantation dance like that in *Princess Nicotine*" (a comic
opera of the moment); Gus Pixley demonstrated "his original manner of walking with his head near his heels"; Mabel
Stephenson told "her familiar stories about Jonah, Daniel,
and the bear." Comedy was furnished by the Tamale Boys;
muscular empathy was excited by the Acrobatic Burlesques
of the Amazons; and the usual response, presumably, was
stirred by Living Pictures and by a "Divertissement on
L'Enfant Prodigue," a brush with art which was made
palatable by the Parisian—i.e., risqué—attire of the dancers.
New York took all this to be something out of the ordinary, though the same diversions, in a somewhat less costly
frame and without the Parisian reference, could be found
wherever vaudeville (as it was coming to be called) and
burlesque sketches were the order of the evening. The
Casino thrived on its first review, and offered another one,
The Merry World (this time anachronistically billed as a
burlesque) in 1895. The formula was the same, and the performance had the help of Dan Daly and David Warfield,
both able players, but the piece lasted only a month. The
third attempt at the Casino, *In Gay New York* (1896), succeeded in spanning the summer, with Warfield, Virginia
Earl, and several other veterans of *The Merry World*. Gustave Kerker wrote the music for *In Gay New York*, and
performed the same service for the fourth Casino summer
review, *All of the Town*, which had a four-month run in
1897. This last piece was hung on a thread of plot involving
the theft of a mermaid from the Aquarium, and it leaned
heavily upon caricatures of familiar figures about town. The

1898 review was known as *Yankee Doodle Dandy*, and fo
the third time Kerker provided the music. The company c
The Merry World had remained something of a fixture unti
now; Edna Wallace Hopper and Thomas Q. Seabrook, however, were new faces in *Yankee Doodle Dandy*.

All of the Casino reviews were devised as hot-weather entertainment, and the house reverted to standard comic
opera and musical-comedy attractions throughout the res
of the year. It was many years before the association between revues (as the word was spelled after the first fev
years) and hot weather ceased to be taken as inevitable
Years later, the *Ziegfeld Follies*, the Shubert *Passing Show*
George White's Scandals, and the *Earl Carroll Vanitie*
continued to be launched in the late spring and early summer, on the apparent assumption that resistance to sucl
frivolities was at its lowest ebb in that season.

In 1898, an autumn review, *In Gotham*, was staged afte
the pattern of the Casino shows, by Coster and Byles. The
were, however, second-rate producers, and their offering wa
a poor man's *Passing Show*, with an old-fashioned burlesque
show olio bringing all the performers on at the end, one b
one, and with the encumbrance of a stupid bit of farce
comedy plot alleging that Rip Van Winkle had come to lif
in 1899, and was moving all over town, accompanied by a
Irish lawyer, in the attempt to prove his identity. Obviousl
Coster and Byles missed the point of the true review, anc
were merely trying to pass off old burlesque and farce
comedy routines in a new guise. Neither *In Gotham* nor it
successor of 1899, *Round New York in Eighty Minute*
(which was notable only for the participation of James J
Corbett in a prize-fight scene), contributed to the progres
of the review. Meanwhile, the Casino, running out of eithe
ideas or patronage, did not continue its series past the tur

of the century. It was a good start, but an abortive one. Not until the Winter Garden opened in 1911 did the review come back to life. For more than a decade it was kept from sight by the more adroit and homelier burlesque-extravaganzas of Weber and Fields, by the growing number of musical comedies, and by the renewed enthusiasm for Viennese comic opera initiated by *The Merry Widow*.

The great new institution of the late 1890s was Weber and Fields' Music Hall, opened by the comedians in 1895. Joe Weber and Lew Fields had grown up together. As boys of eight they had already worked out their first routine, an Irish-comedy act. They were all of sixteen when they obtained their first professional job, in 1884, with the Ada Richmond burlesque company at Miner's Bowery Theatre. Though the boys at that time preferred Irish comedy, they were hired for a Dutch knockabout act—low comedy and horseplay, with a German-English dialect thick enough to cut with a knife. Fields was tall and fairly thin; Weber was short, and as time went on he became exceedingly fat. From their first engagement in burlesque they remained faithful to their Dutch-comedy characters, and it was in this guise that they appeared a decade later in their own productions at their own Music Hall.

Like Tony Pastor thirty years before, Weber and Fields wanted their enterprise to attract the steady patronage and long-term support of the family trade. Though their sketches and dialogue were rough-and-ready, they were never dirty; and the girls of the Music Hall Beauty Chorus, which was thought to live up to its name, refrained from displaying themselves in a prurient manner. Lew Fields, in reminiscences quoted by Bernard Sobel in his entertaining book *Burlycue*, maintained that "we never went back to burlesque"; but the Music Hall shows were in very fact burlesques with the features eliminated that might displease the good folk whom the partners sought to attract to their theatre.

"The Weber and Fields Music Hall shows had girls, but we always avoided dirty material," Fields said. "We had a regular book that was legitimate burlesque of some New York hit such as *The Christian, Heart of Maryland,* or *The Messenger Boy from Mars.* Our first acts were originally written by Edgar Smith and Joseph W. Herbert, and once we were started on travesties we never went back to burlesque. Our company, as everyone knows, included such stars as Lillian Russell and Fay Templeton. Our shows were clean enough for women."

Fields has hinted at the format of his travesties, which was partly borrowed from the structure of the burlesques on which he frowned. The first half of the evening was given over to the travesty itself, more frequently based on a non-musical play than on a current musical hit. The bills changed frequently, and the meaningless titles along with them, but the plan was unchanging. The second half of the performance amounted to an old-fashioned olio, with the performers coming out singly and in combination to offer their song, dance, and comedy specialties, and with a finale involving the girls and the whole company. It was not until Miss Russell appeared at the Music Hall for the first time, in *Whirl-I-Gig* (1899), that the olio was abandoned, in deference to the status her presence conferred upon the bill. While the appearance of Miss Russell was a credit to Weber and Fields, it seems to have been less of one for her, inasmuch as she suffered "a let-down in her style." Be that as it may, from the time of her association with their company, Weber and Fields allowed their shows to rest on their intrinsic merits, without an old-fashioned pendant of scattered variety acts.

The career of the Music Hall under their joint management lasted only nine years, for in 1904 Weber and Fields separated. They renewed their association on the Broadway stage in 1911, when, in a brief flash of their former glory, they achieved a run of 108 performances with their "jubilee revival" of the old type of extravaganza, an entertainment called *Hokey-Pokey and Bunty Bulls and Strings*. (The second half of the title was a parody of Graham Moffat's current comedy hit, *Bunty Pulls the Strings*.) Lillian Russell came back for the occasion, and William Collier was also in the cast. The next year they tempted fate with a less successful sequel, *Roly-Poly and Without the Law*. Their last association in a musical piece, after a lapse of six years, took place in Philadelphia in 1918, in *Back Again*, which they did not bring into New York.

Though they lived to see their project outmoded by changing times and tastes, Weber and Fields made an endearing contribution to the popular musical stage. After the death of Lew Fields in 1941, the New York *Times* carried an affectionate and nostalgic editorial, which must have been written by someone who remembered them in their day of glory:

"Lew was long and Joe Weber was short. They grew up together as if by agreement and for comic effect. Lew and Joe may be said to have learned to act before they felt steady on their legs. Their fun was simpler and heartier than ours.

"You would be bored to read the book of their once famous game of pool or burlesque bank—one finds in some of their scenes such properties as a cigar in the mouth of a bust, and a pig in a canary's cage—those derby hats, like shallow little shells, that tuft of chin beard, those checked suits audible afar were irresistible.

"In their burlesque plays they did finer work and may be said to have anticipated the revue. In the town of their time, their theatre—was it our first little theatre?—was an institution, a temple of drollery, a place where it was 'right' to go, a sight and sound of New York. 'Weber and Fields' was a landmark."

A few footnotes need to be added to the account of the 1890s. There was *The Belle of New York*, Gustave Kerker's first resounding success, a rather conventional cross between comic opera and musical comedy, which for some reason enjoyed greater success in London than here, and was subject to repeated British revivals until as recently as 1940. Apparently the topical allusions to New York life never became dated in London, and retained a flavor as characteristic and exotic as that of a gangster moving picture.

There was also an otherwise obscure musical comedy, in 1897, called *The Good Mr. Beth*, in which "a cinematograph played an active part in the last act." Had the producers been able to gaze into the future, they might have suppressed the satanic invention, which was one day to threaten the entire theatre business, and to rob it of nearly all the road, leaving New York an island of the legitimate theatre in a sea of motion-picture palaces.

The year 1899 also saw the last nail driven into the coffin of musical farce-comedy. Though *My Innocent Boy* was judged to be "one of the best farce-comedies in a long time" (there had been fewer and fewer of them, ever since 1890), it was able to stay open for only a week. Thereafter, nobody was tempted to call a musical piece a farce-comedy, and the genre was officially dead, after twenty years of useful service.

Negro performers finally made the big time, though rather tentatively, in two musical comedies in 1898, A *Trip to Coontown* and *Clorindy, the Origin of the Cakewalk*. The first of these was a short-lived and unimpressive piece. *Clor-*

indy, however, brought Will Marion Cook before the public as a composer, and might have brought Paul Laurence Dunbar into prominence as a librettist if nearly the entire libretto had not been eliminated before the show was finally produced. It was Edward E. Rice who finally, rather to his surprise and somewhat against his will, found himself sponsoring *Clorindy* on the Casino Roof.

In an excerpt from his autobiography published in *Theatre Arts*, Cook gave a vivid account of the tribulations and ultimate triumph of *Clorindy*:

"I went to see Ed Rice, and I saw him every day for a month. Regularly, after interviewing a room full of people, he would say to me (I was always the last): 'Who are you, and what do you want?' On the thirty-first day—and by now I am so discouraged that this is my last try—I heard him tell a knockabout act: 'Come up next Monday to rehearsal, do a show, and if you make good, I'll keep you on all week.'

"I was desperate. . . . On leaving Rice's office, I went at once to the Greasy Front, a Negro club run by Charlie Moore, with a restaurant in the basement managed by Mrs. Moore. There I was sure to find a few members of my ensemble. I told them a most wonderful and welcome story: we were booked at the Casino Roof! . . . That was probably the most beautiful lie I ever told.

"On Monday morning, every man and woman, boy and girl that I had taught to sing my music was at the Casino Roof. . . . Luckily for us, John Braham, the English conductor of the Casino orchestra, was a brick. And, still more luckily for us, Ed Rice did not appear at rehearsal until very late that morning. . . . By this time my singers were grouped on the stage and I started the opening chorus, an orchestral and choral development of *Darktown Is Out To-*

night. I had twenty-six of the finest Negro voices in America. . . . Like a mighty anthem in rhythm, these voices rang out. . . ."

At the opening, "Rice's manager made the simple announcement that the Negro operetta, *Clorindy, the Origin of the Cakewalk,* would now be produced for the first time on any stage. Immediately I struck up the introduction and opening chorus. When I entered the orchestra pit, there were only about fifty people on the Roof. When we finished the opening chorus, the house was packed to suffocation. What had happened was that the show downstairs in the Casino Theatre was just letting out. The big audience heard those heavenly Negro voices and took to the elevators. . . .

"The Darktown finale was of complicated rhythm and bold harmonies, and very taxing on the voice. My chorus sang like Russians, dancing meanwhile like Negroes, and cakewalking like angels, black angels! When the last note was sounded, the audience stood and cheered for at least ten minutes. . . .

"Maybe, when the pearly gates open wide and a multitude of hosts march in, shouting, laughing, singing, emoting, there will be a happiness which slightly resembles that of *Clorindy's* twenty-six participants. I was so delirious that I drank a glass of water, thought it wine and got gloriously drunk. Negroes were at last on Broadway, and there to stay. Gone was the uff-dah of the minstrel! Gone the Massa Linkum stuff! We were artists and we were going a long, long way. We had the world on a string tied to a runnin' red-geared wagon on a downhill pull. Nothing could stop us, and nothing did for a decade."

XI

The Turn of the Century

FASCINATING FLORA is just another musical comedy built along the same lines as scores of its predecessors. Nothing but the expected happens: choruses sing, dance, stand in line, smile, wear colored clothes; principals get into trouble and out of it, burst into song at intervals commensurate with their importance, make jokes about New York, do specialties of more or less cleverness; the curtain falls to divide the evening into two parts; the orchestra plays the air that the promoter hopes will be popular. The whole thing is done according to formula as accurately as a prescription is compounded in a drug store. And the audience, strictly ritualistic as a musical comedy audience always is, is pleased."

Fascinating Flora, the object of the *Dramatic Mirror's* cynicism in this review, appeared above the Broadway horizon in 1907. Although nobody—least of all the producers—knew it then, the next few months were to bring two pieces, the *Follies of 1907* and *The Merry Widow,* that warranted an abandonment of the ritualistic approach on the part of the audience. But in the spring of 1907, the achievements of the New York musical stage, with remarkably few exceptions to prove the rule, constituted a dreary retrospect as far back as the turn of the century.

Instead of bringing fresh life to the popular musical theatre, the twentieth century—let us agree, to circumvent the ancient argument, that the new century began on January 1, 1900—seemed to offer almost no fresh impetus at all. The polite and piquant tradition of the London Gaiety Theatre tapered off in a series of reputable and often successful but unfailingly unoriginal importations from that theatre and others in Britain; the most prosperous and most neatly tailored of these usually had been composed by Monckton and Caryll or Paul Rubens. Gustav Luders and Ludwig Englander provided a series of watered-down replicas of middle-European operetta music, to books garnished by their American adapters with appropriate bits of slang, Tenderloin talk, and references to local people and institutions. Gustave Kerker placed third in a desultory race with Luders and Englander.

The more formal comic operas, few in number, were uniformly poor in quality; and, moreover, it was becoming hard to tell a comic opera from a musical comedy, since most musical comedies were no more than vulgarizations of the comic-opera formula. Except for an occasional piece, once or twice a year, that developed more than the usual momentum, and for the springy, youthful stride of George M. Cohan, the musical theatre was content to bide its time. For the most part nobody made any serious complaint. Times were good, and production costs and salaries were low. Pro-

ducers ran no risk in flooding the theatres with routine attractions—often sumptuously staged, it is true—when a run
of fifty performances or less was sufficient to pay off the initial costs.

Ivan Caryll, who kept the channel of communication with
Britain open by sending over one or two well-mannered
musical comedies each year, divided with Lionel Monckton the claim of being the successor, in his day, to Sir Arthur
Sullivan. This is not to say that Caryll's musical ideas were
a tenth as good as Sullivan's. But by his general competence
and his ability to turn out workmanlike scores on schedule,
he attained a high position in the British musical theatre.
Since he worked with a variety of librettists, most of whom
were largely devoid of a sense of humor, he never had an
opportunity to show what he might have been able to
achieve with the stimulus of so inspired an author and lyricist as W. S. Gilbert. Until *The Pink Lady*, more than a
decade on into the century, Caryll never provided the
American theatre with a major hit, but nearly all his pieces
were successful enough, in terms of the modest expectations
of the day, to make his name on a score a valuable talking-
point.

Caryll was not English by birth. He was born in Liége,
Belgium, in 1861, and his real name was Felix Tilkins. His
musical education was thoroughgoing, if conventional, for
in Liége he studied with the celebrated violinist Eugène
Ysaÿe and in Paris, a little later, with Camille Saint-Saëns.
After a fling at the French stage he moved to London, where
he became conductor at the Gaiety Theatre, and soon
tried his hand at writing the sort of music the purposes of
that theatre required. Until 1911 he remained in England,
commuting across the Atlantic to share in the preparation
of his musical comedies here after they were safely established in London. He took out American citizenship papers

in 1911, and remained here during the last decade of his life. In its obituary of Caryll in 1921, the New York *Herald* provided a moderate and essentially just estimate of the composer, whose works had been almost as identical with one another as the peas in a pod: "Caryll's music combined freshness and lightness with careful workmanship, a knowledge of his medium that is uncommon among musical comedy composers today, and that enabled him to turn out musical hits of enduring merit."

Of the merit of Caryll's *The Ladies' Paradise* (1901), in which Queenie Vassar appeared as Marie Antoinette, there is room for doubt. It deserves to be recorded as a phenomenon, however, for it was the first musical comedy ever produced at the Metropolitan Opera House. Naturally it failed, without operatic voices to fill the vast spaces, at the end of three weeks.

Thereafter Caryll's contributions, in which he often shared musical responsibilities with Monckton (who did not move to the United States) were confined to more seemly surroundings. *The Toreador* (1902) required Francis Wilson to impersonate a footman impersonating a bull-fighter, a device already exploited by De Wolf Hopper in *Panjandrum*. It also required pretty Christie MacDonald to impersonate a boy; the Gaiety Theatre tradition retained a bit of this custom from the days in the 1880s when the house was devoted to burlesque.

Caryll's and Monckton's biggest success of the decade, *The Girl from Kay's* (1903), abandoned a good deal of the typical Gaiety texture in favor of the low comedy of Sam Bernard and Hattie Williams, who attracted a popular audience that normally stayed away from better-bred English works. Part of the evening was given over to such vaudeville repartee as the following passage between Bernard, with his Dutch-comedy dialect, and Miss Williams:

"Vot iss id has two feet, has fedders all ofer id, und barks like a dog?"

"I give it up."

"A chicgen."

"Why, a chicken doesn't bark like a dog!"

"I know id; I chust pud id in to make id difficult."

In *The Girl from Kay's*, Bernard created the character of Mr. Hoggenheimer, an overbearing, uneducated comic Jew who was rotten with money. This characterization, which he carried on in a subsequent musical comedy, *The Rich Mr. Hoggenheimer*, was considered by some to be the apogee of low humor, and gave him his most successful role until the later, non-musical, period of *Potash and Perlmutter*.

The fatuous nature of the plots of the Caryll-Monckton musical comedies was epitomized in *The Orchid* (1907), whose American cast contained Eddie Foy, Trixie Friganza, and Irene Franklin. The action, which was forgotten altogether whenever it became a nuisance, centered upon the quest of a rich American for a $2,000 Peruvian orchid, to be sent, for obscure reasons, to Nice. When foul play kept the orchid from reaching its destination, the stunning discovery was made that a comparable orchid was growing in the garden kept by Eddie Foy, alias Artie Choke. This plot is not cited here as a chamber-of-horrors example, but as a characteristic phenomenon among early twentieth-century musical-comedy books. The opportunities it afforded Artie Choke enabled Foy to captivate his first Broadway audience, and to make a curtain speech in which he asserted that "you can go a long way in this world if you have a weak chin and a sunny disposition."

The musical comedies with scores by Gustav Luders and books by Frank Pixley were, if anything, even more uninviting in content. An academically trained Bremen musician, Luders came to Chicago in 1885, at the age of twenty, to

conduct the orchestra in popular concerts given at the
Schiller Theatre. After a few years spent in conducting
and in composing such orchestral thrillers as *The Cavalry
Charge*, he wrote a musical comedy called *The Burgomaster*
(1900), which received enough praise to encourage him to
continue in the field. *King Dodo*, produced in Chicago in
1901 and brought to New York in 1902, is memorable today
only because it allowed Raymond Hitchcock, as the King of
Dodo Land, to "jump into the front rank of comic opera
comedians." The plot represented Hitchcock as an aging
monarch with a yen for youth. He ordered the calendar set
back thirty years, with rejuvenating results, only to fall in
love with a queen who had an exclusive penchant for old
men.

By virtue of its success on the road rather than its 143
performances in New York, Luders' *The Prince of Pilsen*
(1903) has come to be regarded as one of the historic items
of the American musical stage. This celebrity is not justified
by its thin, conventional score; nor, certainly, is it borne out
by the plot (a Cincinnati brewer is mistaken for a prince
when he lands at Nice), of which one observer wrote, "The
story is worked out—if it is worked out at all—in the wings."
Like half the pieces in the wake of *Florodora* (with which
we shall concern ourselves in due season), it pinned part of
its hopes on a sextette, patriotically entitled "The American
Girl."

May we skip *The Sho-Gun* (1904), with its setting on the
imaginary island of Ka-Choo, even if the book about the
attempt of an American salesman to popularize chewing
gum among the natives was the first attempt at libretto-
writing by the midwestern humorist George Ade? And
may we also skip *The Grand Mogul* (1907)? From our
point of vantage, it is difficult to tell them apart.

Ludwig Englander, like Caryll, had received schooling in

the techniques of the Gaiety Theatre, but his musical style was more conspicuously Teutonic, sounding like memories of the restaurants in his native Vienna. With *The Jewel of Asia* (1903), Englander was taken to task by the *Dramatic Mirror* reviewer for a score that was completely stereotyped, even though "he has the fertile adjunct of Orientalism to assist him in his creations, and the tinkling cymbal and peculiar style and tempo of this sort of music are almost always provocative of successful work." Depending on the impulse of his librettists, Englander's books ranged from such straight comic-opera conceits as this to attempts at the vernacular like *A Madcap Princess* (1904), a musical treatment of Charles Major's novel *When Knighthood Was in Flower*, improved for the times by Harry B. Smith, who required Mary Tudor to speak in Coney Island slang. Only one libretto set by Englander, that of *The Wild Rose* (1902)—in which Smith also had a hand—appears to have commanded respect for its "coherent, consistent plot in these days of tommyrotical libretti."

The contributions of Westphalian-born Gustave Kerker were no more distinguished than those of Luders and Englander. Having climbed up the Broadway ladder from his first assignment as Edward E. Rice's conductor at the Casino Theatre in the 1880s to the triumph of *The Belle of New York* in the 1890s, Kerker's main interest lay in pieces about American situations; and to this extent his output was more homespun than the exotic, royalty-ridden, mistaken-identity pieces his colleagues so often set to music. He was even able to be inspired to a song by a lead-off line (in *The Billionaire*, in 1902) that went, "I will now sing a song written expressly for me by an expressman." On occasion, however, he could ally himself with the lovers of never-never-land as heartily as the next man. *Winsome Winnie* (1903) offered as its heroine a snake-charmer in Monte-negro, and *The Tourists* (1906) took place in Hindustan. The vernacular tone of most of Kerker's pieces may be illustrated by a further reference to *Fascinating Flora*, from the review quoted at the head of this chapter:

"Some of the novel features are a duet between Winnie Wiggles (a girl who has taken vocal culture from a correspondence school) and Caruso (represented by a phonograph record); a Subway Express song, with the chorus impersonating passengers in a subway car; a ballooning episode; and a dancing number by a dozen girls dressed as messenger boys."

Not one of the productions of the best-known light composers of the decade attained the fame and longevity of *Florodora*, which began its American run, exactly a year after its première in London, on November 11, 1900, and continued for 505 performances. It covered the entire nation on the road in the years following, and was successfully revived in New York in 1902, in 1905, and in 1920. It was one of the supreme hits of Broadway's history; and, with the over-simplification wrought by the passage of time, it has come to be remembered as the epitome of all that was delightful about the musical stage at the turn of the century.

For its early prosperity and its abiding fame alike, *Florodora* could thank one number: the famous sextette. Broadway reverberated with excitement after the first appearance of the six Florodora Girls—each one weighing 130 pounds to an ounce, five feet four inches tall, long-waisted, willowy, and either brunette or red-headed. "Tell me, pretty maiden, are there any more at home like you?" inquired their partners, the six Gentle Strangers. "There are a few," confessed the dainty maidens. Nobody believed them, however. How could any other girls match this perfect selection of six— Marie Wilson, Agnes Wayburn, Marjorie Relyea, Vaughn

Texsmith (really Miss Smith from Texas), Daisy Green, and Margaret Walker?

The Florodora Girls were publicized as girls never were again until Florenz Ziegfeld, Jr., began to trade in "the most beautiful girls in the world." They were beset by admirers and besieged with suitors, and three of them set the fashion, not altogether accepted heretofore, of marrying men of wealth and position.

Take the sextette away from *Florodora* and what remained was disillusioning. Neither Leslie Stuart's music nor the book by Owen Hall and Frank Pixley departed from the routine manner of the English stage, whence *Florodora* came, with no outstanding record of success back home. The action took place on an island in the Philippines called Florodora, where Cyrus W. Gilfain, a wealthy American (played by R. H. Graham), manufactured a perfume named after the island. The six Florodora Girls were there to serve as typists ("typewriter girls," they called them then). Gilfain, it transpired, had stolen the island from the deceased father of one Dolores (Fannie Johnston), who now was reduced to working in the factory. A phrenologist, Anthony Tweedlepunch (Willie Edouin) became interested in restoring the island to its proper heiress. In the second act, in Wales of all places, Tweedlepunch invoked a ghost who frightened Gilfain into confessing, and paved the way for the marriage of Dolores to Abercoed (Sydney Deane), who had been around, in supernumerary fashion, all the time. It was a tough-minded audience that could put up with this story, scarcely lightened by its leaden English jokes, for love of the beguiling sextette. Without the droll facial contortions of the veteran Willie Edouin as the phrenologist, and the handsome presence of Edna Wallace Hopper in the peripheral role of Lady Holyrood, the tale might have been unbearably bleak.

But it is necessary to look at the rest of the Broadway scene to realize how grateful the audience felt for that sextette in the fall of 1900. Another English piece, *A Million Dollars*, had just opened at the New York Theatre and been dismissed as "a specific for insomnia." Peter Daly and Christie MacDonald were appearing at the Madison Square Theatre in *Hodge Podge & Co.*, the chief characters of which were named Ledger d'Main (he was a bookkeeper), Rudolph Roastemsum, Minnie Rausmittem, and Ainshee Grayt. *San Toy*, a mediocre though popular English musical comedy set in China, and a labored vaudevillian musical farce, *The Belle of Bridgeport*, with May Irwin and Raymond Hitchcock, were the other principal musical offerings of the moment. Against such a field, *Florodora* could scarcely fail to impress the town.

Not until 1903 was another musical comedy able to jar Broadway out of the doldrums. The magnificent new Majestic Theatre on Columbus Circle opened with *The Wizard of Oz*, adapted from L. Frank Baum's novel. This musical fantasy had been imported from Chicago, where the slipper of its heroine, the lovely Anna Fitzhugh (later, when she sang at the Chicago Opera, Anna Fitziu, and now, in her vocal studio, Anna Fitzu), was likely to be filled with champagne at after-theatre parties. Miss Fitzhugh came to New York with the production, the most celebrated musical comedy ever staged initially in Chicago. So did Fred A. Stone and David C. Montgomery, a pair of comics whose work was not known in legitimate theatres in the East.

The plot, kept alive in our day by the novel and the film version, told, as everyone must know, how Dorothy Gale (and, in the play, her pet cow, Imogene) were blown by a cyclone to the region called Oz, where they consorted with such remarkable folk as the Scarecrow and the Tin Woodman. Five elaborate scenes were required for the first act.

The opening spectacle revealed a Kansas town in the grip of a cyclone. Through the use of stereopticon effects a transformation was managed, with a rainstorm on a gauze screen, to the Country of the Munchkins. Subsequent scenes showed a road in the woods, a poppy field with chorus girls in large hats representing the poppies, and, after another transformation, the poppy field in winter, with the poor girl-poppies dead in the snow. Act II was set in the lavish courtyard of the Wizard's palace, and Act III revealed a lovely grove, "with wisteria vines clambering over everything." The investiture, everyone felt, was rich enough to supply two or three ordinary musical comedies.

The music by Paul Tietjens and A. Baldwin Sloane was something short of memorable. But Julian Mitchell, drawn away from Weber and Fields to demonstrate even more fully in *The Wizard of Oz* how completely he was master of his craft, handled the staging with an ease and security that had seldom been equaled in recent times. And, beyond all else, there were those ingratiating people, Fred Stone, "apparently as boneless as an India-rubber doll," as the Scarecrow, and Dave Montgomery as the Tin Woodman, beginning a career that was to keep their names at the top of the list until Montgomery's death separated them. *The Wizard of Oz* was a joy for children, a delight for adults, a happy thing for everybody.

The Casino Theatre, impressed by the need for keeping its prestige high, brought forward a $75,000 production, *The Runaways*, to compete with *The Wizard of Oz*. Though it was not, technically speaking, a revue, *The Runaways* was a loosely constructed piece thrown together for gasps and laughs. It lacked universal appeal, however, and was intended for those who enjoyed "the conversational style affected by street gamins and loafers." The *Dramatic Mirror* observed bitterly: "To properly estimate it requires the talents of an appraiser rather than those of a dramatic critic. The Casino, which has always been more or less a temple of art, has now become a show room for the exhibition of $75,000 worth of costumes and accessories." The Casino's precipitate fall from grace is made vivid by the following lyric in *The Runaways*:

> "I'm going home, home, home,
> Down to the old plantation where I used to roam, roam, roam;
> With those my coming will be news to, home, home, home.
> To leave the folks again I will refuse to.
> Yes, I'm going back again to fair Dixieland."

Closer to the level of *The Wizard of Oz* was the extravaganza *Mother Goose*, presented by Klaw and Erlanger, a rapidly rising theatrical syndicate, in 1903. This spectacle could not be considered a direct imitation of the successful Chicago importation, for in 1901 Klaw and Erlanger had already offered *The Sleeping Beauty and the Beast*. Moreover, *Mother Goose* was an old-fashioned piece brought over from London, and built along the lines of the London pantomimes, though it involved no harlequinade—nor, in view of the Tenderloinish cast of its dialogue, was it aimed at the juvenile audience. The following year Klaw and Erlanger evoked memories of George L. Fox with *Humpty Dumpty*.

The *Wizard of Oz* was also reflected in *Piff! Paff!! Pouf!!!* (1904)—at least to the extent that Eddie Foy played a role evidently designed to resemble that of the Scarecrow as closely as possible. The force of this influential production was also evident in Victor Herbert's *Babes in Toyland*, one of the great successes of 1903.

Unadulterated comic operas, in contrast to musical comedies and extravaganzas, were relatively rare in the first years of the century, and they were uniformly unsuccessful. The public had lost its taste for French opéra-bouffe (the gifted Claude Terrasse never became known in this country) and for Viennese comic opera of the Millöcker and Strauss variety; they were out-of-date in their external conventions, much as *The Chocolate Soldier* is out-of-date today. English comic opera without admixtures of popular burlesque and musical-comedy elements was all but dead.

The list of comic operas given on Broadway in the first seven years of the twentieth century is pathetic. Sir Arthur Sullivan's last contribution, *The Rose of Persia* (1900), with a book by Captain Basil Hood, closed after twenty-five performances. Johann Strauss' *Vienna Life* (1901), lasted thirty-five, with a cast that held Raymond Hitchcock and Ethel Jackson, who was to remain practically unknown for six years more, until the part of Sonia in *The Merry Widow* fell her way. A contemporary objection to the solemnity of Strauss' treatment of the music in *Vienna Life* pointed out that "in modern works of the same class the song numbers are chiefly, if not entirely, incidental, recitatives are eliminated, and wearisome solo pieces are left out." Ernestine Schumann-Heink, in her only Broadway appearance, kept *Love's Lottery* (1904), a feeble British piece by Julian Edwards, open for fifty performances. Two opéra-comiques composed by André Messager, *Véronique* (1905) and *The Little Michus* (1907), failed to achieve long runs. Times had changed since the heyday of foreign comic opera ten and twenty years earlier. There seemed to be no audience left for pieces that were not colloquialized, at least to some degree.

The most colloquial amusement on the upper-class musical stage was still purveyed by Joe Weber and Lew Fields at their own Music Hall. Even if their yearly extravaganzas were sometimes, as Alan Dale said, "pitchforked publicward without rhyme or reason," Weber and Fields' hearty humor and generous provision of stars, combined with the expensive productions they were now able to afford, made their first nights as brilliant as any in New York. The ladies in the audience strove to outdress Lillian Russell with their Paris gowns and expensive jewels, and the floral offerings to the performers after the final curtain were staggering.

After *Whoop-Dee-Do*, their 1903-04 extravaganza, Weber and Fields determined to follow separate courses. Fields embarked upon a successful career as a producer of musical comedies. Weber, reluctant to change his field of operations, kept the music hall open, calling it Weber's Music Hall. For *Higgledy-Piggledy*, his first solo undertaking—in the fall of 1904—he was shrewd enough to make Flo Ziegfeld the co-producer, for the sake of obtaining the services of Anna Held, then Ziegfeld's wife. The still youthful Marie Dressler also belonged to Weber's first company, enhancing her popularity by her bubbling comedy. Weber continued to operate the music hall, with diminishing prosperity, until 1907, when he called it quits after *Hip! Hip! Hooray!* lasted only sixty-four performances. Leaving the extravaganza field wide open for Ziegfeld, whose first *Follies* had already demonstrated the potentialities of a fresh formula, Weber followed Fields into musical-comedy production.

One of the sincerest tributes of flattery was the persistence of Gus and Max Rogers, from 1898 to 1907, in imitating the Weber and Fields, or Weber, shows with poor man's vaudeville extravaganzas centering upon their own Dutch onslaughts upon the English language. Each year they exploited a new locale—Central Park, Mo. (the joke hung upon the Rogers Brothers' belief that they had bought a tract of land in Central Park, New York), Washington,

Harvard, London, Paris, Ireland, Panama. The fact that they could return year after year is testimony to the inordinate popularity of Dutch-dialect comedy. Theirs was the *reductio ad absurdum,* or perhaps *ad nauseam,* of the Dutch-comedy routine; but their "assaults upon ethics" were an inescapable part of the Broadway scene until 1907.

The historic Hippodrome, which housed a sequence of spectacles for more than thirty years, was opened with great fanfare on April 12, 1905. More than a year in construction, the house cost $1,750,000, and was advertised as "the largest, safest, and costliest playhouse in the world." For once, an opening-night audience forced Weber and Fields to take second honors, for the array of the spectators "would have made Solomon hide his diminished head. The sight on the stage was no less stunning, as a complete circus was transferred from the earth to Mars by airship." This opening transformation scene prompted the title A *Yankee Circus on Mars.* Productions in subsequent years ran a considerable gamut of subject matter. There was a double bill of *Pioneer Days* (replete with cowboys, Mexicans, half-breeds, United States troops, and Sioux Indians in war paint) and *Neptune's Daughter* (including a ballet, "Under the Sea," in which the girls simulated colored fish); there were *The Auto Race,* with a sight-seeing bus driving right onto the stage to bring on the chorus girls, *Sporting Days,* A *Trip to Japan,* and a triple bill of *The International Cup, Ballet of Niagara,* and *The Earthquake.* Each production could be counted on for a year's business, like the ice shows at the Center Theatre in more recent times. A trip to the Hippodrome was as essential an item in the sightseer's itinerary in New York as a visit to the Radio City Music Hall is today.

The Hippodrome was the only new institution founded in the first few years of the century. Two important individual figures in the realm of musical comedy, however, rose to prominence. They could hardly have been more diametrically opposed in every way—the Irish-born, English-bred, German-trained, cosmopolitan Victor Herbert, seeking to compose the American equivalent of the best European comic operas, and succeeding in writing a great many pretty tunes without in any way changing the main course of events; and the Rhode Island-born, New York-bred vaudeville hoofer, George M. Cohan, winning a new audience by refusing to accept the sacredness of European taste and usages.

Before the turn of the century, Herbert had already indicated his gifts in *The Serenade* (1897), which encouraged devotees of a well-turned tune to believe that the bromides of Reginald de Koven need not always continue to set the standard for home-composed scores. Herbert had allowed himself to assimilate American life and tastes so thoroughly that he was generally considered an American composer from the beginning of his Broadway career. Since his entire contribution to the musical-comedy field was made in this country, there was no more reason to harp upon his foreign birth than there is today upon Gian-Carlo Menotti's.

After a few years of silence following the production of *The Serenade,* Herbert reintroduced himself to his audience with *Babes in Toyland* in 1903. This extravaganza was a frank attempt to repeat the success of *The Wizard of Oz* by paralleling it as closely as possible. But despite the resemblance of Toyland to Oz, the Herbert score, with its "March of the Toys" and its adroit use of connecting and incidental music, gave *Babes in Toyland* a musical lift *The Wizard of Oz* had sorely needed.

Now that he was back in harness, Herbert turned out musical comedies at a good clip. Some of them, like *Babette* (1903), which served Fritzi Scheff—fresh from the Metropolitan—for her debut in comic opera, may well be forgotten. In 1905, Herbert gave a helping hand to Lew Fields by writing the music for *It Happened in Nordland*, Fields' first independent producing venture. But until *Mlle. Modiste* opened on Christmas night, 1905, Herbert did not repeat the success of *Babes in Toyland*. With Fritzi Scheff to sing "Kiss Me Again" and to "assault the snare drum" as the Mascot of the Troops, Herbert's music was in good hands. This time, moreover, Henry Blossom, author of the books and lyrics, had provided him with the rarest of advantages by writing dialogue and text that were direct, crisp, fluent, and literate.

Of the plot, set in one of the Parisian shops (a hat shop this time) that were such popular working-places for musical-comedy heroines, less that is pleasant can be said. But at least *Mlle. Modiste* more nearly gave the lie to a sweeping condemnation in the *Dramatic Mirror* than any of the contemporaneous pieces. "No one can long go the rounds of the New York theatres," the reviewer complained, "without becoming a student of theatrical kleptomania. Given from two to five acts which must be filled with material, and having no material scruples as to where or how it may be obtained, once he has discovered the emptiness of his own imagination, the ambitious author naturally takes to intellectual burglary and excuses himself on the time-worn plea of unconscious imitations and coincidences. This is said neither with particular reference to Henry Blossom nor to Victor Herbert, who conscientiously extracts principally from his own earlier works."

In the music for *Mlle. Modiste*, Herbert showed a growing ability to command a variety of styles. There was, of course, the usual sentimental waltz in "Kiss Me Again," but elsewhere in the evening he provided an ultra-Parisian touch in two songs devoted to local color, and was also able to turn with gusto to the task of composing a character song about the Keokuk Culture Club. Even so, most of the music was in his characteristic vein, accurately described by Amy Leslie in the Chicago *Daily News* as nearer Flotow than Audran, Humperdinck than Millöcker. In the countless waltzes he composed in *Mlle. Modiste* and other works, Herbert never captured the Viennese lilt of Strauss or Lehár; his waltzes plod conscientiously through all three beats of the measure, and never seem to get off the ground. His quickstep numbers, for all their dash and their frequently charming melodies, are factual and labored in comparison with those of Offenbach and Audran. But there is no use in thinking of these things. On a relative scale of judgment, Herbert was a marked improvement over Luders and Kerker; and, more important, the American public accepted him as its own composer.

The Red Mill (1906) was one of the gayest and most amusing of the earlier Herbert products. Fred Stone as "Con" Kidder and Dave Montgomery as "Kid" Conner (the quotation marks appear to be integral to their names) appeared as American tourists stranded at an inn in Holland. They were able, by luck, to uncover a plot involving the abduction of the petite Dutch heroine, and to effect her rescue in a scene in which they hung precariously from the arms of a big red windmill as they spirited her through the window. The production was a handsome one, with a Delft-blue setting in the second act that was in more restrained taste than usual.

After seven lesser efforts, Herbert next offered *Naughty Marietta*, under the aegis of Oscar Hammerstein, in 1910. One of the hardiest and most frequently performed of all the Herbert works in the years since its première, *Naughty Marietta* was no more than a mild success at first, attaining a run of only 136 performances. Once again, an operatic singer—Emma Trentini of Hammerstein's Manhattan Opera Company—was engaged as the soprano lead, to impersonate a French countess who ran off to New Orleans, presumably in order to institute enough complications for an operetta plot. One would think, in view of their longevity and continuing popularity, that the "Italian Street Song" and "I'm Falling in Love with Someone" would have been hailed as signal achievements, but their superiority to other songs of the moment was not fully recognized. The most celebrated tune in *Naughty Marietta*, "Ah, Sweet Mystery of Life," was not a song at all in the original production, but an instrumental entr'acte, which recurred in the finale. The familiar words were set to the melody later on, at the instigation of the leading tenor, Orville Harrold, also a member of the Metropolitan Opera.

By 1910, Herbert was just reaching the crest of the wave. By 1910, George M. Cohan was all but finished with his early career as author, composer, producer, director, actor, singer, and dancer of and in musical comedies, and about to begin a second career that kept him either on the speaking stage or writing for it, or both, the larger part of the time until his memorable return in 1937 as President Roosevelt in *I'd Rather Be Right.*

Born in Providence, Rhode Island, not on July 4, as was always said, but on July 3, 1878 (Ward Morehouse examined the city archives), Cohan never knew a life that was not associated with the stage. His father, Jerry J. Cohan, and his mother, Helen F., were itinerant vaudeville performers. As a small child, George learned to help them in their act, and he made his first professional solo appearance at the age of nine. For his own specialty he developed proficiency in the buck-and-wing dancing that was the turn-of-the-century precursor of present-day tap dancing.

As George and his sister Josephine became old enough to take share and share alike, their vaudeville act was billed as "The Four Cohans." In 1899, in an expanded version of one of their vaudeville sketches, the family made a modest bow on Broadway, without exciting much attention. *The Governor's Son*, also an elaboration of a vaudeville playlet, was their first musical comedy, in 1901.

Though no sizable public yet took them to heart, the Cohans began to climb up the ladder. George, in particular, was praised as a "grotesquely agile dancer," and as an actor who could "make the most ordinary lines seem unusually funny, and without a change of facial expression." From the beginning, George M. Cohan would have no traffic with the old-fashioned mugging that, ever since the days of George L. Fox and Willie Edouin and Francis Wilson, had served as a device of prime value in eliciting laughs from the naïve. He was the apostle of breeziness, of up-to-dateness, of Broadway brashness and slang. Straining for effect had no place in the modernized technique he sought to exploit. Speed, directness, and "ginger" were the chief ingredients of his musical plays.

By 1903, when *Running for Office* returned the Four Cohans to New York, their name had begun to spread around, and their opening stimulated a floral offering hardly less suffocating than those at Weber and Fields'. Three generations were represented in the theatre that night, for the daughter of George and his wife, Ethel Levy (who was also a member of the company) watched her parents and grandparents from a box.

George M. Cohan became a star in *Little Johnny Jones*, in 1904. The Four Cohans were no more, for Josephine had left to accept independent engagements. Contemporary observers felt that Cohan had given himself a poor role compared to that of Donald Brian, the future Prince Danilo of *The Merry Widow*. But he had an opportunity to introduce a characteristic Cohan song, "Yankee Doodle Boy," and to recite a sententious sermonette entitled "Life's a Funny Proposition," with which he perhaps justified the snobbish description of him as "the idol of middle-class playgoers." For the first time he was able to afford a production that compared favorably with those of longer-established managers, and to engage his own set of Girls and Boys, à la Florodora, to sing a double sextette, " 'Op in the 'Ansom." (The plot, it should be explained, took Cohan to England as an American jockey riding in the Derby.)

Patriotism and local color having paid off so far, Cohan located his next piece, *Forty-Five Minutes from Broadway* (1906), in New Rochelle, New York. The production was still not expensive; the $10,000 it cost was paid off within a few days after the opening. For the first time, Cohan himself stayed out of the cast, awarding the role of Kid Burns, who spotted and captured the two villains, to a young, tough comedian named Victor Moore, who had not yet evolved the plaintive, slow underplaying with which modern audiences associate his name. Donald Brian appeared as a dapper, rich young man, and the popular Fay Templeton was given the chance to appear in her "first clean play," after twenty years of burlesque and travesty. The play was peopled with two antithetical groups, the native yokels of New Rochelle and the wise guys from Forty-second Street. To the Milwaukee *Press*, "all the froth, the humor, the fatalism, the philosophy, compounded of epicureanism, cynicism, and opportunism, characteristic of the futile little rialto world are perfectly reflected by Mr. Cohan in his songs and slang dialogues." Broadway, in other words, now had a spokesman.

With *George Washington, Jr.*, (1906)—subtitled "an American musical play"—Cohan began to wave the flag in earnest, with the aid of a song entitled "The Grand Old Flag." The plot hinged upon the conflict between an Anglomaniac father and a son so intensely patriotic that he renounced his own name and took that of the Father of Our Country. Cohan's conception of the ideal American youth was by no means universally admired. The dissenting view was strongly put by James S. Metcalfe, critic of the old *Life*:

". . . [He is] a vulgar, cheap, blatant, ill-mannered, flashily-dressed, insolent, smart Aleck, who, for some reason unexplainable on any basis of common sense, good taste, or even ordinary decency, appeals to the imagination and apparent approval of large American audiences. As a living character in any American town or village, it is hardly to be conceived that he would not be driven out as a public nuisance and a pernicious example to the youth of the community. The rounds of applause which greet the efforts of this offensive personality must convey to the minds of ignorant boys a depraving ideal for their inspiration and imitation."

The *Dramatic Mirror*, while baffled by the Cohan phenomenon, took a quieter view:

"Precisely why these Cohan concoctions are so popular with the New York public is a mystery the critic has never succeeded in solving to his personal satisfaction. They are clean; they are spirited; they are inspired with a variety of slang patriotism which may not be the less serious because it is not of superior elevation. Yet, after the last argument has been summarized, they must be classed, so to speak, as high-grade second-grade productions. Perhaps the true secret of Mr. Cohan's unprecedented success, too permanent for mere theatrical luck, consists of his admirable stagecraft. In the art of presenting musical comedy, Mr. Cohan is apparently without a peer."

Against which, almost as though in riposte, *Life* submitted an opposing judgment:

"These combinations of music are curious things, consisting mainly of several bars of well-known patriotic or sentimental songs strung together with connecting links of lively and more or less original musical trash. The words fitted to these curious contraptions are the kind of unmetrical stuff that children compose and call poetry, and are for the most part mawkish appeals to the cheapest kind of patriotism."

Whatever the merits of their content, Cohan's musical comedies introduced a wholly new conception of delivery, tempo, and subject matter into a form of entertainment that was rapidly dying for want of new ideas of any kind. Brushing aside the artificial elegances and the formal developments of the musical comedies based on English and German models, he reproduced successfully the hardness, the compensating sentimentality, the impulsive vulgarity, and the swift movement of New York life, which, except for surface sophistications, has not changed much between then and now. Though the plays might seem dreadful if they were revived today, it is impossible not to grant them validity as interpretations of the whole spirit and tone of life in and around the Broadway sector. "At times," wrote a reviewer in 1907 of *The Honeymooners* (a revision of *Running for Office*), "it goes so fast that it almost bewilders and gives the impression of a great machine shooting out characters, choruses, songs, dances with rapid-fire quickness and precision."

If he had been able to match his ability as a stage director with fresh materials, Cohan need never have temporarily deserted the musical-comedy field. But his plays came more and more to be rehashes—sometimes, as with *The Honeymooners* and *The Man Who Owns Broadway* (1909), reprises of pieces whose initial success had not satisfied him; sometimes, as with *Fifty Miles from Boston* (1908) and *The American Idea* (1908), applications of old recipes to different (yet always the same) characters and circumstances.

XII

The Merry Widow
and the Ziegfeld Follies

PUBLIC INTEREST in Viennese comic opera had declined to
so low an ebb in the early years of the twentieth century
that Henry W. Savage watched the inordinate success of
The Merry Widow in Vienna and Berlin and London for
two years before risking an American production of it, even
though he had obtained the rights many months before.
There was, after all, no reason to be sure that this piece
with a score by an unknown young Hungarian named
Franz Lehár would succeed with a public that had recently
spurned so established a master as Johann Strauss. Savage
had seen *The Merry Widow* in Hamburg and Vienna, and
had been enchanted by what he called its "essence of youth-

fulness"; but perhaps it would look and sound different in English, on the other side of the Atlantic.

On October 21, 1907, he finally presented the operetta in New York. Adrian Ross had already provided idiomatic English lyrics for the London production; George Marion whose youthfulness matched that of the score itself, undertook the stage direction. For the romantic leads, Savage engaged Donald Brian, who had received his chief schooling thus far from George M. Cohan, and Ethel Jackson, a comic-opera soprano so little known that Savage pretended to a gullible press that he had discovered her—though those with good memories could recall her performances on Broadway in *Little Miss Nobody* and *The Runaway Girl* and on the road in *Miss Bob White*, which never reached New York.

To those who were at the New Amsterdam Theatre on that opening night, the enraptured close of the second act has always remained a supreme recollection. The "Merry Widow Waltz" appeared first in hints by the orchestra; Brian and then Miss Jackson began to hum it; tentatively and experimentally at first, then with a crescendo of fervor, the couple moved into the waltz. As their dance continued, they became faster and lighter, until it seemed that their feet scarcely touched the stage at all. With this single dance, this single tune, the aging musical theatre recaptured its youth. The audience was transfixed as it watched the scene. At the end the tumult of applause forced an encore, and another encore, and still another.

For fifty-two weeks, *The Merry Widow* lifted its New York audiences into a heaven of romantic ardor. Ethel Jackson's laughter, which "sounded like water bubbling out of a small bottle," her lovely gowns and fashionable sailor hats, her exquisite singing of the "Vilia" melody; Brian's debonair gallantry and nimble movement; the sauciness of the girls at Maxim's; even the intrigue of the Marsovian plot—all these were delights as fresh and gay as the lilting waltz.

Chicago also saw *The Merry Widow* for the first time on the same evening, with a duplicate production equally lavishly staged and costumed, and with Lina Abarbanell—whom some connoisseurs preferred to Miss Jackson—as Sonia, and George Damarel as Prince Danilo. Other *Merry Widow* companies were organized to take the good news everywhere. *Merry Widow* hats, dresses, and drinks were a reigning fashion. Soon after the New York première, the statement was made—for which, at this late date, there is neither proof nor disproof—that more than a hundred *Merry Widow* companies were performing concurrently on the face of the globe.

Granting that the music of *The Merry Widow* was a considerable cut above most of that of Victor Herbert, and an incalculable improvement upon that of most of his contemporaries, it was not primarily its music that made *The Merry Widow* so transcendent a hit. Nor, certainly, was it the humor, since there was almost none to be discovered. It was the dancing, the animation of the waltz presented in the intimate, gallant terms of the ballroom rather than the formal figurations prescribed by established conventions. In *The Merry Widow* the ballroom dance was glorified as a symbol of romantic love, and placed in the focus of attention. The "Merry Widow Waltz" did in fact start a new era, as the *Dramatic Mirror* hoped it would. It dealt a death blow to the marches, drills, and empty convolutions that had punctuated musical-comedy performances until then. It opened the way for Vernon and Irene Castle, the tango, the turkey-trot, and the fox-trot. It humanized dancing, and made it warm, immediate, and personal.

And so, thanks to Lehár and Savage and Brian and Miss Jackson, comic opera leapt back into favor. A rival to Lehár, Oskar Straus—no relation to the great Strausses with a double "s"—had also set up shop in Vienna, and his *A Waltz Dream* was brought over in 1908 to compete with *The Merry Widow*. A sprightly piece with a good score and an ample supply of humor, *A Waltz Dream* made its way nicely without dislodging its predecessor. Among the performers, the one who received the most generous praise was a young Canadian church and oratorio tenor, Edward Johnson, who made his first stage appearance as the romantic hero. "His voice," one review reported, "is a clear tenor of wide range, and he sings without any apparent effort, even the difficult finale of the last act. His stage presence is good and his acting is natural." *A Waltz Dream* was Johnson's first and last light-opera assignment. At the close of its run he went to Italy, changed his name to Edoardo di Giovanni, returned to the United States, changed his name back to Edward Johnson, sang at the Chicago Opera and then at the Metropolitan, and in 1935 began his fifteen-year tenure as general manager of the Metropolitan Opera Association.

Two more Viennese comic operas attained prosperity in 1909 and 1910. Leo Fall's *The Dollar Princess*, a somewhat bromidic piece about the complications aroused by the attempt of an American millionaire's daughter to purchase the affection of a young Englishman, brought Donald Brian back with "evident consciousness of his own merit." The only remarkable feature of *The Dollar Princess*, apart from an attractive score, was the final curtain, which left the romantic couple alone on the stage—"alone, yes, alone; no swaying chorus around them, no farewell jingle and patter —the lovers find awakening, and a golden curtain, like 'amber-glowing flood of light,' enshrouds them in its love mysteries."

The Chocolate Soldier (1909), by Oskar Straus, offered no amber love-finale, but it was provided with something better—a book, not too greatly watered down, drawn from George Bernard Shaw's *Arms and the Man*. It also rejoiced in the first Viennese waltz that offered competition to the "Merry Widow Waltz," the long-lined, slow-mounting "My Hero." Though its first engagement lasted for only 296 performances, as against *The Merry Widow's* 416, *The Chocolate Soldier* has since proved to be almost as durable an object of public affection.

When all was said and done, however, the Viennese-waltz operas were an exotic importation, a borrowed rapture. The chief really American contribution—apart from Cohan's— to the renewed vigor of the musical stage in this period was made by Florenz Ziegfeld, Jr. The son of a dignified, old-school German musician who became president of the Chicago Musical College, Flo Ziegfeld kicked over the traces while he was still a very young man, and served for a time as the manager of Sandow, the strong man whose muscles Chicago society dowagers liked to feel at the World's Columbian Exposition in 1893. His entry into theatrical production was provoked by his interest in Anna Held, whom he met in London in the late 1890s, placed under contract, and featured in a series of musical comedies, meanwhile marrying her to make the tie doubly binding. Anna Held's daintiness, her delicate accent, her flashing come-hither eyes ("I Just Can't Make My Eyes Behave") carried her to success in De Koven's *The Little Duchess* (1901), Luders' *Mam'selle Napoleon* (1903) ("a transplanted rose that turned out to be a particularly large and offensive cabbage"), and *The Parisian Model* (1906), with music by Max Hoffman and various collaborators. Only the last of these fully displayed the exactions of style and rich displays of feminine beauty which were henceforth to be the marks of every Ziegfeld production. While the chorus sang "A Gown for Each Hour of the Day," Miss Held appeared, disappeared, and reappeared in six costly gowns. In "I'd Like to See a Little More of You" a trick effect made the chorus appear to be nude, when in reality it was merely décolleté. A "pony ballet" of sixteen girls wore bells on their fingers, their toes, and "elsewhere."

In Paris in the summer of 1906, Ziegfeld was seized with the notion of furnishing America with a revue discreetly modeled after the Folies Bergère. He could not appropriate the lascivious features of the French revue, he knew; but he was sure that he could, without half trying, make a group of girls look more beautiful. His plan took tangible shape on July 8, 1907, when he presented an entertainment entitled *Follies of 1907* on the New York Theatre Roof, which he renamed the Jardin de Paris.

Let no dreamer imagine that the original *Follies* was planned with the luxury Ziegfeld promulgated in later years. He was still a struggling, impecunious producer, with only a few moderate successes to his credit, and without a large bank account or ready access to the bank accounts of angels. The whole production cost of the *Follies of 1907* was $13,000, and the entire weekly payroll amounted to $1,800. The cast included no important names, though Helen Broderick's became so later on. The music was picked up here and there, and the production was mounted like a high-class vaudeville show. It was reviewed in the *Dramatic Mirror*, in fact, not among legitimate attractions, but on the inconspicuous page headed "New Vaudeville Acts."

"A musical review of the New York sensations of the past season," and "a succession of incidents and specialties," the *Follies of 1907* was decorated by a large chorus of "girls who had appeared with Anna Held last season," who soon same to be called by the more economical name of Anna Held Girls. Their striking scene was a "motion-picture effect" in which the girls seemed to be splashing in the waves.

At the end, twenty-four drummer girls paraded out into the theatre and back. Before then, Mlle. Dazie had offered her sensational Salome dance; Dave Lewis had sung "I Think I Oughtn't Auto Any More"; and George Bickel and Harry Watson, Jr., had given their already well-known band-leading specialty.

The public supported the *Follies of 1907* so willingly throughout the summer that Ziegfeld decided to move it to the street level, in the Liberty Theatre, for the fall season. The takings immediately dropped to $1,500 in the first week after the move. With great misgivings, the producer packed the show off to Washington, where, although it was housed in a legitimate theatre and not on a roof, it played to land-office business. So did it on the rest of a tour that took it as far as Chicago. The road was even more profitable than the Jardin de Paris for the first *Follies*.

During the winter—on January 28, 1908—Ziegfeld returned to musical-comedy production with *The Soul Kiss*, which he built around the Danish ballerina Adeline Genée, who made her first visit to the United States to appear in it. To the *Dramatic Mirror*, "Genée is a thing apart; a spirit untouched by her all too earthly surroundings; an elf, an angel, a bird, an incarnation of Terpsichore; indescribable in words, impossible of analysis, as intangible as sunbeams, as vapory as moonlight." Four dances were contributed by this lovely paragon, ranging from *ballet blanc* and an aristocratic piece in Empire gown and dancing slippers to a hunting dance in riding habit and boots and—Ziegfeld's *pièce de résistance*—a dance in which she wore a lace-trimmed negligee and very high-heeled slippers.

From the *Follies of 1907* and *The Soul Kiss* Ziegfeld earned enough to enable him to plan the *Follies of 1908* on a somewhat more elaborate, though still decidedly moderate, scale. Nora Bayes and Mae Murray were new luminaries in a revue designed to cast a glance at the entire history of society, politics, and the stage from the time of the Garden of Eden to New York in the summer of 1908. The girls were more pulchritudinous than ever, even when they paraded across the stage representing taxicabs.

Between summers, Ziegfeld again produced a musical comedy, *Miss Innocence*, for the benefit of Anna Held this time; it was his last musical comedy until *Sally* more than a decade later. The score was by Ludwig Englander.

But the *Follies of 1909* were in his mind all the while, and when they were revealed at the Jardin de Paris, they initiated the tradition of lavishness to which Ziegfeld was to remain faithful until the very end of his career. Dearest to the producer's heart in the 1909 edition was the exquisite Lillian Lorraine, for whom Ziegfeld always felt the warmest admiration and genuine affection. Miss Lorraine made her *Follies* debut in a sea of soap bubbles. Later on, she clambered into a flying machine and scattered flowers as she sang "Up, Up, Up, in My Aeroplane." As a foil for her serene beauty, Bessie Clayton, a pert and diverting comedienne, burlesqued a typical London Gaiety dancer, with silk hat, stick, tails, and a nether costume that was part masculine and part feminine.

A ponderable share of the *Follies of 1909* was given over to a rowdy representation of President Theodore Roosevelt on an African hunting trip. Harry Kelly impersonated Roosevelt, teeth, glasses, and all. A two-man elephant made friendly overtures to the hunters, and the chorus girls found diverse occupations as tigers, giraffes, and ostriches. An amiable lion allowed the President to shoot at him, accommodatingly holding a large target between his paws. The President, dissatisfied with such easy game, insisted upon shooting an apple off the lion's head. This done, the scene changed, and Ziegfeld's patriotism was affirmed when the show girls appeared with headdresses shaped like ships. The background showed a harbor variously preted as New York and Hampton Roads; whichever the stage lights were dimmed, the girls turned on lights in their headdresses, and the "greatest navy in the world" was seen riding at anchor. The giddy evening ended with a baseball game among the chorus girls, into which they swept the members of the audience as the curtain fell. Despite all these inventions, however, the audience elected to be most impressed by the Nell Brinkley Bathing Girls.

By the time the *Follies of 1910* took over the Jardin de Paris in June of that year, Miss Lorraine had earned an assured place as a reigning beauty. Never hesitant to make imposing claims when nobody could prove them false, Ziegfeld was quoted in an interview as saying, "It was no unusual thing for her to receive flowers night after night over the footlights, and then upon taking the bouquets to pieces afterwards, to find a diamond ring or a pin fastened to a cluster of American beauties." Obviously it paid to take bouquets apart in those days.

In the *Follies of 1910*, Ziegfeld introduced one of his greatest future stars—Fannie Brice, whom he saw at the Columbia Theatre, a cheap burlesque house, and engaged for an initial salary of $18 a week to sing a character song, "Good-bye, Becky Cohen." Bert Williams, a graduate of such successful Negro musical comedies as *In Dahomey* (1903), *Abyssinia* (1906), and *Mr. Lode of Koal* (1909), made the first of many appearances in the *Follies*. For spectacle, the show girls symbolized various schools in the first-act finale, "Our American Colleges"; and Miss Lorraine brought the second act to a climax by swinging out over the audience as she sang to the accompaniment of eight girls, also in swings, ringing Swiss bells.

The *Follies of 1910* was conceived on a more massive

scale than any of its predecessors. Although three more years were to pass before Ziegfeld adandoned the roof as the home of his revues, the pattern was set, and the *Follies* had "come to be looked upon as the biggest thing of their kind of the season." But the proof of Ziegfeld's triumph, and the triumph of the glorified girls and of the revue idea, had already been vouchsafed in 1908, when the Shuberts sought to parallel the *Follies* with a well-staged extravaganza entitled *The Mimic World*. Ziegfeld almost sued the Shubert brothers when he claimed to have seen a score of the overture to *The Mimic World* which appropriated the subtitle *Follies of 1908*. The *Follies* were his own invention, and even the word "follies" in the title remained his sole property until 1919, when the *Greenwich Village Follies* successfully appropriated it.

XIII

Before and During the
First World War

WHATEVER its faults may be, the American musical theatre has never remained static for long. The peak popularity of each new fashion has inevitably been short and the turn-over of modes and ideas rapid. Weber and Fields' Music Hall, which seemed as permanent as the Rock of Gibraltar in the late 1890s, disappeared as an institution in 1904, only nine years after it was established; by 1912, when the partners staged their "jubilee revival," their art was already a matter for nostalgia and sadness over the passing of the good old days. The Gaiety Girls, the models of feminine vivacity and attractiveness in 1894, were pushed into a back seat by our own native-born Florodora Girls in 1900. George

M. Cohan's swift and brash musical farces of the New York scene were top attractions for less than a decade; the freshness of Cohan's inspiration had deserted him by 1911, when *The Little Millionaire* elicited the comment, "If Cohan's reputation rested on this piece, he would never have come to own his own theatre on Broadway." The inordinate popularity of *The Merry Widow* was quite as much a threat as an encouragement to subsequent waltz operas, and Lehár's own *Gypsy Love*, in 1912, was coolly received.

At the beginning of the second decade of this century, the musical stage had again encountered the doldrums. New hits seemed like repetitions of old ones. Upper-crust patrons who had been devoted to the most artistic comic operas and the best musical comedies found the intense and much-publicized rivalry between Hammerstein's Manhattan Opera and Otto Kahn's Metropolitan Opera far more exciting than any stimulus the lighter musical stage could offer. A gap had opened between the carriage trade and the mass audience, which adored its whirly-girly shows and wanted no traffic with art. During the next few years Broadway kept only an attenuated hold upon its audience of cultivated patrons. In 1913 and 1914 show business fell upon the most evil days it was to experience until the depression of the 1930s. But it is always darkest just before dawn, and from 1915 on American musical comedy began to discover and realize its manifest destiny as a native and genuinely popular expression. A new generation flocked to the theatres, and what with wartime excitement and postwar prosperity, the industry entered upon fifteen years of high flying.

In 1911 and 1912, the beginning of the great four-year decline, there was still some life in the old formulas. *The Quaker Girl*, an importation of the Gaiety species from

George Edwardes' Adelphi Theatre in London, cut off the usual bolt of goods and provided with an urbane and easy-flowing score by Lionel Monckton, ran for 240 performances in 1911-1912. The older generation and the younger one met in the cast. May Vokes, of the once famous Vokes family, and Nellie McHenry, leading lady of Salsbury's Troubadours in the 1870s, shared assignments with Olga Petrova, soon to become an emotional star of the silent screen, and a young girl named Ina Claire, fresh from her first Broadway assignment in *Jumping Jupiter*, who sang in a small, clear voice, and danced in a manner that "entitles her to more than ordinary consideration." The Quaker girl of the title quickly "shed her sectarian prejudices but not her principles," for at the beginning of the second act she had found employment in a dressmaking establishment on the Rue de la Paix. The piece was the politest and most soothing pastime London had yet vouchsafed, and was undisturbed by the slightest tinge of novelty, beyond the fact that the "gentlemen of the chorus" did not all dress alike.

The Gaiety Theatre itself made an equally conventional contribution in *The Sunshine Girl*, presented by Charles Frohman in 1913. It was all about soap and a soap works, and Julia Sanderson was elevated to stardom in these spotless surroundings. The score (and most of the book) was by Paul A. Rubens, but the show-stopping tune, delivered with enormous aplomb by Joseph Cawthorn, called "You Can't Play Every Instrument in the Band," had music by Raymond Hubbell and lyrics by John Golden, who later dreamed up "Poor Butterfly" before moving into a long and successful career as a producer of non-musical plays.

The Sunshine Girl employed as its featured dancers Vernon and Irene Castle. Castle had already appeared on Broadway in *The Hen Pecks* (1911), but this was the first musical-comedy appearance of the husband-and-wife team. The evolutions of the couple left the audience breathless, as they exhibited "the last note in the turkey-trot world." To the *Dramatic Mirror*, "Castle is an acquired taste; but once acquired, his fantastic distortions and India-rubber gyrations exert a decided fascination, while, moreover, he has grown artistically." It was a taste the audience acquired cheerfully and quickly. Castle's turkey-trot with his wife (a new dance, suggesting both wings of a turkey) and his tango with Julia Sanderson presaged a new era in which the waltz would be supplanted by dances from the western hemisphere. By including the Castles in one of its productions, the Gaiety all but committed suicide in America. The contrast between old and new was too striking, and it was obvious that the audience preferred the new.

Franz Lehár's *The Merry Widow*, the supreme hit of the first decade of the century, had tallied up 416 performances in its first run in New York, in 1907-1908, and a great many more than that on the road. Two years later, Oskar Straus' *The Chocolate Soldier* ran for 296 performances, and Leo Fall's *The Dollar Princess* for 288. These were phenomenal records at a time when 100 performances constituted a highly profitable New York engagement. Naturally central European comic opera came to be highly esteemed by producers, and in the next five years the Shuberts, Klaw and Erlanger, Henry W. Savage, Charles Frohman, and even A. H. Woods, the bedroom-farce king, placed a number of their chips on it.

But it stubbornly failed to pay off. Lehár's *Gypsy Love*, in 1911, survived for Woods for only 31 performances. Lehár had over-reached himself, and the score was thought to be too close to grand opera, "too portentous and heavy." Frohman's production of Fall's *The Siren* in the same year did better, and rated technically as a success, since it played

136 times. But Harry B. Smith's adaptation of the German lyrics, according to one critic, "bustled with unsingable words that ill accord with Fall's exquisite melodies," and only the combined talents of Donald Brian (the unforgotten Prince Danilo), Frank Moulan, and the gracious Julia Sanderson kept the piece in favor—along with "costumes that would cause women to leave the theatre with their heads crammed full of sartorial inspirations." Lehár's *The Count of Luxembourg*, presented by Klaw and Erlanger in 1912, achieved 120 performances, thanks partly to Frank Moulan's dry, cutting delivery of his comic lines and lyrics, and the skilled hand of Julian Mitchell as director of the dances and production numbers.

The next three Lehár pieces, presented consecutively by Klaw and Erlanger, the Shuberts, and Savage, all failed to make the mark. *Eva* (1912) was too advanced for its time. The book "resorted to the psychological problems of high drama," and in the score, "Eva says 'Yes' in the first act to discords that Schönberg might be proud to have written." (The New York *Times* drama critic evidently had already heard of *Pierrot Lunaire* in 1912.) *The Man with Three Wives* (1913) went to the opposite extreme, being witless and superficial. Charlotte Greenwood, the future long-legged Letty, carried the burden of the evening, kicking into enjoyment an audience that found little other entertainment. *The Maid of Athens* (1914) was stripped of much of its Lehár score, allotted a poor English adaptation by Carolyn Wells, and provided with a finale, "amazingly realistic," on the gun-deck of an American dreadnought. In 1915, the Shuberts finally hit pay dirt with Lehár's *Alone at Last,* which was conducted by Gaetano Merola, today and for the past quarter-century the director of the San Francisco Opera Association. The cast included Roy Atwell, Marguerite Namara, and John Charles Thomas, fresh out of revue for his first operetta assignment. With a score more inventive than that of *The Merry Widow* and suave singing from Mr. Thomas, *Alone at Last* enjoyed a pseudo-operatic success, although the *Dramatic Mirror* complained that "Miss Namara never suggested a maiden." Thereafter, Lehár's sun went into an eclipse. Anti-German sentiment, as war approached, kept his pieces off the American stage, along with nearly all other German and Austrian items. In 1917, the Shuberts made the misstep of presenting Thomas in Lehár's *The Star Gazer*. Although the score was a good one, the temper of the time was shown by the fact that the operetta was forced to close at the end of the first week. No more Viennese operettas were heard in America until well after the end of the war.

A little earlier, however, three items from Central Europe by composers other than Lehár enjoyed respectable successes. Johann Strauss' *Die Fledermaus* finally came to notice, under the aegis of the Shuberts, in 1912, who offered it as a "London novelty" under the title, *The Merry Countess*. The chief novelty appears to have been Gladys Unger's distortion of the book into the Winter Garden idiom, and the "sacrifice" of Strauss to the Dolly Sisters. In the same year, Bruno Granichstädten's *The Rose Maid*, with a book adapted by the unflagging Harry B. Smith, was similarly metamorphosed into a vehicle for Edward Gallagher and Al Shean, who kept it alive for 176 performances.

Henry Savage's production of *Sari*, in 1914, fortified the reputation of the Hungarian composer, Emmerich Kalman. As early as 1909, when he was only twenty, Kalman had introduced himself with *The Gay Hussars*, but *Sari* was his first hit. The motto of the operetta was "Victorious Ever is Youth." Both the bubbling score and the high spirits of the performers bore the slogan out. For the title role, Savage

brought from Hungary a diminutive singing-actress named
Mitzi Hajos (who later called herself plain Mitzi). Abandoning the conventional French heels, corsets, satin bodices,
and multitudinous petticoats of the comic-opera heroine,
Mitzi wore her plain hair in two straight braids down her
back, and bounced and rollicked through the evening with
capricious and disarming naturalness. Among her accomplishments was a grotesque dance, "Hu-za-za," in which she
won applause for her "comical birdlike hoppings." Though
its waltzes—notable among them "Love's Own Sweet
Song"—offered "no solace for the tangoist and the turkey-
trotter," Kalman succeeded in translating Viennese operetta into lively American terms. He remained active in this
country, to share the field of sentimental operetta with
Victor Herbert, Rudolf Friml, and Sigmund Romberg.

Sari was an oasis in a desert. On October 14, 1914, the
Dramatic Mirror mourned, "Never before in recent history
has there been such a dearth of musical plays." At that
moment, the entire list in New York consisted of *The Girl
from Utah, Pretty Mrs. Smith,* and a revue at the Winter
Garden. "With the exception of Victor Herbert, there is no
one in this country who seems to understand musical
comedy requirements. Foreign composers and librettists are
fighting for their colors. Will the war uncover native composers and librettists with works of merit?"

It soon did, but in the meantime Victor Herbert was obviously doing his best to merit the faith the *Dramatic Mirror* placed in him. Between 1911 and 1917 Herbert turned
out five musical comedies (or operettas, or comic operas,
or musical plays, or musical entertainments) of smash-
hit proportions. In addition, he wrote eight pieces that
achieved runs of from 12 to 71 performances. His services
were in demand by nearly every producer in town, and his

thirteen musical comedies in this period were staged under ten different auspices, ranging from Joe Weber to the Shuberts and the partnership of Ziegfeld and Dillingham.

With *The Lady of the Slipper*, a variant on the Cinderella story presented by Dillingham in 1912, Herbert gave Montgomery and Stone their most satisfactory vehicle since *The Wizard of Oz*. This "musical play" was mounted in the best Dillingham style, with the capable R. H. Burnside in the pit, and Elsie Janis, Vernon Castle, and Peggy Wood sharing billing with Montgomery and Stone. The production was in every way refined and in good taste, and was considered "as artistic as any ever seen on Broadway." Castle, as Prince Charming, and Elsie Janis, as Cinderella, danced a waltz. Fred Stone, as the Straw Man, sang and danced and contorted himself in an acrobatic feature known as the "Punch Bowl Glide." Elsie Janis delighted the audience with her imitations. And, to top things off, there was a Russian ballet with Lydia Lopokova as *première danseuse*. It was as lovely a show as could be found; and though the score is not one of his best, the production was one of the high points in Herbert's career.

Though *Sweethearts*, a Cinderella sequel to *The Lady of the Slipper*, was a lesser success when it was produced in 1913, its music proved to have more longevity, and is still subject to revival in outdoor summer-operetta theatres. The relative standing in their own day of these two allied pieces again shows the difficulty of distinguishing content from presentation, in looking back upon historical events in the theatre. What is done with a musical show can often be more important to its success than the intrinsic qualities of book, score, and lyrics. Had Werba and Luescher possessed Dillingham's professional skill, they might have given *Sweethearts* at the outset the standing it attained only over the years.

Herbert's other hits in this period were *The Only Girl* (1914), *The Princess Pat* (1915), and *The Century Girl* (1916). Surprisingly enough, Joe Weber's production of *Eileen*, with which Herbert realized his dream of composing an operetta of Ireland, ran up only 64 performances. To this day *Eileen* is not as popular as it should be; its music surpasses that of *Naughty Marietta* and *Mlle. Modiste*, and is perhaps the warmest of all Herbert's scores.

It was perhaps an oversight of the *Dramatic Mirror's* editorial-writer not to link the name of Ivan Caryll with that of Herbert. For it was in the years from 1911 to 1914 that the Belgian-born, German-trained, English-veneered, American-adopted composer reached the height of his career. Only six days after the editorial appeared, in fact, Caryll achieved one of his most resounding successes with *Chin-Chin*. And both *The Pink Lady* and *Oh! Oh! Delphine* should still have been fairly fresh in the writer's memory.

The Pink Lady, which opened under Klaw and Erlanger's management on March 13, 1911, broke all records for receipts and attendance at the New Amsterdam Theatre in the course of its 320-performance run. In Baltimore, on tour, it broke all records in that city's history except that of *Ben Hur*. Its whole tour was a triumph—especially in Columbus, where it opened the Hartman Theatre, today the sole remaining legitimate house in the Ohio capital.

The Pink Lady was the *Oklahoma!* or *South Pacific* of its day. Everybody, the country over, had heard of it, and everybody wanted to see it. Earl Derr Biggers, then a drama critic in Boston, said that "everyone should see *The Pink Lady* to discover what a musical comedy should be." Philip Hale, of the Boston *Herald*, wrote: "Here we have, then, an amusing book, pleasing music, a rare combination. Here we have a musical comedy that does not depend upon the antics of an acrobatic comedian, on clowning or the independent display of brazen-faced show girls."

Pink became the rage in women's fashions. On the stage, Hazel Dawn, a Utah girl who had risen to stardom in London, wore a "princess effect, with a *chapeau directoire* of coral Milan straw, trimmed with a soft willow plume drooping softly over the left side of the head." Helen Taft pink supplanted Alice blue.

Audiences swooned pleasurably when Hazel Dawn played the dreamy waltz, "Beautiful Lady," on her violin. They gazed with awe upon the spectacular double stairway in the second act, on which the entire cast ranged itself for the chorus of the catchy comic song, "Donny Did, Donny Didn't," and they swayed with the "Ball of the Nymphs and Satyrs" in the third. It was all very striking, very wholesome and clean. But there was not a thing new about *The Pink Lady*: The Satyr Café in Paris was a lineal descendant of Maxim's in *The Merry Widow*; the pink coloring was a recollection of *Erminie*. Yet nobody had the right to say that Caryll could not write a musical comedy that was pleasing to the American audience—and certainly nobody said that Julian Mitchell did not know how to stage some of the most sumptuous production numbers on the New York stage.

For his next success, Caryll and his librettist, C. M. S. McLellan, turned to the naughty-but-nice school, working an obscure French farce into *Oh! Oh! Delphine,* which gave the first of 248 performances in the Knickerbocker Theatre on September 30, 1912. The basis of the plot was so dismal that it deserves to be told: it concerned the search an artist for a model for the left shoulder of Venus. At the opening, the management instituted the unprecedented rule that nobody should be seated after 8:10. Diamond Jim Brady was forced to wait for an hour at the back of the house. Octavia Brosker, as Bimboula, a carpet-seller from Persia, wore "gorgeous flimsy garments and Turkish trouser-ettes," and sang the hit song, "The Venus Waltz." Frank McIntyre sang "Everything's at Home Except Your Wife." A parrot cried "Oh! Oh! Delphine" at regular intervals. At the beginning of the second act, the chorus sang:

> "Now take them all up to the blue room,
> Or rather the bill and coo room."

Another of McLellan's lyrics employed these inspired rhymes:

> "Oo-la!
> Bimboula!
> Of my heart you are the ruler.
> When you are nigh,
> I only gaze and sigh.
> Oo-la!
> Bimboula!"

After such lesser undertakings as *The Little Café* (1913), which had a "rarely beautiful garden scene, with the Venus familiar as a truss-maker's trade-mark," and *The Belle of Bond Street* (1914), in which Gaby Deslys wore garish gowns and sang "Who Paid the Rent for Mrs. Rip Van Winkle?", Caryll got down to business with *Chin-Chin, or A Modern Aladdin*. Produced by Charles Dillingham as a vehicle for Montgomery and Stone, this oriental "musical fantasy" opened at the Globe Theatre on October 20, 1914, ran for 295 times, and made an extensive junket across the country. True to its subtitle, *Chin-Chin* had a mod-ernized Aladdin plot, but Montgomery and Stone, in coolie costumes, with little round caps and pigtails reaching to the back of their knees, kept interfering with its natural prog-ress. Montgomery was his usual amiable, nimble self. Stone appeared as a ventriloquist, a lady bareback rider, an eccentric dancer. As Paderewski, he left a mechanical piano going while he danced with Violet Zell.

Almost nothing was left out of *Chin-Chin*, which reverted in shameless fashion to the technique of suspending as heavy a weight of entertainment as possible from as tenuous a plot-thread as possible. The advertisement offered "caravans of pretty girls; carloads of novelties; tingling-jingling numbers; gorgeous costumes; wonderful scenes; startling situations; quaint Toy Bazaar; teddy bear dances; the Wishing Lamp; the Rain of Gold; the Inimitable 'Paderiski'; the Flight of the Pagoda; the Flight of the Airship; the Marvelous Ventriloquist; the Clown Band; Mademoiselle Fall-offski, etc. etc." To top it all, the beauteous Marion Davies put in her appearance; and Fred Stone sang "Good-bye, Girls, I'm Through."

In *Jack O'Lantern* (1917), Caryll wrote the score for an almost equally popular extravaganza, in which Fred Stone appeared in partnership not with Montgomery but with Oscar ("Rags") Ragland, the king of burlesque comics, who on this occasion made one of his few ventures into the presence of a legitimate-theatre audience. The following year Caryll wrote a musical comedy in collaboration with Guy Bolton and P. G. Wodehouse, *The Girl Behind the Gun*, in which Donald Brian and Wilda Bennett poked fun at "the godmother craze among French soldiers and the godson craze among French girls."

Among the composers of the older generation, Reginald de Koven had become by now something of a myth. A living myth, to be sure, for he kept right on feeling the impulse to compose. From the eagerness with which producers— even canny ones, like the Shuberts—seized at each new De Koven comic opera over more than twenty years, one would think that *Robin Hood* had been more of an earth-shaking work than it was. In point of fact, the chief use of *Robin*

Hood, after its first far from immoderate run, was as a standard repertory piece for the Bostonians, who throve on the presentation of well-cast, smoothly staged comic operas of traditional stripe, from Gilbert and Sullivan to von Suppé's *Fatinitza.* In the later years of his career, De Koven disappointed producers and audiences who hoped for another "O Promise Me" or "Brown October Ale." Christine Nielson and Dorothy Jardon sang in *Her Wedding Trip* (1911), and Mitzi Hajos and Mae Murray lent their vivacious personalities to *Her Little Highness* (1913), to no avail. *Robin Hood* and *Rob Roy* were revived in 1912 and 1913, and *The Highwayman,* with Bianca Saroya, John Charles Thomas, and Jefferson de Angelis, in 1917; but the pavement was worn down by the footsteps of those who passed by the theatre without pausing to buy tickets.

Two more titles complete this end-of-an-era obituary. Gustav Luders was represented for the last time in 1913, by *Somewhere Else,* which was so harshly criticized that a rumor spread to the effect that Luders' subsequent suicide was caused by its bad reception. Ludwig Englander did not commit suicide after the nine performances of his last comic opera, *Madam Moselle* (1914), but it was obvious that he could no longer win the public that had supported his efforts a decade earlier.

When *The Firefly* opened at the Lyric Theatre, under Arthur Hammerstein's management, in 1912, it was apparent that the son of the former director of the Manhattan Opera had discovered an important new talent in Rudolf Friml, its composer. A young American who had started out as a piano virtuoso, Friml possessed a spontaneous gift for writing operetta tunes with a little more substance than the ordinary musical-comedy song. His sensitive feeling for the voice made his tunes grateful to singers, without taxing their resources. The score of *The Firefly* enabled Emma

Trentini to make a good display of her large soprano voice in the role of an Italian street singer who, for love of a yachtsman, made her way to Bermuda as a cabin boy, and ultimately became a famous prima donna. Despite her voice, comic opera proved not to be Mme. Trentini's forte, for she lacked charm of presence, and she "acted like a jumping-jack and talked like a parrot . . . in bastard English." Other leading ladies, in revivals of *The Firefly*, have supplied qualities Mme. Trentini did not display; and, thanks partly to the "Donkey Serenade," the piece has found a haven in the outdoor operetta stadia.

With the collaboration of Otto Hauerbach, one of the most assured authors of books and lyrics, Friml turned out a succession of money-makers, not all of which matched *The Firefly* in intrinsic merit. *High Jinks* (1913) was more vaude-villian in the tone of its score and performance. But *Katinka* (1915) again justified Hammerstein's faith in the Friml-Hauerbach combination. If anything could revive comic opera in an age of ragtime, *Katinka* could; it ran for 220 performances, offering its customers a feast of exotic scenes—a villa on the Black Sea, Stamboul and its harems, the inevitable café in old Vienna. In the third act the great vaudeville performer, A. Robbins, was invited to demonstrate the act upon which he subsisted his whole life long, which entailed pulling an endless variety of incredible objects, large and small, out of his baggy trousers. Just why he should be an entertainer in a Viennese café was not clear then, and is not now, but nobody who ever saw A. Robbins will doubt that he supplied the funniest moments of the evening.

But comic opera had already become an anachronism. *Katinka* was "not a 1916 model." It was, as Heywood Broun wrote, "the sort of a play in which when a character wishes to sing a song she exclaims, 'What shall I do?' Fortunately, the leader of the orchestra was there to inform her." Broun's observation was typical of the thinking of the time. A split had now taken place in the ranks of the theatre-going public, a split that has remained to our own day. The larger part of the audience preferred to keep up with the times. But there remained a homey, melody-loving public, attuned to less exigeant matters than those of foreign-language grand opera, which had become fixated upon the easy delights of comic opera. For the next two generations, there was no exhausting the loyalty of this audience. Novelty was no longer a requisite of comic opera. The critics and the sophisticated public were seldom going to approve of it anyhow, and its own patient, special audience would continue to adore it— especially when it was given in the open on a hot summer night.

One Friml opera of the period, however, did break through the conventions—not because Friml intended it to, but because a man by the name of Ed Wynn would not let it alone. *Sometime* was what the piece produced by Hammerstein in 1918 was called, but any other title would have done as well. "When Mr. Wynn was on the stage the audience forgot *Sometime*," reported *Theatre* magazine. "In fact, time never occurred to them. But when he was not on the stage things dragged dreadfully. For instance, there was a hectic, pink young thing. She was supposed to be the leading lady—whatever that means nowadays— and did her best to make one forget Mr. Wynn, but, thanks to Mr. Wynn's genuine humor, one managed to live through the periods when the pink young thing was on the stage." The pink young thing, unhappy to relate, was Francine Larrimore. Another member of the cast was not even singled out for mention in *Theatre*. Her name was Mae West.

A rival to Friml soon appeared in Sigmund Romberg, who was responsible a little later on for the two hardiest comic operas of the post-World War I repertory, *Blossom Time* and *The Student Prince*. European-born and educated, Romberg was a more thoroughly trained composer than Friml, and in consequence a more versatile one. Coming to this country in his youth, he found himself a job as staff composer at the Winter Garden, which for four years required his whole energy as a tunesmith for the spicy *Passing Show* and other revues. In 1916, for the Shuberts, he ventured into the comic-opera field for the first time, with *The Girl from Brazil*, which was not much of a success. In the same year he tried an out-and-out musical comedy, *Follow Me*, in which Anna Held, covered with diamonds and still retaining her figure, returned after several years' absence to sing "I Want to be Good but My Eyes Won't Let Me" in milk-white tights. Finally, with *Maytime*, produced by the Shuberts in 1917, Romberg hit upon the vein of refined and warmly spontaneous lyricism for which he is still held in affection. He could turn on the tin-pan-alley style at will, to write music for the Winter Garden or for *Over the Top* (1917), but it is in the style of *Maytime* that he has written his most enduring tunes, which he still plays for audiences of thousands on his annual tours with his orchestra.

XIV

A New Era

On January 16, 1912, Winthrop Ames, an ardent young producer with a passion for the betterment of the theatre, entered the New York arena by bringing to the Casino Theatre the complete company of the Deutsches Theater in Berlin. There was no language difficulty, for their "play in nine tableaux" contained not a single spoken word. The accompanying music was composed by Victor Holländer, and the book—or scenario—was by Friedrich Freska. The piece was *Sumurun,* and it was a long and complicated Oriental fantasy.

Sumurun was by all odds the most challenging theatrical event of the twentieth century so far. It introduced America to Max Reinhardt, a stage director whose creative imagination was gradually to revolutionize much of the craft of theatrical production on the American stage, as it had already begun to in Europe.

Some of the critics were so busy expressing official distaste at the frankly erotic aspects of the pantomime in *Sumurun* that they almost overlooked its epoch-making qualities as sheer theatrical spectacle. The *Dramatic Mirror* observed that "the verb *amare* is conjugated in every form, and especially in the imperative." The *Globe* found it "the last word in erotology." The *Times* reported on "a scene of Oriental wooing which would come as near justifying the ringing down of the asbestos curtain as anything which has been disclosed."

But erotology comes cheap, and can be found almost anywhere one wants to look for it. It was in the practical application of Reinhardt's theories of the unity of all the elements of a lyric-theatre performance that *Sumurun* stood apart from and well above every contemporaneous production—so far, indeed, that only the intellectuals were attracted by it, and the run closed after only 62 performances, which were by no means enough to reimburse Ames for the immense cost of bringing the company over and equipping the Casino Theatre.

The stage settings fell oddly upon the consciousness of playgoers used to fussy, gaudy mélanges that were expensive-looking, cluttered-up, and full of color at every cost. Ernest Stern's scenery for *Sumurun* did not compete with the actors and did not swear at the costumes. It was marked by flat, plain-toned surfaces against which the acting and dancing, closely related to each other, could always be discerned without loss of focus. It was, moreover, scenery devised to permit—no, to require—the illusion of skillful lighting. Design, color, and lighting all conspired to enhance the moods of the fantasy, and to compel attention upon the central action. *Sumurun* was the archetype of all we now take for granted as desirable in modern unified design and presentation.

"The lines are straight," explained the *Dramatic Mirror*, "and crude colors are massed in broad, flat expanses. The closing scene of the first half exemplifies the style most strikingly, for it consists of three colors—a frieze of pure white, with the black, shadowy palace, behind it, against a dark but brilliant blue sky. The fantastic characters cross the stage before this white background like animated decorations on Keats's famous Grecian urn. The yellow harem, with its spiral staircase running up to the two corridor balconies, one above the other, is another example of the same poster style. The sheik's chamber was executed by utilizing light in an identical fashion. A huge lantern, hung from the centre of the ceiling, shed its glow slantingly down filmy white draperies leading from it to the bed. The guidance of the light and the eye left the remainder of the stage in obscurity."

The *Times* rounded out the picture with a description of the first scene, in an Oriental bazaar, "represented in a simple, flat elevation of a creamy color, punctuated here and there by oval windows with lattice work in a peculiar shade of blue, and a general effect both restful and unusual."

It was the *Tribune*, though, which came closest to understanding the point, even if its observation was meant to be grouchy: "The scenery is of the plainest. It suggests rather than illustrates."

In its love for gauche overdisplay and romantic realism, the American theatre had entirely forgotten how to "suggest rather than illustrate." For Reinhardt, the suggestion of a whole mood or concept was a more desirable achievement than the literal illustration of part of one. Instead of conforming to the limitations of the stage as they were then understood, he triumphed over them by violating them. He dared to "break the proscenium" by building a stage apron in front of the usual footlight trough and bringing his actors out onto the apron, in closer contact with the audience. He even instructed one actor to lie down right next to the footlights. Most startling of all, he constructed a runway from the front of the theatre to the orchestra pit, over the orchestra chairs, illuminated it with a blue light, and carried the action out into the house, above the heads of the spectators.

Such unabashed functionalism, so complete a challenge to the established canons of staging, was considerably in advance of its time. During the next decade Reinhardt's innovations were slowly incorporated, one by one—frequently in misunderstood or trivialized fashion—into American productions. It was considerably longer, however, before the basic principles of unity that guided Reinhardt's work were thoroughly apprehended and absorbed by American directors and producers; many, of course, have not apprehended them yet. The most immediate influence of *Sumurun* stemmed from its outward accidents rather than its inward essence.

The aspect of exotic Oriental splendor in *Sumurun* led, in due season, to such splashy displays as *Chu Chin Chow* and *Mecca*. For these evocations of the other side of the globe, however, *Sumurun* was by no means wholly responsible. Orientalism, whether in round-the-world extravaganzas or in such comic operas as *The Mikado*, *Wang*, and *The Geisha*, had long been considered a sure-fire device, if not used too often. And by way of fresh impetus, a new cult of the exotic was derived from Russia in 1911, the year before *Sumurun*. In that year, Klaw and Erlanger imported a Russian balalaika orchestra to make sounds such as had not been heard before. A few months later Gertrude Hoffman, having made due arrangements with Diaghileff, presented

1. The celebrated *pas de démons* in the last act of *The Black Crook*

2. Lydia Thompson, headmistress of the British blondes

3. A poster for *The Tourists in a Pullman Palace Car*

4. James Maffitt as the Lone Fisherman in *Evangeline*

Salsbury's Troubadours, the first American farce-comedy troupe

6. Two showmen: Tony Pastor (*left*) and Edward Harri

7. A poster heralding the 1885 revival of *Evangeline*

8. Fay Templeton as Gabriel in the 1885 *Evangeline* revival

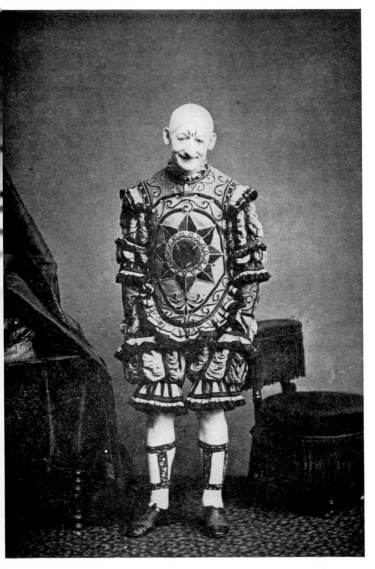

9. George L. Fox as Clown in the pantomime *Humpty Dumpty*

10. James T. Powers in a travesty of the dancer Carmencita

12. The popular matinee idol Henry E. Dixey in *Adonis*

11. The hour-glass figure of Lillian Russell in *Pepita*

13. Francis Wilson in the role of Cadeaux in *Erminie*

14. Edna Wallace and De Wolf Hopper in *Panjandrum*

15. A burlesque of the Florodora Sextette at Weber and Fields'

16. Joe Weber, Marie Dressler, and Harry Morris at the Music Hall

17. George M. Cohan early in his career on Broadway

18. Fred Stone and David Montgomery in *The Wizard of Oz*

19. Bert Williams and George Walker in *Abyssinia*

20. Anna Held, the first Ziegfeld beauty

21. Ethel Jackson in *The Merry Widow*

22. Fritzi Scheff in *Mlle. Modiste*

23. Leopoldine Konstantin in Max Reinhardt's *Sumurun*

24. A lavishly decorated scene in *The Prince of Pilsen*

25. Hazel Dawn and her violin in *The Pink Lady*

26. Leon Errol and a colleague in the *Ziegfeld Follies*

3. Fantasy on Broadway in *Finian's Rainbow* (*above*) and *Brigadoon*

64. Ezio Pinza, Mary Martin, brandy, and romance in *South Pacific*

27. The Gymnasium Girls in *The Passing Show of 1914*

28. F. E. Miller and Aubrey Lyles in *Shuffle Along*

29. Eddie Cantor in his *Ziegfeld Follies* days

30. Willie Howard in *Crazy with the Heat*

31. Marilyn Miller in military semblance in *Rosalie*

32. The Marx Brothers in a lyric moment of *The Cocoanuts*

33. Al Jolson and aboriginal companions in *Robinson Crusoe, Jr.*

34. Charles Winninger greets the river-boat audience in *Show Boat*

35. Tamara Geva, Ray Bolger, and George Church in *On Your Toes*

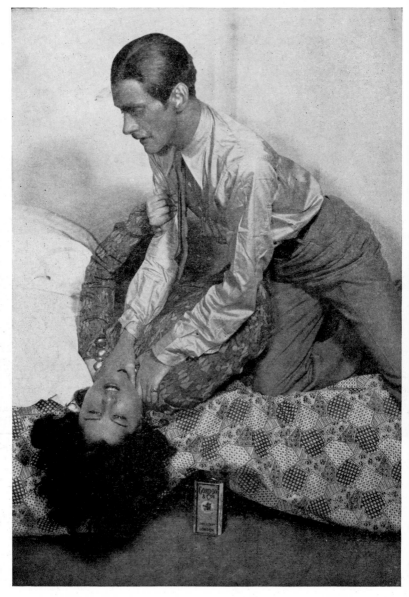

36. Libby Holman and Clifton Webb in *The Little Show*

37. Fred Astaire and his sister Adele in *The Band Wagon*

38. The merry-go-round finale of Act 1 of *The Band Wagon*

39. Victor Moore delivering an address in *Of Thee I Sing*

40. Beatrice Lillie as a traveler in *At Home Abroad*

41. George M. Cohan in *I'd Rather Be Right*

42. Vivienne Segal and Dennis King in *I Married an Angel*

43. Walter Huston in *Knickerbocker Holiday*

44. Jimmy Durante in *Stars in Your Eyes*

45. Bill Robinson in the title role of *The Hot Mikado*

46. Ed Wynn, the Perfect Fool, in *Boys and Girls Togethe*

47. *Porgy and Bess,* with Todd Duncan as Porgy

48. Ethel Waters in a visionary moment of *Cabin in the Sky*

49. A shop window, Gene Kelly, and Leila Ernst in *Pal Joey*

50. Danny Kaye's lightning patter in *Let's Face It*

51. The blaring number "Steam on the Beam" in *Beat the Band*

52. Ethel Merman and Bert Lahr in *Du Barry Was a Lady*

53. Bobby Clark wooing Gypsy Rose Lee in *Star and Garter*

54. Gertrude Lawrence's subliminal life in *Lady in the Dark*

55. Gertrude Lawrence in her office in *Lady in the Dark*

56. Horseplay under rigid military discipline in *This Is the Army*

57. Muriel Smith and Glenn Bryant in *Carmen Jones*

58. Archie Savage, Katherine Dunham, and Talley Beatty

Agnes de Mille's ballets in *Oklahoma!* (*above*) and *Bloomer Girl*

60. Scenes of New York in *Up in Central Park (above)* and *On the*

61. Bertha Belmore, Ray Bolger, Benay Venuta in *By Jupiter*

62. Ethel Merman as Annie Oakley in *Annie Get Your Gu*

her Russian Ballet at the new Winter Garden, dancing the role of Zobéide in *Scheherazade*, with a décor devised after that of Léon Bakst, and engaging Lydia Lopokova and Alexandre Volinine to appear in *Cléopâtre* and *Les Sylphides*.

At the Winter Garden the art of ballet and the old commerce of pleasing the tired business man learned to live together on congenial terms again for the first time since the decline of French ballet in the 1870s. Opened in 1911, the luxurious theatre, which still stands on the former site of the Horse Exchange, was dedicated to revues and extravaganzas. In the summer, the roof was used for the presentation of smaller midnight entertainments, with accompanying food and drink in the cabaret fashion that was at its height then and for a decade afterward.

The first entertainment at the Winter Garden, produced on March 20, 1911, by the Shuberts, who have been its sole owners since the beginning, was a double bill. The first half, *Bow Sing*, was devoted to art. The second half, *La Belle Paree*, concentrated upon frivolity, though the inclusion of the operatic soprano, Dorothy Jardon, who had been engaged mainly for *Bow Sing*, might be termed a concession to art. The new institution was thought to represent "a great outlay of money, energy, and brains," and the first bill left the audience "limp from the exhaustive spectacle and from laughter." Once *Bow Sing*, a Chinese opera in three acts with a score by Manuel Klein and a book by Carroll Fleming, had run its dutiful, and no doubt beautiful, course, the audience was free to enjoy *La Belle Paree*. Described in the program as "a Cook's tour through vaudeville, with a Parisian landscape," the revue was studded with talent on all sides. Jerome Kern and Frank Tours shared responsibility for the music; Edgar Smith, a master of the discreetly dirty phrase and situation, contributed the book and sketches. Melville Ellis, a leading designer of harmonious and fashionable costumes for the musical stage, and Arthur Voegtlin, a scenic designer whose father had devised the visual effects of *The Black Crook*, collaborated in the decorative features. The pert Mitzi Hajos and young Al Jolson, whose days of great popularity still lay ahead, were in the cast. The ballet offered not only the classic graces of Mlle. Dazie and Signor Bonfiglio, but also the more elemental divertissements of Tortajada and sixteen Moorish dancing girls. It is worthy of note that *La Belle Paree* endured for 104 performances, while *Bow Sing* was eliminated after 32.

Success breeds imitation. On April 27, at the Folies Bergère, Henry B. Harris and Jesse L. Lasky launched an entertainment modeled after that of the Winter Garden. The Folies Bergère was a restaurant-theatre, however, and its shows, given at midnight, were shorter than those of the Winter Garden, though hardly less elaborate in conception. The first attraction was a triple bill. It began with a "profane burlesque," *Hell*. Elizabeth Goodall, as the Statue of Liberty, got tired of standing on a pedestal, and decided to go to Hades, "about the only free place nowadays." The Devil and Mrs. Devil introduced her to a variety of people —a Pittsburgh trust magnate looking for a "hot time," Phoebe Snow, a blasé first-nighter. Liberty soon decided that Hell was no better than New York, and returned to her pedestal. The cynicism of *Hell* was counterbalanced by a one-act ballet, *Temptation*, in which Mlle. Britta and Signor Borghini were assigned the choreographic task of showing "how pure love overcame earthly pleasure." One critic complained that the constant manipulation of colored lights distracted from the dancing. The evening was rounded off by *Gaby*, a "satirical revuette," which was again in a riot of color, ending with a "kaleidoscopic assembly of tints."

The Winter Garden, unruffled by the borrowing of its

formula, offered two more entertainments in its first year. *The Revue of Revues* was a collection of three "musical satires." This time the order of things was reversed, and the most popular material came first, with *In the Limelight*, in which grace was sacrificed to grotesquerie in "dancing of the energetic, whirligig kind." *Nel Giappone*, a Japanese pantomime ballet, followed. The order of the program was finally explained by the third piece, a French "comedietta" called *Les Débuts de Chichine*; for Gaby Deslys, making her first American appearance in this, was expected to provide the climax of the evening. She did not create quite the sensation the Shuberts must have hoped for, since, though she was lovely to look upon, she was not much of a singer or dancer. Moreover, the sincerity and directness of Frank Tinney in his humorous monologues, and his quick gift for etching characters, made an impression that tended to obscure the claims of Mlle. Deslys.

Al Jolson came back in *Vera Violetta*, an entertainment that still retained shreds of a German libretto by Leo Stein. His popularity was now decidedly on the upgrade, as was that of Mlle. Deslys, who had begun to be intelligible in English. Mae West, always doomed to receive little notice at this early stage of her career, was also among those present. As a curtain-raiser, a version of *Undine* was written and composed by Manuel Klein and provided with a setting reproducing what was described as a "Claude Manet landscape." Annette Kellermann, bereft of a tank, was able to demonstrate that "her dancing was as marvellous as her diving."

By the end of its first year, the Winter Garden had become an assured operation. The bill on March 5, 1912, started off with *A Night with the Pierrots*, in which the participants in the harlequinade were Al Jolson, Barney Bernard, and a bright young hoofer named George White.

This time the art-item in the middle was frankly played for laughs. Called *Sesostra*, it was a burlesque of the newly arrived *Sumurun*, in which the seemingly bizarre eccentricities of Reinhardt's staging were given a hearty ribbing. Actually, it was to the main piece of the evening, *The Whirl of Society*, that *Sumurun* made its real contribution. Envisaging uses for it of which Reinhardt had not dreamed, the management built a runway across the pit and out into the house. The hoydenish Blossom Seeley used it in a marathon around the aisles of the theatre. But more than this, the girls of the chorus came out on the runway, where the audience could see them much, much better.

With the coming of summer the Shuberts—now incorporated for this special purpose as the Winter Garden Company—revived a great name from the past, and, with the obvious intention of making it an annual affair like the *Ziegfeld Follies*, presented *The Passing Show of 1912*. For the new venture they engaged, or retained from previous assignments, what was to be a fairly permanent production personnel. Ned Wayburn, one of the slickest masters of show-dance routines, became the dance director (nobody called them choreographers in those days). Melville Ellis remained as costume designer. Harold L. Atteridge wrote the lyrics for George Bronson Howard's book; in subsequent editions Atteridge took care of both book and lyrics. Louis A. Hirsch, who did not stay on to do another one, wrote the score.

The chief performers in *The Passing Show* were all new to the Winter Garden, except Jobyna Howland, who had added to the good looks of *The Whirl of Society*. The book was nominally concerned with take-offs on such current theatrical hits as *The Quaker Girl* and *Bunty Pulls the Strings*, for to this extent *The Passing Show of 1912* was conceived in the image of its predecessor of 1894. But the

people in it were more important than its material. The
eighty artfully chosen girls—by whom, according to *Variety*,
"the *Sumurun* runway was again fully tested to its limit"—
answered to three specialized classifications, "show girls"
(the tall, statuesque ones), "mediums," and "ponies."
Longer-legged than the show girls was the future Letty,
Charlotte Greenwood, who swung her legs about and
tangled them up in her usual fashion. Eugene and Willie
Howard graduated from vaudeville into a partnership that
retained its hold upon popular affections for thirty years.
And the first act contained a song, "Ragtime Jockey Man,"
by a young rehearsal pianist named Irving Berlin.

Once the enterprise was under way, the *Passing Show*
arrived like clockwork every year—sometimes as early as
April, sometimes as late as July, depending on other book-
ings at the Winter Garden—and never failed to run for
from fifteen to twenty weeks before setting out on the road.

The second edition, *The Passing Show of 1913*, retained
the runway and Charlotte Greenwood, and introduced John
Charles Thomas, in his first Broadway engagement. Ned
Wayburn provided every variant on the tango and the turkey-trot, and revived the "almost forgotten" cakewalk of
the previous decade. The finale, the most imposing spectacle Voegtlin had yet conceived for the Winter Garden,
showed the steps of the Capitol in Washington, reaching
"from the front of the stage to seventh heaven."

The Passing Show of 1914 was probably never surpassed
in the history of the institution. The two earlier editions had
leaned quite heavily on their stars—the Howards and Charlotte Greenwood. But the third *Passing Show* was in every
way a rounded, balanced, and lavish entertainment. To be
sure, it introduced (for the first time outside vaudeville)
Marilynn Miller, who was to become within a decade the
highest-paid star the American musical theatre had known.

But now she was merely an unknown youngster, though she made an instantaneous hit with her capable dancing and her sprightly imitations of popular actresses.

But the third *Passing Show* went down in history primarily as the moment of final triumph for the slender, modern chorus girl. Gone forever now were the gigantic chorus ladies with their Amazonian marches and drills. "When a Kiralfy show was announced," one old-timer recalled, "managers were wont to look after the bracings under the stage. In the earlier days a chorus person was not considered much of a charmer unless she possessed limbs like barrels, and with a spear in hand, waddled about the stage."

This contrast is, of course, somewhat overdrawn, for fashions do not change overnight, and the choral Amazon had been on the way out for some years. But with *The Passing Show of 1914* the metamorphosis was complete. It signalized the edging-out of the baldheads from the front row, and the usurpation of their places by "unwhipped cubs, the silken sons of dalliance nursed in pleasure's flowery lap." For the benefit of the unwhipped cubs, the girls' legs, which had been emerging from their tights inch by inch for several seasons, were now presented unadorned and *au naturel*, underneath "torsos screened by glittering spangles." Skirts were short and arms were bare, and at one point the glittering spangles were dispensed with, revealing bare midriffs on the upper-class New York stage for the first time. The "winsome witches" gave a new and piquant meaning to the runway; and when they returned to the stage they revealed unwonted energy and talent by engaging in thoroughly professional tap-dancing. In the midst of this "uproarious upheaval of lingerie and laughter," demure little Marilynn Miller (who had not yet cropped the final "n" from her first name) appeared as a Dresden Doll. Nor were the purely spectacular elements overlooked in this carnival of undress. Voegtlin provided a panoramic view of the San Francisco World's Fair and a scene representing the trans-atlantic flight of an airship; and art—not wholly forgotten —was solemnized in a "Beautiful Persian Garden Scene," in the style of Maxfield Parrish.

There is no need to recall subsequent *Passing Shows* in detail, for the pattern was now set. Marilynn Miller, with her adorable smile and happy dancing, was back in 1915, along with the Howards, to grant surcease from a "realistic invasion of London by Zeppelins." The *Globe* commented acidly that bare knees had "ceased to be a *sauce piquante*." But everybody loved Marilynn Miller when she appeared as First Love, opposite John Charles Thomas as Youth.

The 1915 edition showed a falling-off in wit and imagina-tion, though Ed Wynn carried his end of the show, and there were novelties in the form of revivals of clogging and buck-and-wing dancing, an "Olympian ballet" suggesting *Scheherazade*, and a memorable tune by Sigmund Romberg called "Pretty Baby." In 1916, Ed Wynn sought to repair an inner tube with a saw and a hammer in a sketch entitled "A Modern Garage." The humor generally, however, was on the level of cracks about Philadelphia and the Ford car and fighting with one's wife; and the girls who still did boys' parts in the chorus were coming to seem old-fashioned. By 1917 *The Passing Show* had become hardly more than an expensive annual obeisance—this time with De Wolf Hop-per and Jefferson de Angelis as veteran comics, and a "dis-appointingly overdressed" chorus. The 1918 edition had a brighter topical book, with sketches about War Savings Stamps and the new fad of having supper at Childs, and a burlesque showing Salome with the head of the Kaiser. The Howard brothers were back, and the cast also included such newcomers as Fred and Adele Astaire, Sammy White, Marion Stafford, Charles Ruggles, Frank Fay, and Nita Naldi.

In the months when *The Passing Show* was away, the Winter Garden housed other attractions of similar format and appeal. Of one of these, *The Whirl of the World* in 1914, Alan Dale of the New York *American*, describing the "sort of peninsula which separated the stage from the auditorium so that the girls could be touched," wrote pleadingly, "Oh, parents . . . keep tender boys at home. . . . Keep them—aye, keep them from the Winter Garden. It is very, awfully, dangerous." To which Charles Darnton of the *World* added that the Winter Garden was "no place for a man with a weak heart." Plainly people did not come to *The Whirl of the World* with the primary object of seeing Lydia Kyasht and Serge Litavkin in "Harlequin and the Bluebird." A similar situation obtained with *Dancing Around*, later the same year, when the audience had no eyes for Clifton Webb and Eileen Molyneux, an English ballerina, in the "Shepherd Gavotte" and "Silhouette Ballet."

Let the Winter Garden itself provide an evocative finish for our consideration of its early years. How would the late Commissioner Paul Moss have reacted to this throwaway of *A World of Pleasure*, in 1915?

"PERFECT FROM THE PINKY OF THE CUTEST LITTLE PONY TO THE MAJESTIC BATTLESHIP, WHICH, FIRST HEADING TOWARDS THE AUDIENCE, TURNS COMPLETELY ABOUT AND PLOUGHS FORWARD IN THE OPPOSITE DIRECTION. . . . [*A World of Pleasure*] goes to extremes of undress—almost to actual nudity—that would have astounded the unsophisticated audience of five years ago. Unless a girdle of beads be considered a costume, there are scenes in which the chorus may truthfully be described as

wearing no clothes at all. Stockings are as obsolete a
Winter Garden as the steel armor of a mediaeval soldie
A dress not cut to the waist line at the back is a curiosity—
an impudent attempt at unwelcome modesty."

At the time the Winter Garden opened, Flo Ziegfeld in-
directly gave aid and comfort to the project by letting his
Follies decline in quality. The *Follies of 1911* depended
chiefly upon the eccentric behavior of the Dolly Sisters, the
weak ankle of Leon Errol, and the dancing of Bessie McCoy,
"an attractive young woman in a defiant pose, as if of virtue,
able to defend itself, on the aggressively defensive, with
the wind or the movement tossing the skirts above the
shapely ankles." A sketch, "New Year's Eve on the Barbary
Coast," contained an Apache dance, and an elaborate production number required stacks of wheat in a field to turn
into a dancing chorus. But some of the magic was missing.
More still was missing in the following year's edition, for
which Raymond Hubbell wrote music "that went in one
ear and out the other," and Harry B. Smith performed one
of his least inspired jobs of book- and lyric-writing. The
women were now barelegged, though, and in "A Palace of
Beauty," Ziegfeld introduced the device of having the show
girls parade—to the tune of "Beautiful, Beautiful Girl"—
one by one, in a spotlight, to their respective stations.

The fortunes of the *Follies* began to pick up in 1913.
Julian Mitchell surpassed himself in the big picturesque
numbers, beginning the show with an illusive tableau of
Hawkeye and a group of fellow redskins gazing down on
New York, and ending it with a depiction of the opening of
the Panama Canal and the raising of a warship in the
locks. Ann Pennington had now arrived on the scene, happily at a time when it was permissible for her to reveal her
dimpled knees; Frank Tinney was the soul of amiability;
and Leon Errol capsized the audience with an eccentric

kish Trottishness," in which he left the turkey-
a leg to stand on.

Iitchell had not spent the larger part of his
in the theatre for nothing, and in 1914—the
of *The Passing Show*—he brought the *Follies* en-
sembl.. ..o a high level of disciplined sumptuousness. This
time the most striking spectacle revealed the corner of
Fifth Avenue and Forty-second Street after a severe snow-
storm. Leon Errol—who directed the book as well as appearing in the show—chose the tango for his lampoon, and
the graceful, lithe convolutions of Ann Pennington became
the talk of the town.

Channing Pollock, Rennold Wolf, and Gene Buck,
skilled hands all, took hold of the book, sketches and lyrics
in 1915, and gave them more zest. But the greatest improvement of all was Ziegfeld's engagement of Joseph Urban as
his designer. A student of the methods of Gordon Craig
and Reinhardt, Urban gave the décors of his first *Follies*
some of the look of *Sumurun*, making astute use of the
flat colors American designers still disdained, and producing a total of twenty-one different scenes marked by an
imaginativeness and ingenuity of design and color that
neither *The Passing Show* nor any other spectacle could
rival. Against Urban's flat surfaces and plain colors, Ziegfeld's curved beauties developed a fresh appeal, especially
when they appeared in the Elysian Fields.

Urban remained Ziegfeld's designer thereafter, though
not exclusively, for he was in great demand by other producers as well. His designs and Ziegfeld's unerring eye for
the points of a girl remained the constants of subsequent
editions of the *Follies*. The performing talent did not remain fixed, though Ziegfeld was wise enough to keep his
most popular entertainers for as long as he could. One of
these returned to his ranks in 1916—Fannie Brice, who had

been in the *Follies of 1910*, and who now appeared as
Theda Bara and in a burlesque of a burlesque dancer.
Others in the same year were the adroit juggler W. C.
Fields and the handsome, self-collected, clothes-horse
Lilyan Tashman. Ina Claire, Marion Davies, and Justine
Johnstone were in the 1916 edition, too, along with Ziegfeld's droll standby, Bert Williams, and a pert young
hoofer, Carl Randall. In 1917, Ina Claire and Marion
Davies and Justine Johnstone were gone, but Lilyan Tashman was back, along with Fannie Brice, Fields, and Williams. Peggy Hopkins (not yet Joyce) made one of her
intermittent appearances. Eddie Cantor moved from Ziegfeld's cabaret show on the roof down to the street level for
the first time. Will Rogers twirled his lariat as he drawled
homespun Oklahoma philosophies. In 1918, to secure his
permanent triumph over *The Passing Show*, Ziegfeld won
Marilynn Miller away from the Shuberts, discovered a tall,
dark, languid beauty with the single name of Dolores, and
put them both against the luxurious background of Urban's
settings, in the company of Eddie Cantor, W. C. Fields,
Will Rogers, Ann Pennington, and the Fairbanks Twins.

George M. Cohan was quick to make capital of the new
enthusiasm for elaborate revues. After the lukewarm reception of *The Little Millionaire* (1911), he realized that the
time for a change had come. Allying himself with Sam H.
Harris in the producing firm of Cohan and Harris, he
brought to the Astor Theatre in 1914 a "musical crazy
quilt" (Billy Rose appropriated the term for the title of a
revue in the 1930s), *Hello Broadway*. With William Collier
as his partner, Cohan built his first revue more on the pattern of Weber and Fields than of *The Passing Show*, filling
it with broad travesties of current plays and players, stud-
ding it with his own song-and-dance routines, and brighten-
ing it with the presence of Peggy Wood, Louise Dresser,

Roszika (but not Yancsi) Dolly, and Florence Moore, one of the most hard-working and generally-liked comediennes of the decade.

Not until Cohan eliminated himself from the cast in favor of Charles Winninger, in *The Cohan Revue of 1916*, did the substance of the Cohan and Harris revues tend to become modernized, and even here the *Dramatic Mirror* observed that the décors were "not of the new art so much in evidence this season." There was one more Cohan revue, in 1918, before the managers determined to leave the field to Ziegfeld and the Shuberts. Irving Berlin provided some of the songs and Cohan the rest, and Nora Bayes was Winninger's vis-à-vis.

A few other revues cropped up under other managements, but not as many as might have been expected from the consistent prosperity of the established annuals. Klaw and Erlanger seized Joseph Urban immediately after the triumph of his first *Follies*, and had him design *Around the Map* (1915). Louise Groody, who still had several years to wait for *No, No, Nanette*, was the ingenue, but the cast was otherwise undistinguished, compared to those of Ziegfeld and the Shuberts. But the production itself outdid the *Follies of 1915*, amounting to "a gorgeous fashion show which moves in steady procession across three and a half hours." A prescient touch of modernity could be discovered in the chorus girls' dresses in the cabaret scene, which consisted of hoops of empty frames trimmed with fur at the bottom.

Of the rest of the miscellany, none is worth recalling, except perhaps Jack Norworth's "chummy" revue, *Odds and Ends of 1917*, of which Burns Mantle remarked, "The scenery is by someone who plays the Joseph Urban harmonies by ear, and is more or less tone deaf."

As is always the case when innovations come along, the

new fashions did not immediately obliterate the old ones. Of Joe Weber's series of burlesques, and of the return of Weber and Fields in 1911, we have already taken cognizance. The two final Weber and Fields items do, however, deserve a bit more attention, because it was in them, despite their generally outmoded aspect, that the pre-*Tugboat Annie* Marie Dressler gave perhaps the fullest account of her gifts. "In one scene," Alan Dale recounted of *Roly-Poly* (1912), "she appeared in bright green satin, trimmed with a fur rug! She told me she made it herself in the hopes that she would be a laughing stock in it. That hope did not materialize." Her great triumph in *Roly-Poly* was a Spanish gypsy dance, in which "her evolutions caused tremendous laughter." The audience also laughed—the Lord forgive it— at her line, "Father, you are the one thing in Mother's life I can never forgive." A few months later, in 1913, Weber and Fields offered *Marie Dressler's All-Star Gambol*, which included, among a diversity of things, a one-act play by George Arliss. Miss Dressler and Jefferson de Angelis offered a burlesque of *Camille*. They also addressed themselves to "The Evolution of Dancing," in which they were joined by the rest of the company in Ancient Greek Dancing, Old-Fashioned Step Dancing, Original Spanish Dancing (something of a novelty; the first Spanish revue, *The Land of Joy*, did not reach New York until 1917), Classic Toe Dancing, Lightning Turkey Trot, Soft Shoe Dance, Wooden Shoe Dance, Russian Dances, and, to cap the climax, a "classic dance" by Miss Dressler and De Angelis.

Another series of essentially old-fashioned revues was inaugurated by Raymond Hitchcock with *Hitchy-Koo* (1917), to which Cohan and Harris devoted their managerial energies in between the two *Cohan Revues*. Surrounded by Irene Bordoni, Leon Errol, and Florenz Ames, Hitchcock used the revue format to serve the purposes of his informal,

friendly style, greeting the arriving customers out front before the curtain went up, and engaging in confidential, im-
promptu remarks throughout the evening. The same players,
with the addition of Ray Dooley, came back the following
year in *Hitchy-Koo of 1918*, of which Hitchcock himself was
producer and Errol stage director.

Through thick and thin, through fair weather and foul,
the mammoth Hippodrome pursued its own special, spectacular course, still attracting a year's business with each
new production—except in the single case of *Wars of the
World* in 1914, which ran only half the year and caused the
Shuberts to relinquish the house to Charles Dillingham.

Since the site of the Hippodrome, at Forty-fourth Street
and Sixth Avenue, is now no more than a large level scar on
which automobiles are parked, its glories can best be called
to mind by the excited prose of the 1912 souvenir program:

"After passing through the marble lobby, with its circles
of box-offices and staircases leading to the mezzanine floor
and balconies, the visitor reaches the spacious promenade
half encircling the great auditorium. Lined with mirrors
on the outer side, between supports of marble, and on the
inner side, opening to the promenade boxes, it offers a
sight of superb splendor and magnificence.

"The chief ornamentation consists of great and golden
elephant heads, with silvered trappings, and these are
studded with electric lights, of which there are just a few
less than 8,000 from the entrance to the lobby to the dome.
On either side of the stage are boxes of various seating
capacities, some of them holding forty persons, and arranged for parties. Above is the wide sweeping balcony, the
front of which is lined with loges, where smoking is permitted. A second balcony stretches out from above. On one
mezzanine floor are attractive lounging rooms known as
'The Jungles,' where between scenes and during perform-

ances visitors find the comfort and attraction of lounging chairs and cozy corners for a chat, a rest, and refreshments."

The seating capacity at that time was given as 5,200, though in 1917 it was said to be 5,697. Two regulation-size circus rings could be installed on the stage apron. Under the apron was a tank, fourteen feet deep. The stage was 110 feet deep from footlights to back wall, and 200 feet wide, and could be moved up and down on a hydraulic elevator. The dressing rooms accommodated 1,000.

The Hippodrome shows took the whole world and all history as their province, and the mechanical skill of Arthur Voegtlin knew no limitations of time and place. *Around the World* (1911) carried spectators from New York out into mid-ocean, then to England, Switzerland, Constantinople, Egypt, and the Sahara Desert. "The effects in scenery, in distance, depth and height, and light and shade, clouds and storm and other effects impossible to the ordinary theatre, enable the Hippodrome to occupy a field all its own. Mere bigness of spectacle would soon tire the public, so that the success of the venture must be attributed to personal and artistic qualities."

Be that as it may, the "personal and artistic qualities" were bent toward essentially the same ends every year. The thirteen scenes of *Under Many Flags* (1912) included the sight of the White House lawn, the Naval Academy at Annapolis, a fishing village in Brittany, and views of Moscow, Scotland, Berlin, Pekin, and Arizona. The Arizona scene included a herd of deer and a tornado that leveled the town. Not unnaturally, it was felt that "none but a magician can eclipse the genius of Voegtlin in creating illusions such as these." And at Annapolis, Alan Dale reported, "you saw the cadets. These were not chorus girls in a vulgarity of tights, but men—and the baldheads were routed." It was hard going for the baldheads everywhere in these years.

In 1913, with *America,* Voegtlin decided to remain in the western hemisphere. He did not lack materials, however, for in the very opening scene he spanned American history from the landing of Columbus to the rush hour at the newly completed Grand Central Terminal. Later his audience visited a New England farm, the levee at New Orleans, the Alamo Plaza in San Antonio, the East Side of New York, where type characters helped the fire department fight a conflagration, and the Panama Canal, a popular and timely subject for spectacular treatment. At the end, the audience and the hundreds on the stage sang "America."

Wars of the World (1914) was the one half-way success of the series, and the last spectacle presented by the Shuberts. It offered a curious array of conflicts—Robin Hood, the "Holy War," the French Revolution, the Civil War, the taking of Vera Cruz, and the "War of Sport." In one scene soldiers raced down the aisles and were catapulted over the pit onto the stage. The list of the subsequent Hippodrome spectacles becomes redundant. John Philip Sousa and his band played in *Hip-Hip-Hooray,* in 1915. Emanuel List, later the Metropolitan Opera's Baron Ochs in Strauss's *Der Rosenkavalier,* made his first major American appearance in 1917 in *Cheer Up,* which was also egregious because of the freight train, full-size, which chugged up to a rural station at the beginning of the second act. In 1918, for a show patriotically supplied with music by Sousa and Irving Berlin and lyrics by John Golden, Dillingham finally hit upon the ideal title for a Hippodrome spectacle—*Everything.*

New Art and Old Formulas

THE LUSH "new art" movement, engendered in various ways by Reinhardt, the Ballets Russes, and Urban, was sumptuously represented on November 6, 1916, by *The Century Girl*, produced jointly by Dillingham and Ziegfeld to open the handsome new Century Theatre, up above Columbus Circle. Part musical comedy and part revue, *The Century Girl* subsisted on typical Urban-Ziegfeld effects, such as the Celestial Staircase, which Hazel Dawn descended; the Crystal Palace, with a "Procession of the Laces of the World"; and, for spice, a scene in the Garden of a Modern Girls' School. Victor Herbert and Irving Berlin provided the music; Leon Errol and Edward Royce directed; and Ned Wayburn staged the dances and musical numbers. Errol also displayed his comic ankle; Elsie Janis did her bit; Lillian (not Lilyan this time) Tashman offered her sophisticated beauty as a foil for Hazel Dawn's fresh innocence; and comic chores were allotted to Sam Bernard, the classic Dutch comic, Frank Tinney, and—in their first of several ventures out of vaudeville under Ziegfeld's aegis—Gus Van and Joe Schenck, the song-pluggers.

The Century Girl was such a triumph that Ziegfeld and Dillingham spared no expense, even according to their expensive lights, in preparing its successor the following autumn, Miss 1917. Herbert and Jerome Kern, now two of the top names in the business, wrote the score, and Guy Bolton and P. G. Wodehouse, lately established as the brightest littérateurs in the light theatre, devised the book and lyrics. Urban, of course, did the sets, and Wayburn staged the production numbers. Lady Duff Gordon was engaged to design the costumes; and, since there was ballet as well as popular dancing, Adolph Bolm was assigned to the creation of a "choreographic poem, 'Falling Leaves.'" The rehearsal pianist was the teen-age George Gershwin. The cast was nothing short of incredible. Miss Tashman and Van and Schenck were carried over from The Century Girl. Lew Fields replaced Sam Bernard as the apparently indispensable Dutch comic. Young Vivienne Segal sang in her pretty, high lyric-soprano voice. Irene Castle, Ann Pennington, George White, and Bolm all danced. Marion Davies and Peggy Hopkins contributed their beauty. Bert Savoy and Joe Brennan camped. Scarcely an entertainment of the decade was so studded with magic names. But, alas, Ziegfeld and Dillingham quickly discovered what too many cooks can do, and Miss 1917 perished ignominiously after 48 performances.

One other lavish escapist piece lightened the first fall of the war. Morris Gest, William Elliott, and F. Ray Comstock brought the splendor of Bagdad to the Manhattan Opera House on October 22, 1917, in a "musical tale of the

East" called *Chu Chin Chow*. A sort of pageant, with elements of pantomime, ballet, musical comedy, grand opera
and fantasy, *Chu Chin Chow* was the first serious attempt
to recapture the approach of Reinhardt in *Sumurun*. If it
partially failed in its intention, the incompatibility of Reinhardt principles with those of Ziegfeld can be blamed. With
Tyrone Power (Senior, of course), Florence Reed, and
George Rasely taking care of the chief acting and musical
assignments, the central roles were in good hands. Miss
Reed, just beginning the important phase of her career, was
singled out for a performance "in the right key from the
beginning, that never deviated, and was vivid, pulsing, and
vital."

But the production was more commanding than any of
the individual contributions to it. The senses were "wooed,
delighted, ravished, and astounded" by the settings, designed in a manner to "out-Bakst Bakst" by Joseph and
Phil Harker of London, who earlier had designed Henry
Irving's productions. The lighting employed Reinhardt techniques, which were still being overlooked elsewhere in the
American musical theatre: "Only the slave market, which
baked under the midday sun and the steel blue sky, was
diffused with light. In the other acts the concentrated illu-
mination fell directly on the moving character in the picture." To this illusion the music by Frederick Norton also
contributed, for while "original it is not, it has a widely
varied lilt, a salient trick in characterization, and unflagging
vigor." An unwonted device of stagecraft—an application
of moving-picture practices to the Reinhardt device of lighting only part of the stage—was manifested in the use of
"close-ups," or little vignettes, during the changes of the big
scenes. For this purpose the Harkers provided a single Moorish window set in a black curtain.

In this remarkable production, only Oscar Asche's book,

with its pretentious poetry, was out of key in its own time, as can readily be discerned from "The Love Chant of the Wild Women of the Desert":

> "Oh, ye who in walled cities dwell,
>   What do ye know of life?
> Oh, ye who strive to buy and sell,
>   What taste have ye of strife?
> Oh, ye who breathe but reek and dust,
> Who hoard your wealth for moth and rust,
> Whose veins are clogged with lazy lust,
> What can YE feel of Passion's gust?"

These big-budget attractions—*The Passing Show*, the annual *Follies, Chu Chin Chow*, the Century shows, and the Hippodrome extravaganzas—presented no threat to the continuing existence of the bread-and-butter musical productions, the normal-sized musical comedies and operettas. The second decade of the twentieth century may, for purposes of convenient cataloguing, be divided—in oversimplified fashion, to be sure—into two periods. The first period, up to 1915, witnessed constantly diminishing returns from pieces whose style was a hangover from conventions of the previous fifteen years. The second, beginning in 1915, saw the rapid sprouting of new ideas and the appearance of fresh young talents, and laid the groundwork for much that has happened in the musical theatre ever since that time.

The old order, with relatively little admixture of anything novel, was perpetuated by Lew Fields in the three musical comedies he offered in quick succession in 1911. The first of these, *The Hen Pecks*, detailed the trip of the Peck family from Cranberry Cove to New York, where Fields (his Dutch-comedy dialect intact) and Blossom Seeley encountered the debonair Vernon Castle, who sang but did not dance, along with an assortment of chorus girls decked out now in canary yellow, white, and black, now in purple, violet, lavender, and brown against a light green background. The color effects were considered "astonishing," and there can be no doubt that they were.

The Never Homes, Fields' second piece of this busy year, had to get along without its producer's presence in the cast. It might, indeed, readily be forgotten for all eternity, if Helen Hayes, a "talented little girl" of twelve—already a veteran of two previous Fields musical comedies, *Old Dutch* and *The Summer Widowers*—had not raised a singing voice that was never to be heard again until 1946, in *Happy Birthday*. Her principal number was a duet, "There's a Girl in Havana," with "little Will Archie," who was actually twenty-five years old.

The Never Homes was burdened by a plot satirizing woman suffrage. In the election, women won all the offices in the town of Lilydale. Patricia Flynn, the mayor (impersonated by the fat George W. Monroe), ran things with a high hand. In the middle of a conversation with Mrs. Daly Bunn and Mrs. Talkington Louder, the telephone rang. "Girls, what do you think?" said Patricia, toying with her hair. "There's a fire!" Then, into the telephone: "Is it a little one or a big one? If it isn't a very big one we'll come around tomorrow, as it's sort of damp out today, and it wouldn't be good for the horses to go out." Finally the apparatus left, with all the girls but Patricia clinging to the sides. "Gee!" exclaimed Patricia. "The fools have gone to the fire, and I'm the only one who knows the address." This rudimentary comedy took place against settings by Voegtlin, who gave full rein to his usual elaborate taste, using costumes of massed colors in "blazing combinations of red and black or bright green and white" and creating a new effect with "shimmering strips of silvered cloth lighted with various colors." After two more productions, both short-lived—

The Wife Hunters (1911) and *Hanky Panky* (1912)—
Fields withdrew from musical-comedy production.

The low estate of musical comedy in 1911 was further
revealed by *Jumping Jupiter*, whose score by Karl Hoschna,
one ruthless observer said, "hadn't even a tune to keep it
going." Edna Wallace Hopper, "in monkey-hat and accents
strained," was "self-conscious and chorus-girly." It was a ragtime show, with the "Mississippi Dip" and the "Possum
Rag." Like *The Never Homes, Jumping Jupiter's* interest for
posterity resides in its cast, which included Jeanne Eagels,
Helen Broderick, and, for the first time out of vaudeville,
Ina Claire.

The Red Rose, another memento of 1911, was a window-
display for the overdressed Valeska Suratt, who designed
her own innumerable costumes, the most overpowering of
which were a Spanish affair in canary yellow and black (the
fashionable color scheme of the year) and a flaming harem
skirt with the effect of a "perpendicular rainbow." Everybody on the stage wore a red rose from start to finish—in
their buttonholes, on their hats, on their dresses, or between
their lips. Rose-adorned girls handed out roses to first-
nighters at the door. In addition to wearing clothes, Miss
Suratt danced, with "sweeping freedom of movements."
When she opened her mouth, however, her French and
English had "a Chicago accent."

Julian Eltinge, the one human being who could successfully outdress Valeska Suratt, paid her the compliment, a
few weeks after the opening of *The Red Rose*, of imitating
her in *The Fascinating Widow*, a tale in which this most
decorous and ladylike of female impersonators inhabited a
college girls' dormitory. The fad for Eltinge's performances,
which continued long after he could successfully impersonate only matrons and dowagers, is an extraordinary chapter in the history of American taste. The confusion of the

sexes was, of course, a standard feature of earlier burlesques, but in these the male transvestites were always comic characters, while the girls pretended to be boys in order to show off their limbs within a code that frowned on short skirts. About Eltinge's impersonations, however, there was a serious quality that was unique. He avoided all off-color suggestion, and traded exclusively upon his grace, charm and good manners. He endeavored to wear beautiful and modish clothes with the breeding and lack of self-conscious exhibitionism of a well-groomed woman. He never stepped out of character and never drew upon the double entendre used by rougher impersonators of the Savoy and Brennan school. Whole families came to see his eminently decent shows, and the women studied his costumes with all the detached interest they showed toward Valeska Suratt. No other female impersonator has ever equalled Eltinge's quiet dignity about his profession, or gained the same unqualified acceptance from the family trade.

The exposure of feminine anatomy and the exploitation of an unbridled use of color, usually without much taste or restraining sense of color harmony, were aims that in large measure took precedence over all else in the run-of-the-mill musical successes of 1911 and 1912. *Little Boy Blue* (1911) used Gainsborough's painting as a model for the costume of Gertrude Bryan in the title role. Boy Blue was turned into a barmaid from Paris, who found herself—the locale of the plot being Scotland—among a bevy of kilted, bare-kneed chorus girls. The operetta (for so it was designated) added a page to the superstitious lore of the theatre by disposing of its Boy Blues in rapid order. By 1913, when the piece was out on the road, the Detroit *News Tribune* pointed out that the current incumbent, Katherine Clifford, was the sixth in the line, and accounted—I cannot say how reliably—for the disappearance of the first five. Miss Bryan resigned in a dudgeon, because she was refused a raise. Katherine Stevenson was impelled to give the part up because her fiancé, a clergyman, objected to his betrothed's public revelation of her uncovered knees. Eva Fallon fell into the bass drum and had to pay for it, and left in anger. Lottie Engle "ran away with an automobile demonstrator, thinking the machine he drove so gracefully was his own." Florence Martin became increasingly afflicted with "stage fright over seeing the ghosts of her predecessors."

In *The Balkan Princess* (1911) Alice Brady, making her first New York appearance under the stage name of Marie Rose, was not required to make any improper exposure. This task was allotted to Vida Whitmore, who "wore stockings that were black up to about the ankle and then commenced to grow pink all the way to the waist." Miss Whitmore's stockings, which signalized the final phase of indecorum before the ladies began leaving their stockings off altogether, were celebrated by a rash of excited articles in the newspapers and magazines. One writer felt that she was "clad in a manner sensational enough to attract the attention of St. Anthony himself." Nor were all the sensations provided by Miss Whitmore. For Melville Ellis, the costumer, and the unnamed scenic designer went the whole way to make the production a "chromatic Gehenna" of purples, greens, and scarlets.

Flo Ziegfeld, whose taste was always a notch ahead of most other producers', began to bring order out of chaos in *A Winsome Widow* (1912). A modernization of the Charles H. Hoyt hit of the 1890s, *A Trip to Chinatown*, *A Winsome Widow*, having cast an eye at *Sumurun*, employed "bright colors in plain expanses without the aimless kaleidoscopic futility so often found." Leon Errol, Frank Tinney, and the Dolly Sisters provided the entertainment, and business was undoubtedly given a fillip (it ran for 172

performances) by Anna Held's divorce action against Ziegfeld. Nine days after the opening, according to *Variety*,
"Mae West, a 'rag' singer in the *Widow*, abruptly left the
cast and prepared to return to vaudeville."

American musical comedy, obviously in sore need of new
themes, discovered the pioneer country of the West in 1912,
when *The Red Petticoat* opened at Daly's Theatre, under
the wing of the Shuberts. Neither Oklahoma nor Texas was
first honored by Broadway's attention. Lone River, Nevada,
was the scene of *The Red Petticoat*, an outpost that, to the
Dramatic Mirror, "would seem the last place in the world
to furnish local color for a musical play." Rough miners
with beards replaced the customary dandified chorus boys,
and the girls found their way into the plot of this "comic-
opera *Girl of the Golden West*" by becoming manicure
girls in the shop of a lady barber. The score was written by
Jerome Kern, who had now been performing occasional
rather insignificant chores on Broadway for eight years.
Even yet, Kern had not really found his stride, though the
Dramatic Mirror found his tunes "sometimes catchy when
they are reminiscent."

The west was also inspected through the jaundiced eyes
of a pair of German librettists (rendered into English by
Gladys Unger) in Victor Jacobi's "musical play," *The Marriage Market* (1913). Obviously conceived in Vienna and
made over along the pattern of the London Gaiety, *The
Marriage Market* caused Donald Brian, a tailor-made cowboy, to attend a marriage market in distant San Francisco.
Only the first act took place in California, however, among
the cowboys and native Spanish girls. The second act occurred on a yacht, in a manner suggesting *H. M. S. Pinafore*,
and the third managed to get everyone back to the usual
gilded palace.

The motion pictures, just coming into their first real

popularity—with *The Birth of a Nation* just around the corner—provided matter for two satiric musical comedies at this time. It is significant that both pieces originated in central Europe. Apparently the activities of Hollywood had not yet struck any American authors as worth attention. The first, *The Girl on the Film*, was brought from England by the Shuberts at the end of 1913, with a predominantly British cast. The leading comedian was George Grossmith, whose recollections of the Gaiety Theatre we have already encountered. A "capital" technician, Grossmith "brought down the house in a little mimetic scene, when he attempts to make himself understood to the signora and uses the sign language of the cinematograph art to describe a dissolving scene." For the most part, however, *The Girl on the Film* would not strike the modern observer as being very pointed, since it devoted most of its energy to routine entertainment for "the tired business man, his ennuied wife, and blasé children"—loud and lively, with a whirlwind tango by Oy-Ra and Dorma Leigh. A fortnight later, on January 12, 1914, *The Queen of the Movies* touched upon the same subject matter with about the same pungency, and impressed its audience less because of its humor than because of its eight little "powder puff girls."

Nevada gave way to the Mormons of its neighbor state to the east in *The Girl from Utah* (1914). Jerome Kern again had a hand in the music, though most of it was by Paul Rubens and Sydney Jones. Utah was a British discovery, for Ina Claire and Isobel Elsom had played in the musical comedy in London before it was made known here with Julia Sanderson, Donald Brian, and Joseph Cawthorn as the featured performers. The title, while technically accurate, was misleading, for the action took place not in Utah but in London; the heroine, Una Trance, was a Mormon girl who had fled to London to avoid marrying the man to whom she had been "sealed." As the climax of her experiences in the British capital, the sugar-sweet Miss Sanderson, as Una Trance, attended an "arts ball" at which, amid an overload of Moorish settings and trappings, the old-fashioned, buxom girls of the chorus modeled fashionable Oriental styles. All this happened, in the creakiest manner of ancient musical comedy (ancient even then), after Miss Sanderson had wistfully sung, "I'd like to wander with Alice in Wonderland."

A momentary and abortive flirtation with more serious aesthetic concerns was initiated by *The Red Canary* (1914), which ran for only sixteen fainting performances. Its claim to documentary permanence—if not to an audience at the time—lay in its attempt to apply a theory of the effects of color upon the emotions and actions of the characters: blue indicated jealousy, red rage, and so on. The notion was not conclusive, and it buried the story under its abruptly shifting colors. But at least it is pleasant to pay obeisance to a show that recognized how greatly something needed to be done about the color-schemes of the usual musical comedies.

Anticipating the various great doings that were to make 1915 and 1916 the years of the rebirth of the musical stage, Charles Dillingham ushered in an absolutely new era at the New Amsterdam Theatre on December 8, 1914. On this memorable evening the "syncopated musical show," *Watch Your Step*, equipped with music and lyrics by Irving Berlin and a book by Harry B. Smith, gave the American audience a foretaste of the ragtime and jazz delights that lay ahead in the musical theatre in the next decade or more. In this "ragtime riot and dancing delirium," the Castles took possession of the stage with their tangos, fox-trots (the fox had devoured the turkey), and one-steps. As a relief from the brash, nervous Berlin music and the lightning grace of the Castles, Frank Tinney provided periods of quiet hilarity with his confidential, "*entre nous*" patter, which made him the prototype of the modern master of ceremonies. Nothing was sacred to Berlin, who embraced a fashion that still continues when he provided a "rag" version of the *Rigoletto* quartet.

To be sure, one observer found Berlin's music "a little emaciated," and not the equal of his "Alexander's Ragtime Band," and remarked that the lyrics "have the same relation to poetry as limericks in a prize contest." But, he continued, "Mr. Berlin knows how to put the 'go' in tango. *Watch Your Step* has all the allurements of the craze [dancing] that has kept a majority of the populace high stepping in ballrooms and restaurants for the last two or three years. If there were ever a doubt that the tango and the fox-trot would resist becoming a musical-comedy theme it was dispelled by Mr. Dillingham's stroke of genius in making the Castles his two stars." *Theatre* magazine said, "Berlin is now part of America."

Ragtime and fox-trotting held no fascination for the more sedate young Jerome Kern, whose *90 in the Shade*, presented the following month (January, 1915), evoked the Philippine Islands, and remained faithful to "the school of musical comedy which flourished some years ago, which always contained for background a picturesque and romantic country, for its characters bibulous Americans traveling for adventure; and which depended for its action on intrigue and mistaken identities." An important augury for the future—though it offered no aid to the present offering, which was poorly patronized—was the linking of Kern's name for the first time with that of Guy Bolton, who contributed the book. In less than a year, Bolton was again to collaborate with Kern in a full-scale hit. In the meantime Kern had to be satisfied with public commendation not for the score of *o in the Shade,* but for his earlier services "as chief aid to anemic music" in pieces originally composed by others.

Kern spent a busy year in 1915, writing music for four shows. *Nobody Home* was the second one, smartly outfitted by Elsie de Wolfe (later Lady Mendl), given a book by Bolton and Paul Rubens, and presented on a small scale in the tiny Princess Theatre. It was a mild success, which was more than could be said of Kern's third 1915 production, *Miss Information.* Guy Bolton had no hand in this satire of the craze for publicity among society women; the book was not well written, and the combined labors of Elsie Janis and Irene Bordoni could not save it.

The generally agreeable reaction of the public to *Nobody Home* led F. Ray Comstock, its producer, to realize that a musical comedy in a small theatre could be given a special and friendly character that was not possible in a larger house. Joining with Elizabeth Marbury in the Marbury-Comstock Company, he commissioned Kern to prepare a second "intimate" musical comedy, in the light of his experience with the first. Bolton again prepared the book, which he derived from Philip Bartholomae's farce, *Over Night.* Elsie de Wolfe was shifted to the scenic department; Melville Ellis devised the costumes; and Schuyler Green wrote the lyrics. The finished product, called *Very Good Eddie,* opened on December 23, 1915, continued for 341 performances, and spanned a second year on the road.

Every feature of *Very Good Eddie* was scaled to the size of the house and the proximity of the entire audience to the stage. Everything was handled with a light touch, and the tempo of the performance was rapid and zestful. The plot, requiring only two scenes, recounted the contretemps of two honeymooning couples separated on a Hudson River steamboat, each man with the other's wife seeking shelter for the night and searching for his own bride. Elsie de Wolfe's settings were smartly simple and plain, though the hotel scene had "the inevitable symmetrical double staircase" at the back. There were only a dozen chorus girls. Though they were advertised as a "swagger fashion chorus," Ellis designed their clothes with a simplicity of line that accorded with the settings and the general tone of the performance. Their skirts reached down to the top of their high shoes, a style that led Heywood Broun to rejoice that "one is not called upon to gaze at the knees of the world and weep." It was, moreover, an "individualized" chorus. "Each girl has a dress of her own," Broun explained. "No, that's not exactly what we mean. What we intend to convey is that each girl is costumed differently, as suits her style."

Under Edward Royce's direction, the performers pitched their speaking, singing, and acting in an informal low key. Oscar Shaw, said the *World*, "sings just as he might in your own home after dinner." So did Ernest Truex, though nobody thought much of his voice. His bright, clean humor and ingenuous lisp carried the day for him, as the bridegroom of Helen Raymond, a young woman of proportions about twice those of the frail Truex. The second couple presented an opposite contrast, with John Willard big and burly, and Alice Dovey petite and demure. Kern's score, in the main, was "refined ragtime," with a sophisticated reference to Strauss' recent opera, *Der Rosenkavalier*, in a celesta obbligato in the final waltz.

With little or no space separating the players from the audience, *Very Good Eddie* depended upon the ease and credibility of the acting and characterization. Scarcely any previous musical comedy had been favored with a plot and dialogue so coherent, so nearly related to those of well written non-musical plays; "unlike most musical comedies it has a connected story with laughable situations following one another in rapid succession." Dancing was kept to a minimum. There was only enough "to satisfy the audience and incidentally recognize that the 'dancing craze,' as it is now reminiscently called, is a thing of the past."

A few critics, spoiled by the louder and gaudier displays to which they were conditioned, cast aspersive phrases at *Very Good Eddie*. One called it a "kitchenette production," and another characterized it as "pleasing parlor entertainment that has found its way to the stage." But the body of playgoers found its principle acceptable, and the "intimate" musical comedy became established as a suitable and successful genre.

The next partnership of Kern and Bolton was on a larger scale, in *Have a Heart* (1917). P. G. Wodehouse, one of the brightest of all lyric writers, joined the Kern-Bolton combination for the first time. *Have a Heart* was possibly a little ahead of its time, at least as an attraction in one of the larger-sized theatres. In its integration of music, book, and lyrics, it was an improvement over *Very Good Eddie*. Slapstick comedians were eliminated (John E. Hazzard had perpetuated this tradition, as the clerk of the Rip Van Winkle Inn, in *Very Good Eddie*), as were "obvious music cues, irritatingly insipid lyrics, and inane characters."

The Kern-Bolton-Wodehouse triumvirate returned to the Princess, with *Oh, Boy*, on February 20, 1917, to confirm the viability of the "intimate" formula. Discovering that youth can often be a substitute for expensive names, William Elliott and F. Ray Comstock, the co-producers, employed such less-known players as Marion Davies, Justine Johnstone, Tom Powers, and Edna May Oliver. The last-named of these, who was to reach her full Broadway stature in a later Kern musical comedy, *Show Boat*, was cast as "the drunk lady without which no modern musical show could reach a second performance." A sensual pleasure of a different order was vouchsafed by Anna Wheaton, "one of the thousand and one victims of the pajama contagion which is now sweeping our theatres. Judging from recent examples, true artistic distinction in musical comedy can best be achieved by a pair of satin bedroom slippers, a shower of hair, à la Pickford, a pair of blue (or pink) silk pajamas, a smothered yawn, and a lighted candle, à la Lady Macbeth."

But it was not drunk ladies or pajamas and showers of hair that gave artistic distinction to *Oh, Boy* in the minds of those who had collaborated upon it. In the *Dramatic Mirror*, Bolton sought to explain how the Bolton-Wodehouse-Kern musical comedies differed from "those which have had their day on Broadway." The public now demanded realism in musical comedy, Bolton said. The new Princess musicals depended "as much on plot and character development for success as on the music." They also dealt with subjects near to the experience of the audience. "Americans laugh more naturally at a funny hotel clerk or janitor than a crudely drawn cannibal princess," he maintained.

In the outmoded type of musical comedy, he continued, "a prince from some neo-Balkan country, disguised, is in love with a poor maiden. She does not know he is a prince; he does not know she is the daughter of an Albanian Croesus. . . . There is one situation in each act; the rest is gaps. Comedians filled these gaps—with gun scenes, timetable scenes, soda-fountain scenes. . . ." In *Nobody Home*, upon which Wodehouse did not work, Bolton began to overthrow this standard conception. In *Very Good Eddie* "it was easy to have real plot and characters, but difficult to get altogether away from irrelevant scenes, of which there were still two." *Oh, Boy* contained nothing irrelevant. It was a "straight, consistent comedy with the addition of music. Every song and lyric contributed to the action. The humor was based on situation, not interjected by the comedians."

The Princess housed two more intimate "Oh" shows before the project was outmoded by postwar developments. *Oh, Lady, Lady* (1918) involved Constance Binney, Vivienne Segal, Margaret Dale, and Carl Randall in complications in Greenwich Village—a locale that was soon to be subject to wholesale exploitation on Broadway. *Oh, My Dear!* (1918), for which Louis A. Hirsch supplanted Kern as composer, was less adequately supplied with ideas, and fell back upon the "reliable formula of mistaken identity," with Roy Atwell, Joseph Allen, Joseph Santley and Ivy Sawyer to help in the process.

Meanwhile Kern, who could apparently turn out a whole score as fast as the ordinary man can write his name, also busied himself with musical comedies of ordinary proportions. Bolton and Wodehouse were involved in only one of these, an adaptation of George Ade's *The College Widow* (1917), presented under the title *Leave It to Jane*. This was one of two or three pieces that discovered the American college campus at about the same time, and rigged it up with specialized slang, stalwart halfbacks, and co-eds who looked and behaved remarkably like chorus girls. Of the miscellany of other Kern pieces at this stage of his prolific career there is no need to take cognizance, since none of them offered anything new. It is impossible, though, to resist a sample of the literary style of the criticism that appeared in the *Dramatic Mirror* in connection with the performance of Mitzi (originally Mitzi Hajos) in *Head Over Heels* (1918): "Mitzi usually makes a hitzi in whatever bitzi she undertakes."

Under the stimulus of new ideas and wartime prosperity,

the theatres were glutted with musical shows in 1916, 1917, and 1918. Only a few more warrant a momentary backward glance. For fifteen performances, beginning on March 28, 1916, at the Maxine Elliott Theatre, *See America First* ran its wobbly course. The music and—with the aid of T. Lawrason Riggs, the book and lyrics—were by a young unknown from Indianapolis, Cole Porter. A story about a "back-to-nature" debutante and a cowboy-duke underlay Porter's attempt to "combine Gilbert and Sullivan wit with college musical spirit," and the music was held to have "sought inspiration in George M. Cohan." Most of Porter's later shows were considerably more durable, and none of them imitated George M. Cohan.

Among other manifestations of the time, *So Long Letty* (1916) established the gangling Charlotte Greenwood in the character she kept alive for twenty-five years. *Canary Cottage* (1917) had a finale in which the girls tossed oranges at the audience, and employed "futurist" scenery. *Girl o' Mine* (1918), by Frank Tours and Philip Bartholomae, showed how easily an "intimate" musical comedy could fail when Kern, Bolton, and Wodehouse were not around. *Oh, Look!* (1918) opened the Vanderbilt Theatre, and introduced the song, "I'm Always Chasing Rainbows." Jazz took over in *The Rainbow Girl* (1918), in Florence Ware's dance, "The Alimony Blues."

As the war continued, Irving Berlin was inducted into the Army. He returned to Broadway for a month's stay at the Century Theatre, beginning on August 19, 1918, in a soldier show for which he concocted the tunes and lyrics. It was known as *Yip, Yip, Yaphank,* "a musical mess cooked up by the boys of Camp Upton." Sergeant Berlin, in a thin, piping voice, came out alone on the stage to sing "Oh, How I Hate to Get Up in the Morning." Four months later the soldiers of Aberdeen Proving Ground, Maryland, followed suit, at the Lexington Opera House, with *Attaboy*. Their cast included Captain Frank Tinney, and they offered a skirted chorus rivaling that of *Yip, Yip, Yaphank*.

XVI

The Post-War Revue

AFTER THE armistice in 1918, the pleasure-seeking, prohibition-despising, boom-rich American public enabled the musical theatre to revel in a decade of luxury and wastefulness and irresponsibility such as it had never known before, and will probably never know again in our time. Money was available to produce anything with the slightest prospect of success, and audiences were lenient, easily amused, and generous with their patronage. Despite the H. C. L., as the high cost of living was affectionately called, people were making money faster than they could spend it. In the theatre, production costs had not yet risen in ratio to the increased national income. For one mad, magical decade, the Broadway theatre could afford to produce as many musical shows as it wanted to, and to market them at box-office prices that the audience could pay without feeling any pinch.

People wanted their pleasures to be easy-co
swift, and full of kicks, like jazz music and I
For theatregoers in a generation too overstimu'
quieter and sweeter diversions, the revue, a'
developed by Ziegfeld and at the Winter Garden, wu.
ideal format for an evening's gaiety. In attending a revue,
the purest hedonist made no commitment that need deflect him from his course. And so, although a procession of
musical comedies also shared the theatre sector, the revue
was the archetype of post-war jazz-and-prohibition entertainment.

Beyond taking care to keep their visual appeal up-to-date,
Ziegfeld did not tamper with the character of his *Follies*.
Joseph Urban remained his collaborator, designing the
scenery for all the successive annual editions, and in 1919
the costumes as well. Ziegfeld's stable of composers included, at one time or another, Irving Berlin, Victor Herbert, Harry Tierney, Rudolf Friml, Gene Buck, and divers
lesser lights. Marilynn Miller appeared again (for the last
time in the *Follies*) in 1919, as also did Eddie Cantor, who
carried more than his share of the show, Bert Williams (for
the last time before his death), and Eddie Dowling. And,
of course, the "most beautiful girls in the world" passed
before the footlights of the New Amsterdam Theatre.
Fannie Brice, W. C. Fields, Charles Winninger, Ray
Dooley, Van and Schenck, and Carl Randall came back
for the 1920 *Follies*. All except Winninger and Randall
stayed on in the 1921 edition, for which Raymond Hitchcock signed a contract with Ziegfeld, abandoning his endeavor to produce his own revues. Urban provided "masterly perspectives of limitless vastness," and a smaller but
"more select" chorus wore "ventilated cobweb costumes"
by James Reynolds and arranged themselves in living pic-

es under Ben Ali Haggin's direction. Miss Brice sang
Oy, I'm an Indian!"

The Ziegfeld Follies of 1922 returned Will Rogers and
his lariat to public notice, gave Gilda Gray an opportunity
to shimmy, and caused Ed Gallagher and Al Shean to immortalize themselves with their "Mr. Gallagher and Mr.
Shean" number, one of the most insinuating question-and-
answer duos in the memory of the oldest playgoer. The
unending Ziegfeld series continued without essential change
in style or format, whether the production numbers were
staged by Gertrude Hoffman, by Ned Wayburn, or by
Julian Mitchell, and whether the roster included Bert
Wheeler or Will Rogers, Gilda Gray or Ann Pennington,
Fannie Brice or Lina Basquette, Paul Whiteman's band or
George Olsen's. In the 1924 edition, a device later to become a favorite was inaugurated when the lights blacked
out and the Tiller girls jumped rope with luminous ropes.

Through these lush times, the Shubert *Passing Show*
at the Winter Garden continued to give the *Follies* their
stiffest competition. Always more daring and risqué than
the *Follies*, the post-war *Passing Show* pushed undress constantly nearer to absolute nudity; but if clothing was not
abundant at the Winter Garden, it was always expensive.
The Passing Show of 1922 provided a striking indication of
what righteous people thought to be the decline of moral
standards in the early 1920s. A ballet was danced "in the
manner of the Marquis de Sade." Francis Renault, whose
female impersonations had not the decorum of Julian
Eltinge's, swished about as the Diamond Girl. In a parody
of Eugene O'Neill's *The Hairy Ape*, the chorus girls dressed
like stokers and swore without shame.

As had long been their custom, the Shuberts provided
miscellaneously titled collations of froth to fill the months
when *The Passing Show* was away from the Winter Gar-

den. One of these, *Make It Snappy* (1922), found a new use for the runway—of which the audience was beginning to tire—when the girls tossed ice-cream bricks to the orchestra patrons. *Innocent Eyes* (1924) brought the eternal Mistinguette from Paris to the Winter Garden, and, after 31 unsuccessful performances, sent her back to her adoring Parisian following, humiliated by notices that claimed that her voice lacked freshness and that her artistry "seldom rose above the level of mediocrity."

It was with a new annual series called *Artists and Models*, begun in 1923 and usually given in other theatres than the Winter Garden, that the Shuberts made their first unqualified, all-out appeal to what might be termed the baser nature of the public. "Never before," wrote one startled critic, "in an American revue has a similar degree of nudity been obtained." Before what *Variety* called a "75% stag audience," "women with naked breasts promenaded about the stage. . . . A burlesque on *Rain* was the rawest, smuttiest, most shameless misdemeanor ever committed." With content of this kind, it was not necessary for the Shuberts to proffer an expensive cast of principals. The girls were the thing; such comic duties as there were devolved primarily upon Frank Fay. In the 1924 edition—presented, by exception, at the Winter Garden—the beauties revealed their reflections in a lily pool. The runway was abandoned in favor of steps leading directly down into the orchestra. Chorus girls ran down the aisles handing the men in the end seats cords which, when pulled, uncovered examples of living statuary. The 1925 version was even more elaborate. The audience had a wonderful time with noisemakers—metal strips with little clappers on each side. In "The Rotisserie," the Gertrude Hoffman girls impersonated broilers turning on spits above the fire. Name performers, for a change, were numerous. Jay Brennan and Stanley Rogers carried on in the Savoy and Brennan routine, with Rogers taking over the character of the Dame created by Savoy, who had been killed by lightning. Phil Baker was a new and personable master of ceremonies; Aline MacMahon was a fresh young comic; and the future motion-picture star, Jack Oakie, was a member of the chorus.

Even Charles Dillingham's ponderous shows at the Hippodrome developed a fresh postwar aspect, though obviously the huge house was not the place to make the most of the contours of the female body. Abandoning the spectacular travelogues of earlier years, Dillingham transformed his extravaganzas into mammoth vaudeville revues, with circus elements as an added attraction. The old-fashioned flag-waving, geographical titles were supplanted by ones that promised a livelier evening—*Good Times, Get Together,* and *Better Times. Get Together* (1921) depended heavily on elephants and on clowns (who made their first entrance by stepping from posters on the wall), ice-skating (in two scenes billed as "The Red Shoes"), and a ballet, "The Thunder Bird," with Michel Fokine and Vera Fokina. In the course of the evening a moving-picture comedy from the Fox studios, Clyde Cook in *The Toreador,* was shown. *Better Times* (1922) offered a Ladies' Jazz Band, more kinds of animals than ever before, including crows, an old-fashioned "shadowgraph" that threw moving shadows on a screen, and Mark Lawson's spectacle "The Story of a Fan," which evolved "from a fan to fans, to floods of fans, to an electrically lighted fan holding twelve girls in its panels and perched aloft of the whole."

As if it were not enough to have the theatres inundated with revues and extravaganzas between 8:30 and 11:15, the various roof-garden restaurant-theatres did a tremendous after-midnight business. On the Century Roof and the New Amsterdam Roof, in particular, the bright stars of revue

and musical comedy foregathered to give the 𝑟
trons another hour or two of more intimate
their charms and talents. The *Morris Gest M*
which opened, with Urban décors on the Centu𝑟
time for New Year's Eve business in 1919, gave employ.
to two youngsters—George Gershwin for the music, an
Buddy de Sylva for the lyrics. One of their song titles will
serve to suggest their callowness at this early stage of their
careers. It was called "Cutie, Cut Your Cuticle." The *Midnight Whirl* kept memories of the war green by dressing
chorus girls in Salvation Army costumes and sending them
out to distribute doughnuts to the customers.

The most expensive array of midnight cabaret talent was
usually to be found in Ziegfeld's *Midnight Frolic*, a dine-
and-drink corollary to the *Follies* on the New Amsterdam
Roof. Fannie Brice and W. C. Fields were standbys. Urban
was the designer, and Ned Wayburn staged the dances.
The girls were chosen to stand even closer scrutiny than
those of the *Follies*; in 1921 the producer's slogan was
"See New York and Ziegfeld's girls and die." But even with
so generous a provider as Ziegfeld, the vogue for roof entertainment was short. In the early 1920s even the best floor
shows began to descend to the street and basement levels,
and the night club largely supplanted the more formal roof-
garden cabaret.

Some of the favorite performers of war and pre-war days
found it possible, in the first flush of the revue craze, to
promulgate loosely constructed entertainments built around
their special stellar abilities. Elsie Janis, who made herself
a national celebrity by her unflagging efforts to sustain
morale among the soldiers, made periodic appearances
billed as *Elsie Janis and Her Gang* (in 1919 her "gang"
included Eva Le Gallienne). She last appeared under Dillingham's management in 1925 in *Puzzles of 1925*, which

ntained nothing more cryptic than Elsie's imitations of John Barrymore, Lenore Ulric, and—to be up to the moment—Beatrice Lillie, who had recently insinuated herself into the American consciousness in the first *Charlot's Revue*.

Raymond Hitchcock produced for himself two more *Hitchy-Koo* revues, in 1919 and 1920, before hiring himself out to Ziegfeld and other producers. The 1919 edition was "Hitchier than ever in its fun, more Kooey than ever before in its music." For the Kooeyness, Cole Porter, now beginning to pull his lyric and satiric gifts into salable shape, was responsible. Jerome Kern wrote the music for the 1920 edition. A fortnight before the opening of *Hitchy-Koo of 1920*, another one-man-show entertainer, Fred Stone, was given free rein in Dillingham's production, *Tip Top*. When Stone was off the stage, Anna Ludmila, soon to become the partner of Adolph Bolm, pirouetted and arabesqued, and the new sister act of Vivian and Rosetta Duncan also appeared.

Al Jolson was the sole reason for the long run, in 1921, of the Shuberts' *Bombo*. Though Sigmund Romberg was the official composer of *Bombo*, many patrons came primarily to hear Jolson deal with "April Showers," an interpolated song by Lew Silvers. Stirred by the public response to "April Showers," Jolson announced that he would retire from the musical stage after *Bombo*, to devote his whole time to "concert work." Needless to say, he did not, but all his subsequent appearances were in musical comedies rather than in revues.

For Ed Wynn, with his zany carnival of elaborate nonsense, the revue provided a perfect frame. The *Ed Wynn Carnival*, in 1920, took him one rung farther up the ladder of popularity. But it was in *The Perfect Fool*, a title he later appropriated as a description of himself, that he established himself, in 1921, upon a comic eminence from which the public has never been willing to allow him to descend. With constant changes of grotesque costume, Wynn devoted himself mainly to the demonstration of various labor-saving devices. Dragging a toy wagon onto the stage, he extracted from it a safety device for noiseless soup, a coffee cup with a hole in the bottom (to save the labor of pouring the coffee from the cup into the saucer), and a gadget to hold an ear of corn so that the ears would not get covered with butter. In a novelty scene for the chorus, a typewriter took up the larger part of the stage, with the girls' legs as stems for the keys. The commercial plug was now becoming known, for the typewriter was prominently labeled a Corona.

Three years later, in *The Grab Bag*, Wynn integrated his own performance more completely with that of the rest of the company, whose idiocies were the mirror of his own. He summoned forth a "Russian octette" to sing a Cossack folk song called "He Eats French Dressing Every Night So He Can Wake Up Oily in the Morning," and a lament entitled "She Might Have Been a School Teacher, But She Hadn't Any Class." Throughout the evening, music was provided by Spanish singers who plainly were not Spanish, Scottish singers who were not Scottish, and Russian singers who were not Russian. The Wynn touch pervaded the whole show, making *The Grab Bag* in many ways the most successful revue yet built around the idiosyncracies of a single performer.

George White, who had begun his career in the theatre as a musical-comedy juvenile and hoofer, turned entrepreneur in 1919, issuing on June 2 of that year a revue patently modeled after the *Ziegfeld Follies*, and called *Scandals of 1919*. With Ann Pennington as the leading Jazz Baby, dancing, "from the ancient toe whirling of grandpa's time to the shimmie," dominated the first *Scandals*. The score by Richard Whiting was workable if undistinguished; the book, on which White and Arthur Jackson collaborated, was less than that. "Where there was so much money to be spent," one reviewer complained, "Mr. White might have set aside a few dollars for a good scenario writer."

Having established his claim to a share of the takings from the revue-mad public, White continued with annual editions of the *Scandals*, each more fashionable and lavish than the last. George Gershwin became the *Scandals'* composer in 1920, and remained with the project through 1924, though it did not call forth the songs for which he is best remembered today. White himself was a member of the cast for the first four years, after which he withdrew into the producer's office. By 1921, his name meant enough in connection with the *Scandals* to merit incorporation into the title, and from then on the successive versions were always known as *George White's Scandals*. Essentially imitative of ideas and vogues already exploited by more inventive producers, the *Scandals* added nothing new to the over-all theatrical scene, though the elaborate stage pictures, appetizing girls, and generally competent routining of the shows guaranteed them a dependable following.

A fresher note was sounded by the *Greenwich Village Follies*, which began life in the Greenwich Village Theatre on July 15, 1919, remained there for a second edition in 1920, and moved uptown in 1921, where annual versions appeared with diminishing distinction until 1928. The *Greenwich Village Follies* were the brain-child of John Murray Anderson, one of the few designers of his day whose gifts could stand comparison with those of Joseph Urban. Even though the scale of the first edition was restricted by the small dimensions of the theatre, the investiture gave an impression of open-handedness, controlled by a degree of taste and an appeal to cultivated sensibilities which were not part of the basic assumption of the *Ziegfeld Follies* or *George White's Scandals*.

From the first, the *Greenwich Village Follies* were intended to be "sophisticated," which meant that the members of the audience could enter the theatre without checking their brains at the cloakroom. The plays, people, and foibles chosen for lampooning were matters of interest primarily to the intelligentsia. From the first, Anderson understood that the intelligentsia enjoyed a bit of dirt quite as heartily as the commoner folk, as long as it was handled in terms that were not too direct.

In the two years the *Greenwich Village Follies* productions remained in the Village, they faithfully sought to evoke the Village atmosphere—as in the cabaret scene of the 1920 edition, where the characters represented various well-known hotels, restaurants, and haunts of the locality. The move uptown to the Shubert Theatre in 1921 inevitably led to the abandonment of much of the local color, for the larger and more general audience of a Forty-fourth Street theatre could not be expected to understand or react to the fine points of neighborhood satire. Richard Watts found this first uptown *Follies* "as uneven and uncertain as life in Greenwich Village itself, with here a dull stretch and there a spot that gleams like unexpectedly successful homebrew." But Anderson still provided staging that was artistically and technically in advance of all the other revues in New York, and the tone of the production continued, on the whole, to appeal to the intelligent audience, even if it was "dirty without flowers and smeary with smut." At the opening, an unintentional thrill was provided when Bird Millman fell off a tight-rope; but she was not seriously injured, and immediately tried again with success.

By 1922, this "most sophisticated of revues" was marked by a heaviness and coarseness that had been the very

qualities its Village-inspired predecessor had avoided. The
camping of Savoy and Brennan replaced more delicate
humors, and there was a broad burlesque of Nikita Balieff,
recently arrived as master of ceremonies of the *Chauve-
Souris.* An emotional ballad told of a gold-digger who
wanted $5,000 not for a mink coat but to pay for an opera-
tion for her baby. Still, the members of the audience who
were *au courant* were not wholly forgotten. The Swedish
Ballet, the rage of the moment in Paris, was subjected to a
burlesque; Eugene O'Neill was travestied; Oscar Wilde's
"The Nightingale and the Rose" was made the subject of
a ballet; and a *cantatrice* (nobody had yet invented the
peculiar American locution, "chanteuse") named Yvonne
George introduced "Mon Homme."

The *Greenwich Village Follies of 1923* has gone down in
history as the one in which Martha Graham danced—not
in the radically personal style she later evolved, but in her
most girlish, pretty-pretty classical and interpretative manner. Among her fellow-performers were Sammy White and
Eva Puck, whose great day came in *Show Boat* a few seasons
later on; the Flying Cansinos, the parents of Rita Hay-
worth; and Joe E. Brown, who fell downstairs and injured
himself in the opening performance. The première must
have been jinxed, for later on in the evening, one of the
show girls let the metal-cloth fringe of a net cloak trail
into the footlight trough, where it caught fire.

Cole Porter composed the score for the 1924 edition.
With the inclusion of the Dolly Sisters and Moran and
Mack—the "Two Black Crows"—in the cast, the character
of the *Greenwich Village Follies* was now strictly popular.
By 1925, when Hassard Short replaced Anderson as the
director, it had become largely indistinguishable from all the
competing revues. The wit had gone out of the skits, and
the heaviest play for laughs was made by a travesty on

Hamlet, in which Florence Moore, as Ophelia, was determined to drown herself at the Fleischman Baths, but could not, because it was not ladies' day.

The introduction of Ted Lewis and his noisy band, devoted to "Jazz-What-Am," in the 1925 *Greenwich Village Follies* indicated the popularizing treatment to which the project was now being subjected. From this point on, the institution slid steadily downhill—from the point of view of the sophisticated audience for which it was initially conceived—until in its last manifestation in 1928, it was no more than another rough-and-ready, commonplace revue designed to furnish a springtime tenant for the Shuberts' Winter Garden. Its chief performers were funny enough and talented enough in their own right, but the *Greenwich Village Follies* was hardly the place one would have expected to encounter such mass-appeal entertainers as Doctor Rockwell, Blossom Seeley, and Benny Fields. Having become meaningless, the title was now no longer provocative, and it was allowed to drop into limbo.

A couple of efforts to present revues on an intimate scale at the Princess had failed swiftly in 1919 and 1920, because the seating capacity was not sufficient to finance productions more elaborate than the "Oh" musical comedies of the war and pre-war years. But the idea of smaller-scale production, as exemplified by the first two *Greenwich Village Follies* before that entertainment moved uptown, continued to be a tempting one. As an experiment of in-between size, the Music Box Theatre was built by Irving Berlin in 1921. The first *Music Box Revue,* opening on September 22 of that year, was dedicated to the bright, sophisticated, fast-paced entertainment the *Greenwich Village Follies* was about to abandon. The Music Box itself was a tasteful structure with an interior attractively devoid of gewgaws and overdecoration. The first revue in the new house was far from economical, but it was neither vulgar nor naked. For their performers, Berlin and Sam H. Harris, who produced it together, relied largely on such tried-and-true personalities as William Collier, Sam Bernard, Joseph Santley and Ivy Sawyer, Florence Moore, and Wilda Bennett. Though there was little real novelty about either the players or the material, the *Music Box Revue*, by running for 313 performances, showed that an audience existed for a show that relied more on ideas and less on mere displays of the flesh than the *Follies* and *The Passing Show*. It also gave Irving Berlin a showcase for his lively new tunes, among which "Everybody Step" was outstanding.

The second *Music Box Revue*, in 1922, turned to younger talent. Ruth Page, fresh from her first success in Chicago in John Alden Carpenter's ballet, *The Birthday of the Infanta*, was a ravishing *prima ballerina*. Bobby Clark and Paul McCullough started down the path toward comic fame, and so did William Gaxton. One of the spectacle scenes made use for the first time of the effect in which a line of girls seemed to be dancing in front of mirrors, until it was revealed that the images were actually a second line of girls.

Grace Moore appeared in the *Music Box Revue* of 1923, along with Florence Moore, to whom she was not related. Grace was a member of an operatic sextet which delivered "Yes, We Have No Bananas," in the course of which incandescent oranges glowed on the stage and orange-blossom perfume suffused the theatre. Florence paid tribute to the Denishawn Dancers, then at the height of their popularity, by appearing as Flo O'Denishawn in a pantomime that required her to impersonate a starfish.

The fourth and last *Music Box Revue*, in 1924, suggested that the original formula must be wearing thin, for it was loaded with name performers, old and young; and John

Murray Anderson took over the direction from [   ]
Short. Irving Berlin, of course, continued to pr[ ]
music. Tamiris, who today, as Helen Tamiris, is [   ]
musical-comedy choreographer, was the leading [   ]
Grace Moore was again the prima donna. Fannie [   ], as
a bewildered Russian immigrant, and Bobby Clark, as a
prize-fighter, led the comic contingent, and such folk as
Oscar Shaw, Carl Randall, and Hal Sherman were men-of-
all-work in the sketches, songs and dances. Despite its
hardworking personnel, the fourth *Music Box Revue* ran
only half as long as the first, and the project was abandoned.

Earl Carroll was the next to initiate a series of revues.
The *Earl Carroll Vanities*, begun in 1923, were a little more
low-brow than the *Scandals*, and more completely dependent upon sumptuous girls, overdone scenic effects, and
standard comic routines. Though the *Vanities* lasted, with
interruptions, clear through the 1930s, they never developed
a genuinely distinctive character. Carroll always seemed
merely to elaborate needlessly upon themes already more
than adequately taken care of in the *Follies*, *The Passing
Show*, and the *Scandals*. But the *Vanities* were just the
dish for the weary 1924 seeker after beauty who could be
satisfied by a finale in which 108 Vanities Girls stood on a
revolving staircase and revolved.

A particular joy to the intellectual audience from its
first appearance in 1922 was the *Grand Street Follies*.
Produced in a family manner on the little stage of the
Neighborhood Playhouse down on the East Side, the *Grand
Street Follies* remained, on a far more inexpensive scale,
what the *Greenwich Village Follies* started out to be: a
conceit in which ideas were more important than surfaces.
The first edition was labelled on the program "A Low-Brow
Show for High-Grade Morons; Music by the Great Com-
posers, mostly arranged by Lily M. Hyland; Book by Every-

ɔdy." Since elaborate production numbers were out of the question for the small company, satire—usually with sharp fangs—provided the whole substance of the bill. From a beginning laid in the home of the first dramatic critic, Adam Stale (with Aline MacMahon as Eve), the first *Grand Street Follies* proceeded to a satire on Walt Whitman's poetry; a series of dance travesties, "The Royal Damn Fango, or All Change Places," in which Albert Carroll impersonated a Lady with Fan; and burlesques of the inevitable Balieff, John Barrymore, Pavlowa, Elsie Janis, Anna Duncan, Irene Castle, Feodor Chaliapin, and Maria Jeritza. Carroll, with his economical, sharply etched style and his facility for wearing either male or female attire, immediately became the king-pin of the Grand Street Follies, and remained indispensable to it all the way to the end, in 1929.

The next year, Dorothy Sands, as pointed and witty an imitator of acting styles as the American stage has known, joined the *Grand Street* entourage, and stayed with it through the rest of its eight-season history. In 1924, she made light of the manners of a recitalist at the newly opened Town Hall. Aline Bernstein became costume designer for this third edition, revealing her bright mind and powers of observation in her conceits for "The South Sea Islands According to Broadway."

For two more seasons, the *Grand Street Follies* continued its *succès d'estime* at the Neighborhood Playhouse. Among satires too numerous to detail, there were—in the 1925 edition—"The Wild Duck of the 18th Century (as Ibsen would have treated the theme had he really been born before his time)," and a gala performance of the opera, "L'Irlandesa Rosa dell' Abie." In 1926 two composers of future distinction, Randall Thompson and Arthur Schwartz, contributed some of the music.

In 1927, the *Grand Street Follies* moved uptown to the

Little Theatre, after giving a few preliminary performances in the Neighborhood Playhouse. The 1928 and 1929 *Follies* were tenants of the Booth Theatre (with James Cagney a tap dancer in the latter one). While the sodden story of the *Greenwich Village Follies* was not repeated, since no essential change in style occurred, the undertaking was unable to thrive as a Broadway production. By the spring of 1930, the effects of the Wall Street crash the previous October were beginning to be felt all through the theatre, and there was no possibility of continuing. But throughout the noisy, nervous, coarse boom days of the 1920s, the *Grand Street Follies* had quietly and modestly served the valuable function of reminding the theatre audience that everything did not have to be big and costly and vulgar in order to be genuinely amusing. As the most persistent counterirritant to the prevailing diseases of megalomania and big noise, the enterprise had a significance that far exceeded the slender, and sometimes precious, values of its materials.

Moved by the example of the Neighborhood Playhouse, a group of youngsters in the Theatre Guild put together in 1925 their own intimate revue, which they styled the *Garrick Gaieties*. With Philip Loeb and Sterling Holloway among its leading lights, the first edition won an affectionate reception for its naïve high spirits, although, as Percy Hammond remarked, "It seemed to be saying, 'Ain't I cute, I'm only six.'" The second edition, in 1926, retained the same "bizarre ambition to please," but this time Hammond found "the Theatre Guild's precious bambino . . . a wise and flippant ingenue." Loeb appeared as a Broadway mortician, embalming such Theatre Guild "failures" as Shaw's *Arms and the Man* and *Androcles and the Lion*. Everyone from O'Neill to Gilbert and Sullivan was subjected to a ribbing, with *The Dybbuk* and *Lulu Belle* singled out for special treatment. The frayed conventions of musical comedy were ruthlessly exposed in "The Rose of Arizona," a richly devised sketch put together from all the current clichés. In this, a bevy of nasal chorus girls appeared dressed as flowers—each a different one. The heroine was introduced by a chorus girl, who observed, in the intonation of a shopgirl, "Why, here comes Rose now, with her horse." After a romantic duet to end all romantic duets, the cast marched off to war singing, "Hurrah for Pershing and Coolidge! To hell with Mexico!" Not only "The Rose of Arizona," but both editions of the Garrick Gaieties *in toto*, were decked out with the bright tunes and lyrics of Richard Rodgers and Lorenz Hart.

After four years, in 1930, the Theatre Guild offered a third set of *Garrick Gaieties*. But the time for it was past. The youngsters were not so young any more, and failed to recapture their earlier insouciance; and moreover *The Little Show* had now come along to show how to do the job better. Even Marc Blitzstein's "Triple Sec," a hilarious parody of the Frederick Lonsdale school of drawing-room comedy, and contributions by Aaron Copland and Vernon Duke were not enough to keep the revue alive in New York. The Guild salvaged it, however, by putting together a touring *Garrick Gaieties*, fabricated from snippets of all three editions, with the addition of a few items purchased from *The Little Show*.

After *Mr. Lode of Koal*, the last of the Williams and Walker shows before the war, all-Negro attractions were entirely absent from Broadway until Noble Sissle and Eubie Blake brought *Shuffle Along* down from Harlem to the Sixty-third Street Music Hall in 1921. Sissle's musical score was full of vim and vitality, and the choral arrangements were spectacular. The dancing was as swift and tricky as any to be seen in the standard houses. Yet *Shuffle Along*, which had already exhausted some of its potential business by luring patrons up to Harlem, lasted for only 27 performances. This is an important statistic, for the misconception still exists that Harlem-bred Negro shows have frequently enjoyed success on Broadway. Actually, all-Negro musicals have not often succeeded at all, and the Negro has found his rightful place on the New York musical stage—with only a few exceptions—in mixed-cast productions, from *Show Boat* to *Finian's Rainbow*. The venture of taking *Shuffle Along* downtown stimulated several other unrewarded efforts, but it was not until Lew Leslie presented Florence Mills and Hamtree Harrington in *Dixie to Broadway* (1924) that a Negro revue kept open long enough (77 performances) to pay back its cost.

England made its first major contribution to the gaiety of Broadway since the original Gaiety days when Arch Selwyn brought over *André Charlot's Revue* in 1924. It was a small revue, by current American standards, but its three leading performers burst out of its frame in all directions. They were Beatrice Lillie, Gertrude Lawrence, and Jack Buchanan. The music and lyrics were predominantly the work of Noel Coward. The songs and sketches glorified "not the English girl but the English joke"—if the Coward twist may be considered typical of the English joke in general. The whole entertainment was given, most economically, in front of a single set that was hardly more than a white drop upon which lights could play. But nobody looked for settings—or for undraped girls—when Beatrice Lillie undertook to give a song recital, with all the manners of the concert platform but a voice that went back on her, or impersonated with dry brutality a tea-shop waitress or a faded ingenue; or when Gertrude Lawrence gave her characteristic pathetic turn to a sentimental ballad, or showed that she could be equally believable as a Chinese girl in Limehouse and as a super-smart Cowardesque Mayfair wife. Jack Buchanan was a trifle overlooked in the overwhelming experience of making the acquaintance of both Miss Lillie and Miss Lawrence on the same night; but he should not have been, for a suaver song-and-dance man has never existed, and he partnered both ladies with complete technical versatility. Two years later a second edition of *Charlot's Revue* arrived, with the same principals, Miss Lillie being provided with a travesty on ballet dancing in which she was supported by an invisible wire. Buchanan was not to pursue an American career further, though he returned in 1929 in *Wake Up and Dream*. Miss Lillie and Miss Lawrence found unmistakably that they could appear here whenever they wished, and from now on—to the continual benefit of the musical stage—they often did.

XVII

Musical Comedy from
1919 to 1925

THE ART movement, which invaded the revue field in the *Greenwich Village Follies* and the Joseph Urban décors for the *Ziegfeld Follies*, was also expensively manifest in several pretentious and serious-minded exotic spectacles. F. Ray Comstock and Morris Gest made a contribution in the way of Oriental pageantry in *Aphrodite*, which occupied the Century Theatre for 148 performances in 1919-20. Henri Février, composer of *Monna Vanna*, an opera that gave Mary Garden one of her most scarlet roles, wrote part of the music, along with Anselm Goetzl. Michel Fokine devised the choreography, and Léon Bakst had a hand in designing the costumes. A "drama of profane love," *Aphrodite* displayed a gorgeous exterior, but was hollow inside. It reached its climax in a bacchanalian ballet, to Moussorgsky music, danced on a floor of rose leaves. *Mecca* (1920), staged by the same producers shortly after the closing of *Aphrodite*, had even less impressive music by Percy Fletcher, but the touch of Fokine and Bakst was again in evidence. Considered the most stunning extravaganza of its time, *Mecca* exploited Egypt and the Arabian Nights terrain. As a "blaze of color," nothing like it had been seen on the American stage since *Scheherazade*.

On a smaller scale, but no less exciting to the eye, was the Gest-Comstock production of *The Rose of China* (1919), set by Joseph Urban and provided with music by Armand Vecsey, lyrics by P. G. Wodehouse, and book by Guy Bolton. Straying far from their earlier element, Wodehouse and Bolton created a variant of the *Madama Butterfly* theme, recounting the poignant tale of a Chinese girl who lost caste by letting herself be kissed in public. The kiss took place in a singularly luxuriant Chinese garden.

One or two other musical plays of the day also sought to make use of advanced artistic materials. John Murray Anderson found time, in the midst of his preoccupation with the *Greenwich Village Follies,* to produce and direct a musical comedy, *What's in a Name* (1920), in which he used the classic Greek device of an inner and an outer stage, and decorated the scenes with draperies and screens in the manner of Gordon Craig and Reinhardt. He experimented extensively with overhead and side lighting, reducing the use of footlights to a minimum; but many observers found the production too dark. Lee Shubert paid obeisance to modern staging in *The Rose Girl,* an otherwise undistinguished musical comedy in which Lydia Lopokova and the ballet were carried up and down in elevators. More resourceful was the Selwyns' production of *Johannes Kreisler* (1922), a 'fantastic melodrama" from German sources. The plot and music were thin enough; but the staging required forty-one changes of scene. Quick shifts were made possible partly by the artful use of lighting, and partly by using different segments and levels of the stage, and wagons on which rooms rolled out toward the audience.

Norman Bel Geddes entered the Broadway arena as director and co-producer with Richard Herndon of *Arabesque* (1925). The action took place on a single unit setting with three strata. Sometimes all three levels were brought into use at once. The book suffered from the vacuity that afflicted those of *Aphrodite* and *Mecca*. Bela Lugosi appeared as a shiek (pronounced "sheck"). The role may not have been too unpalatable at the moment when "a Bedouin girl, dressed down to the utmost finesse of nakedness, straddles a sheik, who lies full-length on a cloak on the floor of a savage tent at midnight, alone with her."

Conservative theatregoers by the thousands spurned these empty essays in beauty and contemporary stagecraft, and persisted in preferring the conventional, sentimental operettas and musical comedies whose charm, however attenuated, did not require so great an outlay of cultural energy. In the first half of the 1920s, old-fashioned operettas and musical comedies that were pretty and tuneful and entirely orthodox continued to attract a large following. Such pieces as Fritz Kreisler's *Apple Blossoms* (1919), the Cinderella story called *Irene* (1919), *Always You* (1920), *Mary* (1920), *Tangerine* (1921), *The Gingham Girl* (1922), *Sally, Irene and Mary* (1922), *The Lady in Ermine* (1922), and *Poppy* (1923)—all great successes—deserve mention here only because someone might look at the index and object to their omission. All were presented in tasteful, high-class fashion. All were supplied with music that rippled along lyrically, and plots that employed the expected clichés at the right time. None rose above the humo: typified by Oscar Hammerstein 2d's book for *Always You* "What," says the *jeune premier*, "do you say to a tramp in the park?" And the ingenue retorts, "I never speak to one." *Mary*, staged by George M. Cohan, was brisker than most of its old-fashioned contemporaries, and contained an especially well-favored ditty called "The Love Nest."

A number of musical comedies were frankly designed to serve as vehicles for popular performers. The Duncan Sisters Rosetta and Vivian, enjoyed their moment of glory in *Topsy and Eva* (1924), a musical version of *Uncle Tom's Cabin* including a good many incidents by Catherine Chisholm Cushing that could not be found in Mrs. Stowe's original, and a tearful song by Topsy (Rosetta), "I Never Had a Mammy." *Kid Boots* (1923) was a tribute by Flo Ziegfeld to Eddie Cantor, who dominated the production when George Olsen's band was not plugging its unusual jazz arrangements. The piece was the result of one of Ziegfeld's recurrent decisions—always revoked until toward the end of the decade—not to produce another *Follies*. The Shuberts made *Big Boy* (1925) a similar vehicle for Al Jolson.

Meanwhile the inexhaustible Victor Herbert continued to turn out scores, from *The Velvet Lady* (1919), in which young Eddie Dowling was featured, to his last work, *The Dream Girl* (1924), a romance of fifteenth-century England, with Fay Bainter and Walter Woolf as principals. But Herbert's great days were past, and much of his energy was being drained off into workaday songs for the revues. He never again produced another *Mlle. Modiste* or *Naughty Marietta*.

Rudolf Friml, however, was approaching the brief zenith at which he could be taken for a latter-day Herbert. In 1919 he was not yet able to write his own ticket, and in *Tumble In*, an adaptation of a farce by Avery Hopwood and Mary

Roberts Rinehart, he was called upon to supply the score for "a 'chicken' song, a pajama scene, a fashion parade, and a number in which appeals and promises are somewhat embarrassingly made to the most centrally situated bald man in Row A." Friml's temperament was not suited to this sort of modishness, and it must have been with relief that he settled back into the saccharine requirements of *The Little Whopper* later in the same year, secure in the knowledge that Vivienne Segal would sing his melodies as prettily as anyone could. *The Blue Kitten* (1924), taken from a French farce, sent him back to accompanying shimmies and "blue" lines. But this was only a momentary aberration.

With *Rose Marie*, presented by Arthur Hammerstein in 1924, Friml finally reached the promised land of every sentimental operetta composer, for his tunes—particularly the "Indian Love Call," with its wordless mating-call—became part of the corpus of enduring light music. The plot, with its manly members of the Canadian Mounted Police, was no more refreshing than those of comparable pieces, but nobody cared, when Dennis King and Mary Ellis were on hand to sing the tunes. A better dramaturgical effort was *The Vagabond King* (1925). As full of tunes as *Rose Marie*, this adaptation of Justin Huntly McCarthy's *If I Were King* (in which E. H. Sothern had acted) gave Dennis King one of the best swashbuckling, romantic roles of his ardent career.

The peak of Sigmund Romberg's success coincided with that of Friml. After a couple of mildly successful tries— *The Magic Melody* (1919) and *Love Birds* (1921)—he delved into the music of Franz Schubert in an alleged biography of the composer, *Blossom Time*. The operetta was first given in central Europe under the title *Lilac Time*, but to avoid confusion with Jane Cowl's earlier play, the name was changed for the American première, under Shubert (Lee and J. J., not Franz) sponsorship, in 1921. The New York run of 295 performances did not begin to tell the whole story of *Blossom Time*. Bertram Peacock took his lachrymose impersonation of the near-sighted, bumbling composer out on the road, and, with his colleagues—Olga Cook, Howard Marsh, William Danforth, and Roy Cropper—created an audience that retains its fealty to this day. The "Song of Love," in which a theme from the Unfinished Symphony is turned into a singularly banal waltz, and the overwrought treatment of "Ave Maria" have become treasured staples of the American repertory of light music.

Blossom Time, with its phenomenal power to withstand bargain-counter casting, is probably one of the two most valuable musical properties the Shubert organization possesses. The other is *The Student Prince* (1924), for which Romberg was also responsible, this time without aid from Franz Schubert. *The Student Prince in Heidelberg* (to give its cumbersome original title) was a work of far greater integrity than *Blossom Time*. Homogeneous in musical style, reasonably well plotted and characterized, and free from the appalling mawkishness to which Schubert's airy melodies were subjected, *The Student Prince*, unlike its predecessor, has deserved the permanent acceptance it has gained. Musically it is one of the strongest compositions of its kind, both in the intrinsic merit of the songs themselves and in the highly professional handling of the solo voices and the ubiquitous chorus of male students. Nor is the general tone of the university capers nearly as repellent as it might be— or, indeed, as it has been in a good many musical pieces laid on American college campuses. Not until *Best Foot Forward* and *Too Many Girls* was school life again presented as agreeably.

Meanwhile a tunesmith with friendlier and more vernacular gifts, Jerome Kern, was busily consolidating and improving upon his past experience, although his best days were still five and ten years ahead. Because the pieces whose scores he contributed occupied a twilight zone between the older sentimental musical comedies and the up-to-date jazz ones, Kern's métier for some time remained somewhat ambiguous. For this reason, perhaps, his producers seldom supplied him with singers of a caliber equal to that of the best participants in the Friml, Herbert, and Romberg operettas. This deficiency was cause for complaint when Joseph Santley and Ivy Sawyer appeared in *She's A Good Fellow* in 1919: "As everybody knows, musical comedy has practically dispensed with the singing voice as an essential, most of the singers nowadays being engaged according to their ability to dance."

This objection could also have been leveled with justice at the otherwise enchanting Marilyn Miller, who became a star in Florenz Ziegfeld's sumptuous production of *Sally* in 1920. Victor Herbert and Jerome Kern collaborated on the score, but it was Kern who gave Miss Miller "Look for the Silver Lining." Her performance of the song provided an instance of the extent to which the public hears what it wants to, when it is enamored of a performer. Miss Miller possessed a wiry little voice, sometimes hardly audible, except for a single enormous tone on F (the climactic note of 'Look for the Silver Lining"), which threw the whole song out of scale. But the little Ohio girl who had worked her way up through the *Follies* was gifted with a personality 'like a burst of sunshine," with blue eyes and blond hair and a lovely, friendly face, and with exquisite airiness as a dancer. The stage of the New Amsterdam Theatre was raised above the footlights so that everyone could see her twinkling toes; singer or no singer, she was every inch a star. With *Sally*, Marilyn Miller became the dearest love of the musical-comedy audience of the 1920s. When Ziegfeld put her in its sequel, *Sunny* (1925), he paid her the highest salary—reported to be $3,000 a week—ever known in American musical comedy until Gertrude Lawrence signed her contract for *Lady in the Dark*.

In his book of memoirs, *G. G.*, George Grossmith preserved his recollections of the composer of *Sally*:

"*Sally* has been conceived, written and produced almost entirely by English brains. Guy Bolton and Clifford Grey made the story and lyrics and Edward Royce (son of the old Gaiety comedian . . .) had made the most gorgeous presentation of the play. [This was the English production, which antedated Ziegfeld's.] He it was who staged the long series of Daly's successes, beginning with *The Merry Widow*. And the music of Sally! . . .

"Somewhere between the years 1905-1910 there was a penniless little song writer who hailed from America, but made his home in London. I knew him as Jerry Kern and liked him immensely. He often came to my house and played to us. He played divinely like nearly all of his kind, with a tremendous gift of 'tune.' He was the only one I could detect in a barren field likely to fill the shoes of Monckton, Paul Rubens, and Leslie Stuart. In my dressing-room at the Gaiety was a tiny yacht piano on which Rubens had composed his first song that was sung in a London theatre—'Trixie from the Town of Upper Tooting.'

" 'Give me a lyric,' one night asked Jerry, 'and let me try what I can do on the same instrument'; and together we wrote and composed 'Rosalie,' which I sang in, I think, *The Spring Chicken*. . . .

"Kern wrote several things for George Edwardes, but had no outstanding success until his return to America a year or two before the War, when he married a little English bride."

After *Sally*, Kern attached himself principally to the office of Charles B. Dillingham, whose productions, while less plushy than those of Ziegfeld, were consistently as handsome as any Broadway had to offer. Kern's major status was thus assured, since everything he wrote was presented with discretion and technical mastery. *Stepping Stones* (1923), a Little Red Riding Hood piece, provided volatile and likeable music for three dancing Stones—Fred and his daughters Dorothy and Allene. Except for *Sunny*, whose value was enhanced more by the bounding Jack Donahue and the Tiller Girls (billed as Eight Marilyn Miller Cocktails) than by any superior qualities in the score, the Kern pieces of this era are now all obscured by the more impressive quality of his later output.

The composers of rowdier character were kept busy by the demands of revue producers. Irving Berlin did not return to musical comedy until 1925, when he wrote a run-of-the-mill score for the Marx Brothers—who were easily able to demolish anybody's music—in *The Cocoanuts* (1925), which might as well have been a revue, for all the plot meant by the time the unbridled brothers and the stately Margaret Dumont got through with it.

Vincent Youmans, whose achievements would have warranted comparison with those of the best musicians in the field if his career had not been cut short by illness, first made his mark with *Wildflower* (1923), a colorful and richly orchestrated score. His chef d'oeuvre, however, was *No! No! Nanette*, in which Louise Groody and Charles Winninger appeared in 1925. Entirely conventional in scope, *No! No! Nanette* rode to popularity with two deft and refreshing tunes, "Tea for Two" and "I Want to Be Happy."

Almost indistinguishable in title from *No! No! Nanette* was George Gershwin's first musical comedy, *La! La! Lucille,* presented six years earlier, on May 26, 1919, at Henry Miller's Theatre. It was an unassuming little bedroom farce, full of people opening the wrong door at the wrong time. The music, described by one critic as "tinkly and sentimental as Kern at his best" scarcely identified the future composer of *Of Thee I Sing* and *Porgy and Bess*. Gershwin was new in show business, and had received almost no instruction beyond the mechanics he had been able to pick up in backstage jobs. He learned his craft in the full public gaze, making some mistakes as he went along, but adding to his own stature consistently, as his technique came to approach his talent. Probably no first-rank composer of musical comedies ever began with less preparation. A part of the idolizing attachment of his audiences probably sprang from their feeling that Gershwin had no secrets from them, that he was a local boy making good before their very eyes.

Gershwin kept so busy earning his living at the piano and making incidental contributions to revues that four and a half years passed before he composed his next musical comedy, *Sweet Little Devil* (1924). He still had not defined his own formula. But in *Lady, Be Good,* later in the same year, his rhythmic ebullience and light-hearted, unorthodox word-scansion began to make their point. With Fred and Adele Astaire to translate the music into visual movement, its freshness and verve were doubly apparent. And now Gershwin had found a lyricist able to support and encourage his most spontaneous qualities—his brother Ira, who from now on had a hand in almost every Gershwin piece, through the final grand-opera phase of *Porgy and Bess.*

In Gershwin's *Tell Me More* (1925), Lou Holtz's low comedy and the unwonted sophistication of the music and lyrics canceled each other out. Holtz deserves to be forgiven, though, in view of his definition of pantomime, as observed in a Russian ballet—"pantomime, from the Greek *pantomimus*: *panto*, meaning pants, and *mimus*, without." Gershwin's *Tip-Toes* (1925) likewise failed to create a stir, though Jeanette MacDonald adorned the cast. The same year, in a strange assignment, Gershwin collaborated with Herbert Stothart in the music for an operetta, *Song of the Flame*, for which Arthur Hammerstein imported the Russian Art Chorus. But this was merely a passing chore for Gershwin, who was to ride a skyrocket for the next decade.

Another celebrated musical artisan, Richard Rodgers, made his modest entry into the field on July 27, 1920, with *The Poor Little Ritz Girl*, for which Sigmund Romberg also wrote some of the music. Lorenz Hart wrote Rodgers' lyrics, and Alex Gerber wrote Romberg's. Though the piece had a piffling plot, it was an unusually successful first try, for it lasted through 119 performances. After a five-year lapse, Rodgers and Hart resumed their partnership to begin work in earnest in an American Revolution item known as *Dearest Enemy*, and also the Theatre Guild's first *Garrick Gaieties*. But as with Gershwin, their day was still in the future.

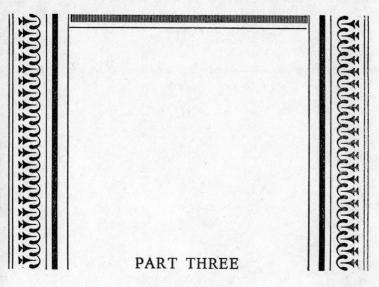

PART THREE

1926-1950

THE REVUE BECOMES CIVILIZED
MUSICAL COMEDY DISCOVERS CONTEMPORARY LIFE
THE DEPRESSION DECADE
THE NEW AUDIENCE
WAR AND POST-WAR YEARS
THE PAST, THE PRESENT, AND THE FUTURE

XVIII

The Revue Becomes Civilized

THE EASY money of the middle 1920s was not an unmixed blessing. With an angel in every speakeasy and an almost inexhaustible supply of box-office patrons, Broadway's stages were uncritically hospitable to almost anyone who thought he could produce a revue and knew he could finance its production. From the distance of a quarter-century, it seems incredible that 104 audiences would have been willing to attend something called *Bunk of 1926*; but they did, and applauded Gene Lockhart as an American variant of Balieff in a piece that offered little else in the way of humor or invention. *Bad Habits of 1926* fared less well, reaching only nineteen showings, with Robert Montgomery in the cast; its title should have been more appealing, signifying as it did that its patrons could expect to see bare bodies and hear dirty jokes. A similar orientation was evidenced by *Great*

Temptations (1926), produced by the Shuberts, of which the *World* said, "There are probably more chorus girls, more pink feathers, more high notes on the cornet, and more sets of steps than in any two shows ever given." The *Herald Tribune* noted the presence in the cast of a newcomer, Jack Benny, "a pleasant imitation of Phil Baker."

Why go on through *Bare Facts of 1926, Nic Nax of 1926, Padlocks of 1927* (with Texas Guinan galloping onto the stage on a white horse), and *Delmar's Revels* (1927)? These were the manifestations of a jaded mood, the soiled playthings of people tired of the very diversions they thought they wanted most. Since there was no more dramatic way of ending the revue craze, it was allowed to die by inches, of inanition.

By the end of 1927, the revue was all but dead. Fly-by-night producers no longer found support for their sleazy smut-fests. The only survivors in the once glutted field were the masters of the craft, who had fairly consistently given value received when the others were merely trying to make quick money. George White was able to maintain his annual *Scandals,* Earl Carroll his *Vanities,* and the Shuberts their variously titled extravaganzas. Probably White never offered a better *Scandals* than that of 1926, when it was still important for him to reiterate the difference between his productions and those of his parvenu competitors. On opening night he charged $50 for a seat in the first seven rows of the orchestra. He offered his $27,000 audience the ebullient Harry Richman as singer, master of ceremonies, and general liaison officer. Ann Pennington danced the "Black Bottom," the name of which, for the sake of decorum, was said to come from the black mud of the Mississippi River delta. Willie Howard—a perennial fixture of the *Scandals,* along with his brother Eugene—ran the gamut from a portrait of a feuding Southern mountaineer to a prediction of the effete behavior of the hero of a "drama of tomorrow." The production was in every way attractive to look at; the chorus girls "gave the impression of wearing less than usual," relying mainly on brassières that were "not opaque." Subsequent *Scandals*, after 1926, while not unfailingly as well supplied with ideas as this one, never slipped far below its level of presentable material and zestful performance. Between 1927 and 1931, when Ziegfeld temporarily abandoned the *Follies* in favor of musical comedies, the *Scandals* were without a peer among the expensive revues.

The *Earl Carroll Vanities* were seldom as strikingly studded with performing talent as the *Scandals*. They were aimed at an audience that was entirely satisfied by extensive and sleek revelations of female skin. Seeking a touch of variety in 1927, Carroll called his *Vanities* an "international edition," and incorporated features from André Charlot's current London revue, bringing over Jessie Matthews as leading lady. The result was an odd mixture, for Moran and Mack, the Two Black Crows, were hardly at home in a Mayfair environment. Carroll, moreover, made the mistake of experimenting with a show in which there was no nudity. He did not make the same mistake twice. In 1928, he returned to his usual predilection, and threw in W. C. Fields, the knockabout team of Barto and Mann, and Vincent Lopez's band for good measure. Reinstated in the favor of the patrons with whose tastes he had tampered, he was able in 1929 to cut down his salary list again, and to rely on the one formula he had been able to bring to perfection. This time, for some reason, he abandoned the name *Vanities*, and called his show *Earl Carroll's Sketch Book*. In 1930, he returned to his trademark, and never again relinquished it until he abandoned Broadway for his modernistic theatre-restaurant in Hollywood.

Apparently finding it easier to rent the Winter Garden to other producers than to produce shows for it themselves, the Shuberts had given up *The Passing Show*. The stock title of *Artists and Models*, however, they applied to two more revues of their own, in 1927 and 1930. To justify the title, the chorus boys were dressed as artists, in smocks and other appropriate vestments of that calling. The girls posed no costume problem whatever when they impersonated models.

In 1926, 1927, and 1929, the Shuberts also offered a triumvirate of exotica, *A Night in Paris*, *A Night in Spain*, and *A Night in Venice*. Yvonne George, who had sung "Mon Homme" in the *Greenwich Village Follies*, provided almost the only perceptible Parisian note in *A Night in Paris*, with imitations of Mistinguette and Raquel Meller. Jack Pearl, with his guttural German dialect, was hardly a typical exponent of Gallic style. Phil Baker, Ted Healy, Helen Kane (the Boop-Boop-a-Doop girl), and Rogers and Brennan were the featured Spaniards in the second revue of the series, which had the fastest and best dancing and the least nakedness of the three. The Venetian evocation, the biggest and most expensive of all, reverted to nakedness as its central article of faith.

Meanwhile the old master, Flo Ziegfeld, was largely distracted by his multiple interests as a producer of musical comedies. The *Ziegfeld Follies of 1927* was followed by a four-year gap before he returned to the revue field. Engaging Eddie Cantor as the top player in the 1927 *Follies*, he made much of the fact that the enterprise, having reached its twenty-first edition, had now come of age. The program carried the slogan, "He who glorifies beauty glorifies truth," inadvertently placed immediately ahead of Cantor's name. Crammed full of Albertina Rasch Girls, show girls, and Ziegfeld Dancing Girls who performed more complicated steps than before, the last *Follies* of the prosperity era lived up to the reputation of its twenty predecessors. As Brooks Atkinson observed, "In the art of handling groups of chorus girls on the stage amid whirls of dancing and costuming all through an evening, Mr. Ziegfeld has no equal." Percy Hammond thought the finale "the best of the thousands of revue finales" he had seen, as the chorus girls danced complex patterns and played on such diverse instruments as the banjo, the flute, the xylophone, the piccolo, the trombone, the cornet, and the snare drum.

One of the gayest revues of the late 1920s was a hands-across-the-sea affair, *This Year of Grace* (1928), in which the author and composer, Noel Coward, appeared in the company of his irresistible compatriot, Beatrice Lillie. Two years earlier Miss Lillie had saved a witless revue, *Oh, Please!* by her inspired clowning. So far, she had not found materials comparable to those of the two *Charlot's Revues* in which she had first appeared here. In *This Year of Grace* she was supplied with them. Covered with grease, she emerged from the water as a triumphant channel swimmer, and disrupted the welcoming crowd by her predatory attempts to require everyone to accept her autograph. She caroled songs with such refrains as "Whoops, girls, up and at 'em" and "A-ding, a-ding-a-dong." She sat pathetically on a bookkeeper's stool and ate her heart out in a song called "World Weary." As La Flamme, the Queen of Bohemia, in a *boîte* called La Chatte Vierge, she told of her acquaintance with an American named "Mr. Higginderrière." But Miss Lillie did not have to carry *This Year of Grace* alone. Mr. Coward was able to turn from an urbane ditty to the macabre "Dance, Little Lady," as bitter a satiric comment on the jazz age as the musical stage ever vouchsafed. This was, said the *Journal,* "a taut and jazz-strained piece, itched to a frenzy of saxophones as Mr. Coward chants out a deathly song to a girl almost tranced in the vacancy of the hypnotic music. As the rhythm leaps, a group of shiny mannequins shuffles onto the stage, with faces twisted into vapid masks, and presently the girl emerges with them, and becomes, with them, a dummy, treading out the crazy measure in the empty movement of automatons."

The British touch was also manifest in Charles B. Cochran's revue, *Wake Up and Dream* (1929), for which the American-born Cole Porter had been commissioned to write the music. Arch Selwyn brought the London production over lock, stock, and barrel, with Jessie Matthews, Jack Buchanan, and Tilly Losch as featured performers. The piece had taste, refinement, and intelligence, but too little material. The sensation of the evening was Miss Losch in "Arabesque," to Ravel music—"a dance of the hands," wrote Arthur Pollock in the Brooklyn *Eagle*, "which she does fascinatingly while crouched in plain black silk on a black dais, her fingers and hands and wrists and arms only moving, her body occasionally in response to them." John Mason Brown was an unbeliever in Miss Losch and in the revue as a whole, for the best thing he could find to say in the *Post* was that "Pogo, the performing horse of the Griffiths Brothers, was the drollest and most convulsing human horse that has capered on any stage within or before recent memory."

Another transatlantic gesture, Lew Leslie's *The International Review* (1930), was markedly less successful. Leslie made the mistake of trying to crowd too much into a super-variety entertainment; and he also erred in picking so mismated a batch of foreign folk as Gertrude Lawrence, Argentinita, Anton Dolin, Viola Dobos of the Budapest Opera Ballet, and Robert Conche, a Parisian child prodigy, who played the violin and the concertina, conducted the orchestra, and then disappeared from sight forever. Dolin made his mark sufficiently in an Apache dance, "The Pet of Montmartre," but Argentinita, whose modest Spanish folk dancing required special care, was so badly stage-managed that she was unable to win an American audience for several years afterward. The show ended at 12:15, with six numbers omitted, and with "exhaustion on the part of all concerned."

Leslie's inept planning was only partly responsible for the failure of *The International Review*. It was badly timed, for only a few months earlier—on April 30, 1929, at the Music Box—the whole course of the revue had been remapped by *The Little Show*, produced jointly by William A. Brady, Jr., Dwight Deere Wiman, and Tom Weatherly. From the first measures of a paean to the celebrated hardware store that ran "Hammacher Schlemmer, I love you," it was evident that *The Little Show* cherished a purpose far removed from that of the various *Follies*, *Scandals*, and *Vanities*. In it, the viewpoint of the *Grand Street Follies* was elevated to the highest Broadway level, and a piece for an audience with a reasonable I. Q. was given the advantage of the skilled presentation usually reserved for revues of less aristocratic pretensions. *The Little Show* offered no "dream appearances of all the lovely ladies of antiquity," nor did it employ more of a chorus than it needed for a sketch purporting to show the home life of the Tiller Girls. It was a fast show, but it also knew the value of slow tempo and quiet tone, as was demonstrated by a beautifully underplayed scene showing, as Richard Lockridge described it in the *Sun*, two bums sitting on a park bench, "singing of the market reports and welcoming a street sweeper and a policeman, who stop to assist them in assuring the listening world that 'money is easier today.' " Fred Allen's monologues before the curtain held the audience transfixed, especially one about a little boy who shot both parents in order to be entitled to go to the orphans' picnic. Clifton Webb was fleet of foot and tongue, and superbly sartorial. Libby Holman penetrated deep under the hide of a tough first-night audience with her dusky, throaty, throbbing delivery of "Moanin' Low." The grace and wit of Jo Mielziner's settings marked the beginning of a post-Urban, and from the modern point of view a super-Urban, conception of stage design.

Naturally the first *Little Show* was not the last. But it takes more than a general conception to keep an idea alive from one edition of a revue to the next; and except for the new Mielziner scenery and the artless delivery of Ruth Tester in "Sing Something Simple," a protest against the tricky rhyme-schemes that had come into vogue, the *Second Little Show* (1930) gave its audience less to remember. By the time the *Third Little Show* came along in 1931, Wiman and Weatherly—now its sole producers—were tempted to make it less intimate, and to rely heavily on the overpowering personality of Beatrice Lillie. It was no longer a real *Little Show*, but thanks to Miss Lillie, everyone had a fine time. Seated in a rickshaw, she intoned Noel Coward's charge that only mad dogs and Englishmen go out in the midday sun. She dealt ruthlessly with the behavior of a late comer at the theatre—a theme Iva Kitchell, whether consciously or unconsciously imitative, has treated in a similar vein in recent years. She introduced a parody of Ruth Draper's "Railway Station on the Western Plains" by telling the audience, "In this little sketch, ladies and gentlemen, I want you to imagine far too much." For the benefit of what has sometimes euphemistically been called the "intellectual audience," she exhumed and reinterpreted a ballad of the 1890s by Liza Lehmann, entitled "There Are Fairies at the Bottom of Our Garden."

The true successor to the first *Little Show* was Max Gordon's production, *Three's a Crowd* (1930). Even more assured in every department than its predecessor, it ran for 272 performances, whereas the first *Little Show*, in spite of a warmly favorable critical reception, closed after 55. Fred Allen, Portland Hoffa, Clifton Webb, and Libby Holman moved directly into *Three's a Crowd*, in which they were joined by Tamara Geva, Fred MacMurray, and Allan Jones. This revue, wrote Arthur Pollock, "has beauty and grace without effort, and high polish and a civilized sophistication and a little good, clean-cut, gentlemanly dirt unmarred by vulgarity or exhibitionism." It was a grown-up revue, entirely free from banality and largely free from routine usages; the first act, for instance, "ended so quietly you'd hardly know it was over." The Allen monologues, the Webb feet, and the Arthur Schwartz-Howard Dietz songs were major assets, and Libby Holman sang Johnny Green's torch song "Body and Soul," to which she gave an intensity of inward emotion that is rare on the light musical stage—or, for that matter, on any stage at all.

The reputation of *Three's a Crowd* was eclipsed, however, by Max Gordon's *The Band Wagon*, which arrived at the New Amsterdam Theatre on June 3, 1931. Twenty years later, unless memory bears exceedingly false testimony, it is still possible to believe that *The Band Wagon* was one of the most perfect revues in the history of Broadway. Schwartz and Dietz were again composer and lyricist, and Dietz collaborated with George S. Kaufman on the book. Hassard Short directed, and Albertina Rasch staged the group dances. The personnel on the stage was entirely different, however, from that of *Three's a Crowd*. Fred and Adele Astaire were the romantic singing and dancing leads. Tilly Losch contributed her individual compositions, which were as modern as Broadway could then tolerate. The major comedy assignments went to Frank Morgan, drawn away from the non-musical stage for the first time; Philip Loeb, experienced from the *Garrick Gaieties*; and the dry, tough, economical Helen Broderick.

A part of the delight of *The Band Wagon* lay in its transmutation of stage machinery into something approaching lyric poetry. The first American revue to take full cognizance of the revolving stage, it had two of them, and used them in all sorts of imaginative ways as an integral part of the bright Albert Johnson settings and the action and business devised by Short. The Astaires danced on them as they revolved; in the first-act finale the turntables turned in opposite directions as the entire cast waved from a merry-go-round. The sketches, bearing the imprint of Kaufman's typewriter, were wonderfully malicious. In a manner far more telling than that of the *Garrick Gaieties*, a travesty of the set pieces of formula shows revealed in their true light the moonlight serenade, the waltz sequence, the uninspired dance routine, the close harmony of a male quartet, and the overworked device of the blackout. The last of these was handled memorably in a sketch, "Pour le Bain," portraying Miss Broderick as a Westchester matron in search of bathroom appliances in an especially cultivated sales salon. Having satisfied her interest in washbowls and bathtubs, she intimated that no mention of another type of fixture had passed between them. The salesman, who obviously always had a line from Keats on the tip of his tongue, replied, "Heard melodies are sweet, but those unheard are sweeter." Blackout. Elsewhere in the evening, Frank Morgan appeared as a southern colonel in "The Pride of the Claghornes," in which the Claghorne daughter was thrown out of the house because she had violated Southern canons by never going wrong. The chorus girls were "not made of wood," and their comely freshness enabled Percy Hammond to bring out one of his most frequently repeated lines: "They look, as Miss Laurette Taylor used to say, as if they all had mothers."

The prescient Brooks Atkinson, of the *Times*, recognized that *The Band Wagon* had established a new era. "After the appearance of *The Band Wagon*," he predicted, "it will be difficult for the old-time musical show to hold up its head. George S. Kaufman and Howard Dietz have put the stigmata on stupid display by creating a thoroughly modern revue. It is both funny and lovely; it has wit, gaiety, and splendor."

The ascendancy of the intimate revue posed a challenge to Flo Ziegfeld. In 1931 he determined to revive the *Follies*, even though production money was hard to get and the public pocketbook had shrunk to a fraction of its pre-1929 thickness. On July 1, 1931, accordingly, he opened the *Ziegfeld Follies of 1931* at his own Ziegfeld Theatre, assigning the chief tasks to such experts as Harry Richman, Jack Pearl, Albert Carroll, and Helen Morgan, and exerting his special spell of glorification upon the beautiful Gladys Glad. Though the public supported him, Ziegfeld's triumph was a questionable one. Without Joseph Urban, the décors were less consistent, and the performance seemed to move sluggishly because it lacked the crispness and brisk projection of the more up-to-date revues. Ziegfeld would have done well to let the 1927 edition be his last, instead of indulging in this anachronistic effort.

Ziegfeld's continuing belief in the big, or non-intimate, revue was shared by a young producer, Billy Rose, who threw his hat in the ring with *Sweet and Low* (1930). A whole-hearted believer in "belly laughs," and also the lucky possessor of a wife named Fannie Brice, Rose already mani-

his first Broadway endeavor, a gift for assembling
edy revue in a fashion that concealed a keen ana-
igence. With Moss and Fontana to give the proceedings a ballroom lift, and with George Jessel, James Bar-
ton (with his perennial drunk act), and Arthur Treacher
to share the comic chores with Miss Brice, *Sweet and Low*
attained the very solid early-depression figure of 184 performances in New York. In 1931, Rose devised *Billy Rose's
Crazy Quilt* as a further vehicle for his wife, whom he placed
in the company of Phil Baker, Ted Healy, and their assorted
stooges. The long run and extensive tour of *Crazy Quilt*
effectively established Rose as a new major producer, though
his output in subsequent years was never large.

During these years a continuing procession of all-Negro
revues made its way from Harlem to Broadway, though few
of them were ever really assimilated in the Broadway scene.
The most successful producer of Negro revues was Lew Leslie, whose series of *Blackbirds*, beginning in 1928, established
a pattern of high-pressure delivery, musical pandemonium,
and incessant tap dancing. Bill Robinson came to Broadway
in *Blackbirds of 1928*; and Ethel Waters, having previously
appeared in Earl Dancer's revue *Africana* in 1927, was the
undebated star of *Blackbirds of 1930*. With *Rhapsody in
Black* (1931), Leslie tried to take a more elevated view of
the potentialities of a Negro show, and fell into the abyss
of cultural pretense. Miss Waters, the Cecil Mack Choir,
and the Berry Brothers carried the burden of a show in
which dancing was minimal and "symphonic" montages
predominated. "A sort of Harlem *Chauve-Souris*," wrote
Howard Barnes in the *Herald Tribune*, "it dispenses with
choruses and in large measure with the ecstatic shuffling that
has marked sepia offerings in the past." When a Negro choir
began singing Jewish and Russian music, the racial reason
for presenting the show evaporated; and it was not until

Porgy and Bess that the all-Negro show was restored to a position of importance. Meanwhile Miss Waters moved on to *As Thousands Cheer* and *At Home Abroad,* to conquer new provinces.

Musical Comedy Discovers
Contemporary Life

As THE revue wore out its welcome, musical comedy moved back into a dominating position on Broadway. But these were still the mad 1920s, and an exclusive diet of moonlight-and-honeysuckle themes was not to the liking of an increasingly hysterical generation. Obviously musical comedy, which had been gradually catching up with the times for a decade or so, would have to complete the process if it hoped to recapture the attention of the audience that had been kept up to the minute by the satiric sketches of the revues. After all, there was no binding reason for avoiding current topics and fads as subject matter for musical comedies, merely because most (though, as we have seen, not quite all) past examples of the form had dealt chiefly in romantic intrigues. Accordingly, the topical musical comedy became one of the standard types of the late 1920s, and as time went on it tended to become the ruling type.

For sheer efficiency in handling a topical book in a manner that was intelligible and diverting to a large public, no team surpassed the trio of De Sylva, Brown, and Henderson. Beginning with *Good News* (1927), their names were listed together so inextricably that it was difficult to tell who did what. In point of fact, Ray Henderson wrote the music, Lew Brown and B. G. de Sylva worked together on the lyrics, and De Sylva took care of the book, sometimes alone and sometimes with the aid of a collaborator. In six years, from 1927 to 1932, they turned out an unbroken series of six hits, and they could probably have continued longer if the depression and Hollywood contracts had not disrupted their team.

Good News (1927) was a college comedy. In those days, as Chancellor Robert M. Hutchins of the University of Chicago has pointed out, the colleges confused themselves with country clubs. Since any resemblance between De Sylva's imaginary Tait College and any real college was largely accidental, *Good News* was two steps removed from everything we associate with the seats of higher learning today. The orchestra began the evening with a cheer, "Rah! Rah! Rah!", before launching into the overture, and the ushers in the theatre wore dirty old jerseys. At Tait, college rhymed with knowledge, but bore no further relation to it. With George Olsen's band to play the "Varsity Drag," the collegians had a hot time of it, and to hell with studies.

Perhaps the most perplexed member of the first-night audience was Alexander Woollcott, whose reaction was a study in kid-glove detachment from the whole rowdy antic: "I confess that I had not precisely expected to attend this season a musical comedy of which the plot would turn on whether Tom Marlowe would pass his astronomy exam, and so be able to go into the big game on Saturday and win for dear old Tait. I had not expected to hear a theatre hushed by Tom's big, manly resolve not to cheat in the exam, but to play fair and square. I certainly had not expected to see a cluster of chorus girls, led by a fair and writhing maiden with implausible hair, lift their approximately assembled voices in soprano fealty to Pi Beta Phi."

After taking time out to work on *Manhattan Mary* (1927), a "vast, bewildered, gorgeous extravaganza" produced by George White (in which he himself returned to the stage), the De Sylva, Brown, and Henderson triumvirate returned to more mundane interests with *Hold Everything* (1928), a fast and funny saga of the prize-fight ring. Bert Lahr, hailed as the best addition to the roster of comics since the advent of Ed Wynn, played the role of a pug who usually wound up on the floor. A high moment occurred when Nina Olivette, his vis-à-vis, said angrily, "For two cents I'd knock you out." "You're mercenary! You're mercenary!" howled Lahr.

Having disposed of prize-fighting, De Sylva, Brown, and Henderson turned to golf in *Follow Thru* (1929). Eleanor Powell offered some of her cleanest and fleetest tap dancing to "Button Up Your Overcoat," one of Henderson's most felicitous and easy-moving songs. Jack Haley invaded a swanky country club, and commented to one of the golfers, "The trouble with your game is that you stand too close to the ball—after you hit it."

By refraining from digging very deep into the subjects they treated, the trio managed to avoid alienating any of their patrons. They had their formula down pat by now; it was easy to deal with aviation successfully in *Flying High* (1930), with the aid of Bert Lahr as an addled pilot. *Hot-*

Cha, written for Flo Ziegfeld in 1932, enabled Lahr to be a fake matador in Mexico.

In 1932, De Sylva left his partners to team up with Vincent Youmans in *Take a Chance*. A somewhat nondescript show that had failed on the road as *Humpty Dumpty*, *Take a Chance* made history principally by adding luster to the reputation of Ethel Merman, who had emerged from the night clubs two years earlier in *Girl Crazy*. Youmans gave her two of the best songs anyone ever wrote for an American musical comedy—"Eadie Was a Lady" ("though her past was shady"), an evocation of pre-prohibition New Orleans; and a rousing pseudo-revivalist hymn, "Rise and Shine," which brought the first-act curtain down in the midst of pandemonium. It would have taken no more than these two songs to establish, if *Girl Crazy* had not already done so, that Miss Merman was one performer the Broadway stage could not do without. Until now, happily, it has not had to. While *Take a Chance* was making its mark, Ray Henderson worked with Lew Brown and Mack Gordon on a vehicle for Jimmy Durante, *Strike Me Pink* (1933).

Take a Chance was the last Broadway score to which Youmans contributed before illness struck him. His loss was a deprivation for the musical stage, for in his time he alone deserved to be ranked with Gershwin, Porter, Rodgers, and Kern. Another of his notable achievements was the naval musical comedy, *Hit the Deck* (1927), which contained one of the unforgotten classics of the 1920s, "Hallelujah." *Great Day* (1929) included "Without a Song"; but the show deferred its opening so many times that in the end it did not become a success. Youmans' only other musical comedies of the 1930s were *Smiles* (1930), a Ziegfeld production in which Marilyn Miller and the Astaires appeared, and *Through the Years* (1932).

As a result of *Oh, Kay* (1926), George Gershwin finally

enjoyed the pleasure of hearing himself called "the premier music-maker." Never before had he cördinated his powers so well, or joined the staff of so inviting a production as this one, mounted by the "freshman impresarios," Alex Aarons and Vinton Freedley (whose partnership is symbolized today by the name of the Alvin Theatre, made out of the first syllables of their first names). *Oh, Kay* dealt with the most overworked subject of the day, bootlegging; but the collaboration of first-class experts in every department lifted the treatment high above the ordinary. Gertrude Lawrence returned from England to play the role of the sister of a titled British bootlegger. Guy Bolton worked out a tight, amusing book; P. G. Wodehouse, the lyricist, was also credited with such high-voltage lines as "Never criticize a bootlegger's English if his Scotch is all right." Miss Lawrence displayed even more versatility as a mimic than the *Charlot's Revues* had led her audience to expect, and she "wrung the withers" of Percy Hammond's heart with her throbbing performance of "Someone to Watch over Me." The score, which also included "Clap Yo' Hands," "Fidgety Feet," and "Do-Do-Do Like You Done-Done-Done Before," reinforced Gershwin's reputation as a composer ready and able to deal with a wide range of situations, moods, and sentiments.

In *Funny Face* (1927), Gershwin returned to partnership with his brother Ira, who fitted out Victor Moore with the lyrics of " 'S Wonderful." The next year (1928), Ziegfeld lured both Gershwins away from Aarons and Freedley, to coöperate with Sigmund Romberg and P. G. Wodehouse in *Rosalie*, the most richly caparisoned piece the master ever produced for Marilyn Miller. With glowing Urban sets representing West Point, conveniently turned co-educational for the occasion, and the usual outlay of glorified girls, *Rosalie* buried the Gershwin music deep under its visual appeals.

But at least the collaboration of Gershwin and Romberg was an amusing and unlikely idea, which made Woollcott "think we shall soon have a novel written by Harold Bell Wright and Ernest Hemingway." Woollcott's account of Miss Miller's entrée is too savorous to pass by:

"There comes a time once in every two or three years when the vast stage of that playhouse [the New Amsterdam Theatre] begins to show signs of a deep and familiar agitation. Down in the orchestra pit the violins chitter with excitement and the brasses blare. The spotlight turns white with expectation. Fifty beautiful girls in simple peasant costumes of satin and chiffon rush pellmell onto the stage, all squealing simple peasant outcries of "Here she comes!" Fifty hussars in fatigue uniform of ivory white and tomato bisque march on in column of fours and kneel to express an emotion too strong for words. The lights swing to the gateway at the back and settle there. The house holds its breath. And on walks Marilyn Miller."

Ziegfeld and the exploitation of Marilyn Miller were not up Gershwin's alley. After writing two minor items for other producers—*Treasure Girl* (1928) and *Show Girl* (1929)—George and Ira Gershwin, with the help of Morrie Ryskind, turned their energies to the preparation of the most uncompromising musical comedy the American stage had yet tolerated. After *Strike Up the Band* opened in 1930, William Bolitho wrote in the *World*: "I don't remember ever before in a musical comedy having noticed or understood what it was all about. Here all is not only clear but really startling. Of all things in the world, here is a bitter, rather good, satirical attack on war, genuine propaganda at times, sung and danced on Broadway, to standing room only."

Not only war, but the Babbittry that had complacently led the country into a parlous financial and political situation, were the targets of Ryskind's book. Cushioning his story by telling it within a dream context, Ryskind detailed the events in a mock war between the United States and Switzerland over the high tariff on chocolate. Victor Moore, already recognized as ideally suited to political satire, was "the man behind the President," engaged in fixing up a peace treaty that involved the illegitimate annexing of territory, renaming Baluchistan Jugo-Slavia, and partitioning Russia. The miracle of *Strike Up the Band* was its ability to present its argument without losing its good nature, and without sacrificing opportunities for such ebullient Gershwin tunes as "Strike Up the Band" and "Mademoiselle from New Rochelle." *Strike Up the Band* was the precursor of the musical satires of the depression period, most notably of *Of Thee I Sing*. It was the first real token of liberalism and a social conscience in the American musical theatre.

Gershwin did not, however, immediately pursue the implications of *Strike Up the Band*. In *Girl Crazy*, his other product of 1930, he reverted to a light-minded plot, provided by Guy Bolton and John McGowan, which told of the adventures in Custerville, Arizona, of a girl-crazy Eastern youth who had been sent there to keep out of trouble. The theme apparently inspired little tenderness in Gershwin, for although *Girl Crazy* was one of his most inventive scores, it was also one of his coldest. There was softness, it is true, about "Embraceable You," and there was a melting languor in the ministrations of a male quartet, the Foursome, who covered the scene changes by returning again and again to sing in close harmony, "I'm bidin' my time; That's the kinda guy I'm." But for Ethel Merman, fresh from the night clubs, Gershwin wrote two of his hardest-hitting songs, the kinetic fury called "I Got Rhythm" and the western dance-hall torch song, "Sam and Delilah," a Barbary Coast satire on the Frankie and Johnny ballad. With its stern humors, *Girl Crazy* more than ever marked its composer as a man of strong personal idiosyncrasy, with nothing but contempt for the tired clichés of his trade.

It would be unjust to imply that Cole Porter was less willing than Gershwin to deal satirically with social and political issues. His method, however, was different from the outset. He made use of satirically oriented books, but preferred to employ as his weapon the barbed shaft of an individual line or song. Moreover, he developed his technique of acid comment only slowly, contenting himself at first with a special urbanity of manner that was the reflex of one intent upon forgetting his Hoosier origins.

Fifty Million Frenchmen (1929), concentrated its attention in both music and lyrics (Porter, as always thereafter, wrote both) upon one matter—sex—somewhat to the discomfiture of Richard Watts, who complained, "The lyrics he devised for the new musical comedy once more discussed learnedly and wittily the sex habits of the beaver, oyster, armadillo, gnu, aardvark and kindred exhibits in zoölogy and proved again that their author is the most definitely individual and completely brilliant deviser of song words, but it also made some of us wish that Mr. Porter wouldn't pound at one theme so constantly." In William Gaxton, Porter found an abettor so engaging that Robert Littell of the *World* thought it would be all right to "take nearly all other musical comedy heroes and throw them into the Seine." Since the story provided by Herbert Fields was laid in Paris, Norman Bel Geddes was called upon for handsome sets of the proper places—the Ritz Bar, the American Express, the Café de la Paix, the races. It was all very chic, very brittle, and without much trace of the warmth of sentiment which middle age was to bring to its composer later on.

Porter claimed that *The New Yorkers* (1930) was a "sociological musical satire," but this phrase may have been no more than an obeisance to *Strike Up the Band*. At any rate, *The New Yorkers* offered no profounder social revelation than the sight of Hope Williams as a resident of Park Avenue, "the street where bad women walk with good dogs." Such satiric impact as the piece might have had was effectually shattered by Jimmy Durante, who was appearing in his first musical comedy, in the company of the irrepressible Lou Clayton and Eddie Jackson. Durante won the hearts of his sophisticated audience with an engagingly crude song entitled "The Hot Potata"; and at the close of the first act proceeded to an anthem in praise of wood and its place in American history, illustrating his meaning with exhibits in the form of miscellaneous trees, boxes, violins, and express wagons. In his comic play with Clayton and Jackson, wrote Brooks Atkinson, "Jimmy the superman burns his way across the stage, splintering the English language, assaulting his companions, hurling hats into the orchestra pit, whirling around to confront an imagined adversary, bursting with undisciplined energy." Porter lost this round to Durante.

Richard Rodgers and Lorenz Hart first adventured into the realm of satire by indirection. In 1927, Herbert Fields— son of Lew Fields—supplied them with a book inspired by Mark Twain, and on November 3 of that year, *A Connecticut Yankee* lifted the reputation of its collaborators to the top of the profession. Fields brought Mark Twain up to date with a host of 1927 references and slogans and slang expressions, and Hart followed suit with the lyrics of "Thou Swell." In the second act, as King Arthur's courtiers began to find their way around in the language of their American visitors, they could be heard remarking, "Methinks yon damsel is a lovely broad," or "I would fain walk a furlong for a Camel." A whole evening of this became a bit taxing, but the insouciant and unexpected rhymes of Hart's lyrics and the lift of such melodies as "On a Desert Isle" and "My

Heart Stood Still," along with the tireless affability of William Gaxton as the Yankee, kept the interest of the audience from flagging. During the intermission the spirit of the occasion was kept intact by a curtain decorated by Robert Benchley's wondrous map of Camelot and its environs. The sentimental hit song, "My Heart Stood Still," incidentally, was not written for or first used in A Connecticut Yankee. Rodgers had composed it for a Cochran revue in London, One Damned Thing After Another. Flo Ziegfeld wanted to buy the song for the Follies, but Rodgers and Hart, having their own use for it, would not sell it.

Having entered the field of topical humor through the back gate, Rodgers and Hart, and Fields along with them, remained in it for Present Arms (1928). A patent imitation of Hit the Deck and Good News, it was a vehement and blary depiction of the behavior of the Marines in the Hawaiian Islands, made especially salable by the elaborate tableaux and evolutions dreamed up by Busby Berkeley. Hart's lyrics assumed even more of the cast that set them apart from all others, with such personalized end-rhymes as "Egypt" with "he gypped" and "Scotland" with "what land."

Neither Present Arms nor the other musical comedy Rodgers and Hart wrote early in 1928 represented Rodgers at his most inspired. Beatrice Lillie and Clifton Webb took the spotlight away from both the composer and the lyricist in She's My Baby, though Rodgers and Hart were no less responsible than Miss Lillie for the supernal bathos of the song that ran, "You can have another friend, another lover; A baby's best friend is its mother." The shopworn book by Bert Kalmar and Harry Ruby required the combined genius of Miss Lillie and Webb to make anything out of such repartee as this:

WEBB: "Let us ensconce ourselves upon the sofa."
LILLIE: "No, I prefer to sit down."

Still relatively young practitioners of their craft, Rodgers and Hart spent most of the 1920s searching for their best métier, without quite finding it. Until they returned to Broadway with *Jumbo* in 1935, after a four-year absence, they remained hardly more than bright and fluent workmen, able to turn out attractive and moderately successful work without again tapping the rich lode they had momentarily uncovered in *A Connecticut Yankee*. They moved from one assignment to another, with no special conviction as to the direction in which their best usefulness might lie. There were moments of real distinction, it is true, in Rodgers' score for *Spring Is Here*—especially in the song bearing the title of the show. But *Heads Up* (1929), a spoof of life on a yacht, and *America's Sweetheart* (1931), a poorly aimed attempt to repeat the Hollywood satire of George S. Kaufman's *Once in a Lifetime*, were swiftly forgotten; and so would Ziegfeld's production of *Simple Simon* (1930) have been without Ed Wynn. In his familiar hornrimmed spectacles, with his omnipresent lisp and giggle, Wynn ventured on a picnic. Admiring the canvas trees, he exclaimed, "I love the woods! Ah, how I love the woods!" Whereupon the woods, including a huge green frog which was one of the residents, proceeded to show Wynn that his sentiment was not reciprocated.

While Rodgers and Hart were engaging upon these early and inconclusive endeavors, the older and more experienced Jerome Kern came into the fullness of his powers. Although he supplied the music in 1927 for Charles Dillingham's musical-comedy-revue, *Lucky*, in which Paul Whiteman's band interpreted the score in the latest jazz arrangements, Kern appeared to realize that his real gift lay in the direction of sentimental and nostalgic evocations bordering upon the province of operetta.

Everything that was most persuasive and endearing about

Kern as a melodist was summoned forth by Flo Ziegfeld's commission to write the score for Oscar Hammerstein 2d's dramatization of Edna Ferber's novel *Show Boat*. The production, presented at the Ziegfeld Theatre on December 27, 1927, proved to be one of those rare convocations of talent in which everyone concerned—authors, directors, and performers—was protected by a lucky star. Hammerstein suddenly found himself in possession of gracious and expert powers as a lyricist at which his earlier verses had only hinted. His easy, natural handling of dialogue gave life and credibility to a book that would have seemed in less skillful hands to be too slow-moving in the first half, and too rambling in the thirty-four-year span covered by the second half. Charles Winninger as the bluff and merry Cap'n Andy; the starchy Edna May Oliver as Parthy Ann; Helen Morgan, with her brave little sob, as the half-caste Julie; Howard Marsh as a dashing Ravenal; Norma Terris as a fresh and pretty Magnolia—these were among the truest people the musical stage had ever represented. Filled with period devices as it now seems, *Show Boat* in its day was perhaps the only musical comedy to achieve a dramatic verisimilitude that seemed comparable to that of the speaking stage.

Because the play itself was so honest, the Kern-Hammerstein songs took on a double force. But in their own right they formed an astonishing procession—"Old Man River," "Only Make Believe," "Can't Help Lovin' That Man," "Why Do I Love You?", "Bill" (with words by P. G. Wodehouse). No other American piece of its vintage left so large a permanent musical legacy, and certainly no other surpassed it in quality.

Since masterpieces seldom come in quick succession, Kern slipped somewhat below the level of *Show Boat* in the succeeding *Sweet Adeline* (1929), perhaps partly because he was too intent on continuing the *Leitmotiv* plan of providing each character with his own theme, with which he had experimented unobtrusively in the earlier score. For *The Cat and the Fiddle* (1931) he again conceived a rich and lovely score (including "The Night Was Made for Love" and "She Didn't Say Yes"), but the effect of the piece as a whole was lessened by Otto Harbach's inordinately dull book about the love affair between musicians of disparate tastes—a sophomoric composer of serious intentions and an American girl devoted to popular music.

The plot of *Music in the Air* (1932)—dealing with a four-way intrigue absorbing two members of a Bavarian choral society, a prima donna, and a famous playwright—was scarcely more invigorating, but the smooth touch of Oscar Hammerstein 2d took some of the curse off. It followed the way pointed by *Show Boat,* moreover, in seeking to achieve honorable characterization and dramaturgy. Whether or not the story was worth attending to, the treatment of it was made significant by Hammerstein's exorcising of the precision dancing, the knock-about comics, and the overelaborate staging and costuming that had still related *Show Boat* to the conventions of its time. In everything except its plot materials, *Music in the Air* was thoroughly modern in conception. The integrity of its form required the music to be so intimately related to the circumstances of the book that even so charming a song as "Egern on the Tegern See" did not mean enough outside its context to become especially popular in its own right.

Though its composer is less celebrated than Rodgers or Kern, one other Ziegfeld musical cannot be left out of this chronicle. On February 2, 1927, *Rio Rita*, with a book by Guy Bolton and music by Fred Thompson, opened the producer's new "cathedral," the Ziegfeld Theatre. Today the proud possession of Billy Rose, the Joseph Urban façade and interior may still be inspected, in their original state, at the corner of Fifty-fourth Street and Sixth Avenue. *Rio Rita* was an extremely ordinary affair with a villain and a tenor and an ingenue. To match it to the occasion it celebrated, Ziegfeld borrowed the beauteous Gladys Glad from the *Follies*, and gave Urban an even more than usually free hand to design a bewildering array of vermilion and black and turquoise costumes for the hundred girls who adorned the stage. Bert Wheeler and Robert Woolsey were the comics, and much of the dancing was allotted to the Albertina Rasch Girls, then a new ensemble, addicted to unison bending and swaying of a sleek and stylish kind.

Despite the rapid rise to favor of the younger practitioners, the composers of old-hat operetta also retained their hold over a portion of the Broadway public. Sigmund Romberg still had two robust and tuneful romances to offer— *The Desert Song* (1926) and *The New Moon* (1928)—as well as the more modestly successful *Nina Rosa* (1930). After this he lapsed into a fifteen years' silence which he broke only twice, with *May Wine* (1935) and *Sunny River* (1941), before writing *Up in Central Park* (1947). Emmerich Kalman made his best impression with *Countess Maritza* (1926), in which Odette Myrtil fiddled "Play, Gypsies, Dance, Gypsies" whenever she was permitted to. *The Circus Princess* (1927), a weaker story and score, was aided at the box office by the great clown, Poodles Hanneford, and a variety of equestrians and aerialists. Rudolf Friml composed his last hit in *The Three Musketeers* (1928), produced with splendor by Ziegfeld. Alexander Woollcott confessed that he "did greatly enjoy the first few years of Act I."

Viennese operetta, which has a way of coming back to life precisely when it looks deadest, put in a reappearance in 1929, when the Shuberts staged a sumptuous revival of Johann Strauss' *Die Fledermaus*, under the title *A Wonderful Night*. They stole a march on Max Gordon and *The*

Band Wagon by making extensive use of a revolving stage. In its whole tone, the production was elegant, graceful, and faithful to the period. The libretto was much too faithful, for its "wormy" text was a source of universal ennui. The leading man was a young British actor named Archie Leach. In view of his later celebrity in the motion pictures as Cary Grant, Arthur Pollock's impression of his callow American debut is worth repeating: "Archie Leach, who feels that acting in something by Johann Strauss calls for distinction, is somewhat at a loss as to how to achieve it. The result is a mixture of John Barrymore and Cockney. He makes a handsome hero, though."

Largely neglected by American producers in the first few decades of its history, *Die Fledermaus* now came to be regarded as the most dependable of all Viennese products. As *Champagne Sec* (1933), Dwight Deere Wiman provided it with an attractively modernized book by Robert A. Simon, and Monty Woolley's direction taught the actors to treat their assignments in gay, posturing, period-satire fashion. As *Rosalinda* (1942), the New Opera Company offered a version that was both beautiful and modish, with Felix Brentano adapting Max Reinhardt's direction to Broadway needs, and with George Balanchine as choreographer, Oliver Smith as scene designer, and Ladislas Czettel as costume designer. In 1950, *Die Fledermaus* was awarded the ultimate accolade by being welcomed into the repertory of the Metropolitan Opera.

A Wonderful Night cannot be said, however, to have initiated a trend toward the general restoration of Viennese operetta to the American stage. The only other Broadway manifestation of it at this time was a production of Karl Millöcker's *The Dubarry*, undertaken in order to win Grace Moore away from the Metropolitan for a season. Otherwise Viennese music was still neglected except at that august house, where on January 2, 1931, von Suppé's *Boccaccio* was mounted for Maria Jeritza, who "cut a fine figure" in it.

The record of transatlantic curiosa can be completed with two more items. *The Wonder Bar*, a cabaret drama imported from Berlin, was unsuccessfully broached in 1931, with Al Jolson as its continental star. Noel Coward's delicately tasteful *Bitter Sweet*, a memento of the sixty-year incursion of British musical attractions, was the last musical importation from Britain, except the D'Oyly Carte Company, to reach Broadway for a decade—until Coward's *Set to Music* arrived in 1939, with Beatrice Lillie on hand to sing "Mad about the Boy," and a withering sketch, "The Stately Homes of England," to put the decaying upper classes in their place.

XX

The Depression Decade

A QUICKSTEP march tune sounded from the orchestra pit. The curtain rose upon a crowded stage of excitedly moving people. "The marchers, with their torchlights and banners, move against a shadowy background of skyscrapers, churches, and—almost certainly—speakeasies. Across this background is thrown a huge election banner on which are Gargantuan reproductions of the faces of the party's candidates. Highlit and prominent is the party's battlecry: 'FOR PRESIDENT, JOHN P. WINTERGREEN.' The name of the vice-presidential candidate, however, is lost in shadow. As for the countenances of the candidates, it is a little hard to pick them out in the general blur, and the chances are that that's a break for the party."

In this fashion, as the authors described it, musical comedy entered politics on the opening night of *Of Thee I Sing,* at the Music Box Theatre, on December 26, 1931. The election that lost the Republicans their lease on the White House was still almost a year in the future. But two years had passed since the great stock-market crash of 1929; and how many chickens were there in every pot now, and how many cars in every garage?

George S. Kaufman and Morrie Ryskind, and also George and Ira Gershwin, took a look at the calamitous state of affairs. They did not like what they saw, and they thought it would be good to do something about it. American musical comedy had never fully learned from Gilbert and Sullivan the art of arguing about public issues by means of laughter. With another election—and a crucial one—just around the corner, it was time, they felt, for Broadway to develop a sense of political responsibility.

Kaufman and Ryskind had made a start in this direction with *Strike Up the Band*, and the Gershwins had borne out their intentions with hardy, straight-punching tunes and lyrics. But *Strike Up the Band*, in retrospect, was hardly more than a tentative foreshadowing of the relentless yet incomparably funny unfrocking of American politics accomplished by *Of Thee I Sing*.

Kaufman and Ryskind hung their plot on two central pegs. The President was an unqualified nonentity, elected merely because the voters were stampeded by the party's platform of Love; and the Vice-President was a pathetic figure, a man nobody cared about and everybody forgot. Throughout the evening Victor Moore, a melancholy little bundle of sadness as Alexander Throttlebottom, the Vice-President, tried without much success to discover what he was supposed to do in order to fill his office. William Gaxton, as President John P. Wintergreen, talked glibly and constantly out of both sides of his face at once, and nearly plunged the country into war with France by refusing to marry the winner of a beauty contest held to select a bride for him; she was, it transpired, "the illegitimate daughter of the illegitimate son of the illegitimate nephew of Napoleon," and the French ambassador considered Wintergreen's attitude an insult to the French nation. Congress was likewise overwrought, and after some months of deliberation came to the brink of impeachment proceedings. But by this time Wintergreen was able to extricate himself. The girl of his heart, whom he had meanwhile married, was now in an interesting condition. As Vice-President Throttlebottom pointed out, shortly before the final curtain, "the United States has never impeached an expectant President."

Upon this improbable complication of incidents, worthy of the contrapuntal imagination of W. S. Gilbert, the authors festooned a profusion of colorful jests about national affairs and the behavior of politicians. By the end of the evening neither political party was left with a leg to stand on. But at least Love still reigned, as Wintergreen joined with the rest in the reprise of his love song to Mary, who now carried a twin on each arm:

> "Of thee I sing, baby,
> Summer, autumn, winter, spring, baby—
> Shining star and inspiration,
> Worthy of a mighty nation,
> Of thee I sing!"

In the spring of 1932, the Pulitzer Prize, for the first time in its history, was awarded to the authors of a musical play—for "the original American play performed in New York which shall best represent the educational value and power of the stage." If there had been a way to do so, the committee should have included George Gershwin in the citation. The songs and the accompanimental music were much more than the frosting on the cake: to a degree hitherto unknown in the musical-comedy theatre, the mood, pace, and placing of the musical numbers was an integral part of the construction of the play as a whole. If the music were removed, the structure would collapse. In its loud and raw way, *Of Thee I Sing* was a genuine music drama.

The creators of *Of Thee I Sing* were persuaded by Sam H. Harris, its producer, to go to work on a sequel. Nearly two more depression years had idled by before *Let 'Em Eat Cake* was ready to be offered to the public, on October 21, 1933. Life had certainly become no more amusing, and Kaufman and Ryskind made the mistake of letting their bitterness find too plain an expression. "Their hatreds have triumphed over their sense of humor," wrote Brooks Atkinson. Then, too, Gershwin had begun to picture himself as a serious composer, and the score of *Let 'Em Eat Cake* was self-consciously modern and somewhat lacking in the spontaneity that had been the priceless asset of his music for *Of Thee I Sing*.

In between the two satires, George and Ira Gershwin picked up a bit of money by writing, with Herbert Fields, what turned out to be a routine and old-fashioned musical comedy, *Pardon My English* (1933). Gershwin's mind was now beginning to focus itself upon a distant goal, and except for *Let 'Em Eat Cake* this was his last musical comedy. He was determined to write an opera, and he had selected *Porgy*, DuBose and Dorothy Heyward's play of Catfish Row in Charleston, as his subject. Knowing that his technique was inadequate to the requirements of serious composition, he concentrated upon the disciplines of counterpoint and orchestration. The result of his labors, the "American folk opera," *Porgy and Bess*, was staged by the Theatre Guild, who had also presented the play in its original form—it was the Guild's first musical production, except for the *Garrick Gaieties* and *Parade*—at the Alvin Theatre on October 10,

1935. Rouben Mamoulian staged it, and Sergei Soudeikine designed the settings. The cast, which seems notable today largely because their participation in *Porgy and Bess* lifted so many of its members to prominence, included Abbie Mitchell (a veteran from the early Broadway days of Will Marion Cook, her husband), Todd Duncan (as Porgy), Ann Wiggins Brown, later known as Anne Brown (as Bess), Ruby Elzy, Georgette Harvey, Edward Matthews, Warren Coleman, J. Rosamond Johnson, and the dancers Buck and Bubbles. Eva Jessye directed the sonorous choral ensembles. Mamoulian's staging was resourceful and reasonably appropriate, though it ran more to trick effects than Robert Ross' direction of Cheryl Crawford's revival in 1942, which was in many ways superior to the earlier version.

Porgy and Bess has been so thoroughly assimilated into our folkways that discussion of it is hazardous. Certainly it has become the best-loved American opera—if it is, indeed, an opera. But with due regard for its appealing features, it is a blemished masterpiece. More a Singspiel than an opera, it does not maintain a consistent tone or treatment. It lurches abruptly into vaudevillian clichés of the popular stage, and deserts them with equal suddenness when the time to be serious seems to have arrived. Musically most of the most expressive sections of the score are those allotted to the chorus; and the most felicitous instances of musical characterization are attached not to the central characters, but to Sportin' Life and Serena. Such pieces as Bess' "Summertime" and Porgy's "I Got Plenty o' Nuttin' " and "Bess, You Is My Woman Now" are decorative operetta divertissements, pure and simple, and serve little or no valuable end in advancing the plot or clarifying the characters.

The musical idiom of *Porgy and Bess* is a curious and unique amalgam of Broadway parlance and figures suggested by Hebraic and Oriental chants, with a surface sprinkling of Negro or pseudo-Negro jazz, religious, and minstrel-show elements. Because Gershwin's sincerity was so apparent, and because the context was so engrossing, audiences from the beginning have always been willing to suspend disbelief, and to accept *Porgy and Bess* as an authentic example of Negro music. As a result, its musical vocabulary has tended to become the official idiom of Negro music in the theatre, much as Aaron Copland's highly personal style in *Rodeo* and *Billy the Kid* has become the official way of suggesting the plains.

These considerations, however, are pertinent only if one chooses to regard *Porgy and Bess* as a full-fledged opera, and to subject it to the rigorous tests of excellence and consistency which that branch of art imposes. If it is viewed—as perhaps it should be—as an upreach of the light lyric stage, both its integrity and the viability of its songs entitle it to a high position. Its qualities serve to emphasize the width of the gap separating opera from music of lighter genre. As an opera, Gershwin's last work is an interesting but inconclusive first try by a stranger to the métier. As a Broadway musical play, it is one of the important mileposts in the developing craft of light musical composition.

Having poked its finger into politics and pulled out a plum, the musical theatre could not stay away from the savory mess. Irving Berlin and Moss Hart were the next to survey the current lot of man, with *Face the Music* (1932), of which Sam H. Harris was again producer. Hart was not satisfied with a Gilbertian contrivance of plot; he was intent upon coming closer to names, dates, and places. The Seabury investigation had just revealed evidence of corruption among the New York police. Hart therefore made the police force the target of his fiercest satire—with Hugh O'Connell as the chief of police, and Mary Boland as his wife. The depression in general and the sorry state of show business in particular also received his attention.

A less sustained piece of work than *Of Thee I Sing*, *Face the Music*, by its references to actual people and events—in the manner of a revue—aimed its punches closer to the belt-line. The opening sketch portrayed a group of Wall Street captains at the Automat, eating the regular five-cent dinner and singing at the finish, "Let's Have Another Cup of Coffee." Times were really bad: the Roxy was offering four films and a room and bath for ten cents; the Palace had become a nickelodeon, with a bill including Dr. Einstein, Ethel Barrymore, Aimee Semple McPherson, Eddie Cantor, Al Jolson, and a free lunch. Nobody had any money to invest in the production of a musical show—except the police, who, embarrassed by the bulging contents of their "tin boxes," rose enthusiastically to the proposal that they should be angels for a piece called *The Rhinestone Girl*. The first-act finale of *Face the Music* revealed the splendors of that production, which included a mirror dance (there proved, of course, to be no mirrors, but a second row of dancing girls reversing the movements of those in the first row) and a pretty production number, "Dear Old Crinoline Days," in which the hoop skirts were only a façade, as the audience discovered when the girls turned around.

In the second act, some of the offending police were brought to trial and convicted for ten years—Miss Boland with them. At this tense moment somebody offered her an immortal word of consolation: "Never mind, Mary; when you get out, the Lux soap people will still think you are thirty-nine." In due season she did get out, in time to bring down the final curtain by riding onto the stage upon a genuine, full-sized elephant.

Berlin's music possessed the right journalistic touch to carry off the hocus-pocus of *Face the Music*. When he and Harris and Hart contemplated a successor to it, they determined to abandon all attempt at a consecutive plot, and to incorporate their satire within the more flexible format of a revue. The result was *As Thousands Cheer* (1933), a topical revue that has never since been surpassed in hilarity, vitality, or the encompassing talent of all those involved. Except for *The Band Wagon*, no musical piece of its period received such unqualified approval; Brooks Atkinson wrote that he could "only give meek approval to every item on the program."

Curtains with newspaper headlines introduced the various numbers. Most startling of all was the sketch headed "Franklin D. Roosevelt Inaugurated Tomorrow." Never before had the White House been exposed to shafts of such pointedness. The action occurred on the last night of the Hoovers' tenancy, with Helen Broderick, as Mrs. Hoover, putting the final touches on their preparations for moving out, and commenting acidly to her family and the servants about the Roosevelts and their entourage.

"World's Wealthiest Man Celebrates 94th Birthday" showed John D. Rockefeller, Jr., endeavoring vainly to press Radio City upon his father as a birthday gift, and fleeing for his bodily safety at the end. Clifton Webb demonstrated unsuspected gifts of impersonation as the older Rockefeller, and, elsewhere in the evening, as Mahatma Gandhi. "Metropolitan Opera Opens in Old-Time Splendor" depicted the way in which, allegedly, the new radio sponsor stole the show from the boxholders of the Diamond Horseshoe. "Heat Wave Strikes New York" enabled Ethel Waters, in the most notable assignment of her career thus far, to deliver the couplet that ran "She started a heat wave, By making her seat wave." Later on, Miss Waters struck a deeper note with an affecting song, "Supper Time," in which her man did not come to share her supper because a lynching had taken place. "Noel Coward, Noted Playwright, Returns to England" reported the effect of the Mayfair author's stay in New York upon the behavior and diction of the employees of the hotel in which he had lived.

The cast was scarcely less than a miracle. Webb plunged a sharp-edged rapier home in every scene. Marilyn Miller, in her last appearance on Broadway, was still all effulgence and humor and sweet loveliness, but she also showed a new aptitude for mimicry in her pat and hilarious imitation of Joan Crawford. Helen Broderick "never missed a chance to put poison in the soup," whether as Mrs. Hoover, as Aimee Semple McPherson (whose "foursquare gospel" was attaining its first notoriety), or as an acidulous Statue of Liberty. Charles Weidman's dancers—José Limón, Letitia Ide, and Bill Matons among them—employed choreography that made genuinely pertinent comment, and Albert Johnson's costumes had "meaning as well as beauty." Throughout the evening everyone behaved with wit and gaiety and grace, refusing to be tempted to the anger that had ruined a short-lived revue of similar intentions, *Americana*, the year before. Even unadulterated sentiment was not ruled out, for the first act closed with a colorful Easter parade on Fifth Avenue, to the strains of Berlin's nostalgic "Easter Parade." After so transcendent an achievement as *As Thousands Cheer*, Berlin felt justified in listening to the call of Hollywood, and his services were lost to Broadway until he returned for *Louisiana Purchase* in 1940.

As the national economy sank deeper and deeper into the miasma of the depression, the theatre was increasingly preempted by authors and producers who wanted to use it as a means of protest. With a few notable exceptions, however, it cannot be said that the musical branch of the Broadway stage covered itself with great glory as an agent of propa-

symphonic composition and Berlin's departure for Holly-
wood, there was no commercially produced sequel to *Of
Thee I Sing* and *As Thousands Cheer* until *I'd Rather Be
Right*, in 1937.

On a smaller scale, the Theatre Guild endeavored to
prove its social consciousness with *Parade* (1935), a "satirical revue" equipped with music by Jerome Moross and literary components by George Sklar, George Peters, and several
others. Philip Loeb, erstwhile director of the *Garrick Gaieties*, staged the revue, and Robert Alton, later one of Broadway's breeziest choreographers, directed the dances. But
Sklar and Peters tended to view the objects of their derision
more as enemies than as humorous figures, and like *Americana* three years earlier, *Parade* died of a bad temper, in spite
of Jimmy Savo's attempt to save it with his funny and touching pantomime.

Two seasons later, on November 27, 1937, the one truly
memorable revue of the late depression, *Pins and Needles*,
was presented by a cast composed entirely of members of the
singing, acting, and dancing classes of the International
Ladies Garment Workers' Union. Conceived in the first
place primarily as an entertainment for the union member-
ship, *Pins and Needles*, thanks to the expertness and freshness of Harold Rome's music and lyrics and the high intelligence quotient revealed in the satiric sketches, quickly
became one of the ruling successes of Broadway. Naturally,
its point of view was what we should call "leftist"—though
certainly not Red—today. Its burden was indicated by the
opening number, "Sing Us a Song of Social Significance."
The most celebrated, and the most violent, comment in the
entire evening was made in a sketch, "Four Little Angels of
Peace," which showed Chamberlain, Mussolini, Hitler, and
an undesignated Japanese statesman in a highly unflattering
light. Taking a leaf from the book of *As Thousands Cheer*,

Rome did not forget to provide a touch of quiet sentiment as a foil for the prevailing tone of vehemence. Paralleling the "Easter Parade" finale of the Irving Berlin revue, *Pins and Needles* ended its first half with a genre scene, "Sunday in the Park," staged by Charles Friedman with exquisite reticence.

Pins and Needles became a quasi-permanent fixture, replacing old ideas with new ones when the timeliness wore off, and revising its title from time to time to *Pins and Needles 1939* and *New Pins and Needles.* The 1939 version introduced "The Red Mikado," in which the Russian Lord High Executioner chopped off the heads of the Three Little Maids, who then went into a dance while Gilbert and Sullivan rose in consternation from their graves. The skit was intended, it must be explained to readers in this remote age, as a double-barreled jibe at Russian dictatorship and at the pair of jazzed-up versions of *The Mikado* (*The Hot Mikado* and *The Swing Mikado*) that had recently swept Broadway off its feet. Elsewhere in *Pins and Needles 1939* the international scene was dealt with in a biting number called "Britannia Waives the Rules," while union interests were mirrored in a portrayal of the home life of Papa Lewis and Mama Green, and capitalistic promotion was given its comeuppance in "Cream of Mush," a burlesque of radio commercials. By now, the acting members of the ILGWU had forgotten how to operate their machines; and with the time occupied by the tour of *New Pins and Needles* they were kept away from the dressmaking business for three years. Many of them, having developed thoroughgoing professional competence, remained in show business.

Spurred by the surprise success of *Pins and Needles*, Max Gordon, George S. Kaufman, and Moss Hart joined together in producing a similar revue, *Sing Out the News*, in 1938. Full of comments about prominent people and expositions of New Deal philosophy, *Sing Out the News* amounted to "*Pins and Needles* in a Broadway tailor's dress suit." Harold Rome was its composer, turning out such well-wrought songs as "Just an Ordinary Guy" and "Franklin D. Roosevelt Jones." Jo Mielziner's fanciful scenery certainly did not hurt the chances of the show; but it did not help them, either. The point of view was no longer quite as fresh as it had been with the ILGWU, nor was it altogether consonant with an expensive production. The revue attained only a moderate run—105 performances.

The other side of the picture, the upper-class, rightist attitude, was set forth in 1939 by an expensive and beautiful little revue, *One for the Money*. For those who had approved of the liberal orientation of *Pins and Needles*, the piece, devised with a kind of super-amateur gaiety by Nancy Hamilton and supplied with naïvely fresh tunes by Morgan Lewis, was a "sleek and glossy vacuum," an "orchid and patent-leather bore." Actually it was more than this, and probably would have been better appreciated in post-depression years for the smartness of Raoul Pène du Bois' Parisian-Park Avenue sets, Robert Alton's blithe choreography, and John Murray Anderson's smart staging. Presented without a chorus, its youthful cast of twelve included several performers who later made names for themselves—Alfred Drake, Gene Kelly, Nadine Gae, Brenda Forbes, Ruth Matteson, Philip Bourneuf, Don Loper, Keenan Wynn, and William Archibald.

The title of *One for the Money* indicated that Nancy Hamilton had a succession of revues in mind. In 1940, *Two for the Show* duly came along, with Eve Arden and the inexhaustible Betty Hutton as new members of the company. Less well stocked with bright ideas, but closer to the Broadway pulse, it prospered somewhat better. Its success was not sufficient, however, for Miss Hamilton to obtain support for *Three to Make Ready* until six years later (1946). This third edition turned out to be a larger, more conventional show, dominated by the dancing of Ray Bolger and Harold Lang, neither of whom was given opportunities commensurate with his gifts. The whole original point of the series was lost, and to this day no word has been heard of plans for *Four to Go*.

Less pretentious than *One for the Money*, but similarly dedicated to the exploitation of youth, had been Charles Dillingham's *New Faces*, presented five years earlier, in 1934. Assembled by Leonard Sillman, a company including Imogene Coca, O. Z. Whitehead, and Henry Fonda modeled their performance on what was still remembered of the *Garrick Gaieties*, of which Miss Coca had been a charter member. Sergei Soudeikine designed cute little miniature sets. Nancy Hamilton tried out her literary hand with a sketch purporting to reveal Katharine Hepburn working herself into the appropriate mood for *Little Women*.

Sillman himself produced a second edition, *New Faces of 1936*, introducing Van Johnson and Helen Craig, and retaining the ever-present Miss Coca, whom one reviewer described as "a new face from a fairish way back." After a seven-year lapse, Sillman brought out *New Faces of 1943* (actually on December 22, 1942), without adding as much as before to the sum total of human merriment.

In the meantime, Miss Coca had moved into *The Straw Hat Revue* (1939), picked up by Harry Kaufman and the Shuberts on the summer theatre circuit and brought into Broadway for a fall engagement. In this breezy enterprise, the rapid-fire delivery of Danny Kaye fell on Broadway ears for the first time, preparing the way for his rise to the top of the profession in *Lady in the Dark*. Alfred Drake was al-

emphasis was on dancing, with a roster including Jerome Andrews (the choreographer of the show), Jerome Robbins, Ruthanna Boris, William Bales, and Richard Reed.

The cycle of intimate revues designed to give unknown youngsters a chance was closed for the time by the most successful one of all, *Meet the People,* which pitted itself against a Broadway opening-night audience on Christmas night, 1940, after a year and a half in Hollywood and San Francisco. The first Hollywood musical production to make its way to New York, *Meet the People* was not particularly modish. But it was warm, informal, and friendly, and Jay Gorney had given it a spate of likeable, if sometimes rather sprawling and poorly organized, tunes. A vivacious little girl named Nanette Fabares, who later phoneticized her name to Fabray, charmed the audience no end; and Marion Colby set a brief fashion by intoning emotion-charged torch songs with deadpan colorlessness and unyielding metricality.

During the years of the depression, the United States was too preoccupied with its own ills to care much about Europe and its theatrical products; and, moreover, nobody had any money to risk upon steamship passage for foreign players. A single exception was *Continental Varieties* (1934), actually a sophisticated vaudeville show employing Nikita Balieff as master of ceremonies, and Lucienne Boyer, the exponent of "Parlez-moi d'Amour," and Vicente Escudero, the greatest of Spanish male dancers, as its headliners. No further European touch was to be discerned on the revue stage until 1939, when a group of indigent refugees offered their specialties in a pathetically ineffectual collation called *From Vienna,* and were sufficiently encouraged by the response of a sympathetic public to continue with *Reunion in New York* the following year.

The Federal Theatre Project of the WPA might have been expected to make some arresting contribution to the musical stage, since it occasionally did so in other areas. But the record of the New York unit was wholly undistinguished. A Negro revue, *Swing It* (1937), added nothing to what had already been offered earlier by Lew Leslie's companies. *A Hero Is Born* (1937), an extravaganza with music by Lehman Engel and a book by Theresa Helburn, went above, or around, the heads of the audience. *Sing for Your Supper* (1939), an elaborate revue that took a year and a half in preparation, succeeded in inverse ratio to the time spent on it.

The one historic production of the musical branch of the New York WPA Theatre was rejected by government officials before it opened. Marc Blitzstein's musical drama *The Cradle Will Rock*, a social-consciousness document written at white heat to expose the mistreatment of the honorable Larry Foreman by the capitalist big-shot Mister Mister, with subsequent repercussions throughout the entire social structure, was scheduled to open under Federal Theatre auspices on the evening of January 3, 1938. That day word came through that Washington disapproved of the ultra-liberal tone of the piece, and would not permit its presentation. Hastily the directors of Orson Welles' Mercury Theatre scurried to find a theatre that would be available that night. As the members of the audience assembled at the Venice Theatre, they were told the circumstances and asked to troop up to the Windsor Theatre. Once there, they saw a unique representation. Neither Actors' Equity nor the Federation of Musicians, in view of the controversial nature of the situation, would allow its members to go through with their share in the performance. Blitzstein sat alone on the stage at a piano, playing the score and singing some of the songs. The more daring members of the cast sang their parts from the orchestra pit or from seats in the house, while some instrumentalists tootled from scattered seats in the balcony. Later on, *The Cradle Will Rock* was given in more orthodox fashion, but a little of the first excitement was inevitably missing.

In *The Cradle Will Rock* and its subsequent companion piece, *No for an Answer* (1941), Blitzstein (who wrote music, book, and lyrics) created another of those in-between pieces which, like *Porgy and Bess*, defies pigeonholing. The materials—songs, ensembles, and dialogue—were essentially those of any light-hearted musical comedy. But the composer's treatment of them was wholly serious, employing advanced devices of dissonance and instrumentation to give them a sardonic edge. These two works moved one step farther in the direction of a conciliation between Broadway and the soberer reaches of the lyric theatre.

The only other noteworthy accomplishment of the WPA in the musical theatre originated not in New York but in Chicago, in the fall of 1938. On March 1, 1939, the New York audience finally saw *The Swing Mikado*, in which Harry Minturn and Sammy Dyer had turned Gilbert and Sullivan's opera into a fiesta of fast trucking and hot vocalizing. John Pratt decked out the singing, dancing actors in Caribbean outfits of unbridled flamboyance. The opposing polarities of Gilbert's lines, most of which were kept intact, and the tropical brilliance of the production constituted a cosmic accident that could never be repeated.

By comparison, Michael Todd's production entitled *The Hot Mikado*, mounted in competition three weeks later, seemed effete and calculated, even with Nat Karson's blinding costumes and sets and the incomparable tapping of Bill Robinson as an adornment for the title role. But Todd's attempt to Harlemize a classic was not the last. Later in 1939, Erik Charell presented at the Center Theatre, at vast expense, one of the most confused failures of all time, a "musical variation" of Shakespeare's *A Midsummer Night's*

Dream called *Swingin' the Dream*. A mixed-cast production, this abortive piece of nonsense enlisted the services of Dorothy McGuire, Ruth Ford, Butterfly McQueen, Maxine Sullivan, Bill Bailey, Benny Goodman, Louis Armstrong, Eddie Condon, and a variety of other jazz celebrities. Agnes de Mille created the statelier features of the choreography, and Herbert White directed the jitterbugs. The settings were designed after Walt Disney cartoons by Herbert Andrews and Walter Jageman. Never were so many unrelated people and ideas crammed into a single show. It closed after the thirteenth performance.

XXI

The New Audience

THE STANDARD Broadway musical stage, as opposed to these aberrant efforts, pursued an increasingly cautious course as the depression deepened and lengthened. The theatre industry had received not one body blow but two at the end of the 1920s. Precisely when abundant free money for production all but disappeared, the motion-picture screen developed a voice. By the beginning of the 1930s it was clear that the flesh-and-blood theatre would henceforth occupy a far more restricted corner of the entertainment field than it had in the past. The musical stage was especially hard hit by the perfection of the rival medium, for the first all-talking picture, Al Jolson in *The Jazz Singer*, made use of music; and the host of cinema musical comedies and extravaganzas that followed this first experiment took away from the living musical stage a large audience that never came back.

The audience that remained faithful to the musical stage and was able to continue supporting it was relatively aristocratic in its tastes. Those who sought no more than a rowdy good time and a chance to hear some lively songs and see some splashy production numbers were now quite content with Hollywood provender. Broadway producers quickly learned that they might as well spare their energy and save the money of their backers if their shows were not equipped to outwit the motion pictures with more intelligent and fresher ideas, more pungent or subtle wit, better casting and direction, and superior taste in costumes and stage designs. *The Band Wagon* established a new level of discrimination. Along with the Gershwin and Berlin satires, it was fully attuned to the new, small, and demanding audience of the 1930s. Henceforth, the successful Broadway musical productions paid ever greater attention to art as well as to craft. The ascendancy of the stage designer, the costumer, and the choreographer were at hand. Generally speaking, only the most gifted composers were able to continue at their jobs; book-writers were no longer permitted to commit the indiscretion of being dull, and lyricists were expected to find some other rhyme for "June" than "moon."

Max Gordon fully understood the change that had come over the musical branch of show business when he commissioned Arthur Schwartz and Howard Dietz to write the music and lyrics for the revue, *Flying Colors* (1932). But business was so bad that he was afraid to risk another intimate and restricted piece like *The Band Wagon*. For the sake of success—which he achieved in reasonable degree—he decided to make *Flying Colors* a bigger affair, spectacular in mounting yet stylish and "modernistic," as they used to say, in treatment. Charles Butterworth, the melancholy dancer Tamara Geva, the hoofing Buddy and Vilma Ebsen, and Clifton Webb were the leading entertainers. In the face of Webb's subsequent transformation in the moving pictures, it is well to recall, in Percy Hammond's words, the qualities that made and kept him one of the most favored revue performers in this earlier period:

"Mr. Clifton Webb is the Town's pet dancer, tragedian, buffoon, vocalist and dude. The fastidious Mr. Webb, clad in garments now somber, then oriant, but always form-fitting and scrupulously in the mood of the moment, dominated the ceremonies by the rhythm of his movements, the music of his voice, the sadness of his pathos and the fun of his burlesque. Little or no scenery is needed by any play in which Mr. Webb appears, for he is his own production, combining in his appearance all the eleven arts of Joseph Urban and Norman Bel Geddes." (Geddes was the creator of the splendors of *Flying High*.)

Parting company with Gordon, Schwartz and Dietz attempted in 1934 to create for Arch Selwyn and Harold B. Franklin a modern parallel of *The Three-Cornered Hat*, the Spanish short story by Pedro Alarcón which Manuel de Falla, Léonide Massine, and Pablo Picasso had earlier turned into one of the rarest of ballets. *Revenge with Music*, as the paraphrase was called, turned out to be neither flesh nor fowl. In an unmistakably Broadway show, the book seemed tepid, and the whole undertaking is now memorable chiefly because it gave Libby Holman and Georges Metaxa one of the finest and sultriest of the Schwartz-Dietz songs, "You and the Night and the Music."

Closer to the focus of their original success was the revue, *At Home Abroad* (1935), written by Schwartz and Dietz and produced by the Shuberts as a co-starring vehicle for Beatrice Lillie and Ethel Waters. For Miss Waters, in her first Broadway appearance since *As Thousands Cheer*, they provided the sizzling, shouting "Hottentot Potentate." Hung on the around-the-world formula familiar in extravaganzas ever since the Kiralfys' version of Jules Verne's *Around the World in Eighty Days* in the 1870s, *At Home Abroad* gave Miss Lillie scope for action against a variety of exotic settings, freshly and gaily devised by the new young designer of the moment, Vincente Minnelli. It was in *At Home Abroad* that Miss Lillie twisted her tongue in endeavoring to order "two dozen double damask dinner napkins," impersonated Mitzi of Old Vienna and a Russian ballerina who could not "face the mujik," exploited to the hilt the Parisian grisette's motto, "L'amour the merrier," and popped out of the second line of a chorus of geisha girls to cry, "It's better with your shoes off."

The Show Is On (1936), another revue for Miss Lillie, also enlisted Schwartz and Dietz, though in this case the Shuberts, wanting to be sure that enough authors were involved, also obtained contributions from Richard Rodgers, Lorenz Hart, Vernon Duke, Moss Hart, and others. Minnelli both designed and directed the show. A crane carried Miss Lillie out over the heads of the audience on a property moon, whence she tossed garters (many more than two) to men in the front rows. The comedienne's supremacy was challenged by Bert Lahr, who rendered—there is no other word—the "Song of a Woodchopper," complete with a small fir tree, a property ax, chips flying into the air from an unseen hand in the wings, and, on the chopper's rotund head, a toupee which "took on a new personality every time it shifted to a new angle."

The last Schwartz-Dietz collaboration until *Inside U.S.A.* (1948) was *Between the Devil* (1937), in which Jack Buchanan again returned from England, this time in the company of Evelyn Laye. For *Stars in Your Eyes* (1939), a sumptuous outlay sponsored by Dwight Deere Wiman, Schwartz wrote tunes to lyrics by Dorothy Fields and music for the extensive ballets choreographed by Carl Randall. A name-heavy cast included Ethel Merman, Walter Cassel, Mildred Natwick, and Jimmy Durante in singing and speaking parts, and a roster of dancers headed by Tamara Toumanova, Alicia Alonso, Nora Kaye, Maria Karniloff, Jerome Robbins, Fernando Alonso, Dwight Godwin, and Richard Reed. Jo Mielziner was given a free hand, and—since the action took place on a Hollywood sound stage—had a field day, making use of moving cameras, a treadmill across the front of the stage, and shifting scenery that never required the curtain to be run down. There was also a dream ballet —not the first of its kind, since George Balanchine had already used the idea in Wiman's production of Rodgers and Hart's *I Married an Angel*. After this expensive failure, Schwartz remained away from Broadway until 1946, when he and Ira Gershwin wrote *Park Avenue*, another failure, smaller but scarcely less expensive. Dietz was represented in the ill-fated *Sadie Thompson* (1944), a musical version of Somerset Maugham's story, for which Vernon Duke wrote the music. More recently he made an English adaptation of the lyrics of *Die Fledermaus* for the Metropolitan Opera.

Though satire and smartness and modernity were the order of the day in the 1930s, Jerome Kern remained true to his essentially lyric temperament. His last triumph on Broadway, before he assigned his talents to the motion pictures, was *Roberta* (1933). Nobody cared a fig about the book, based on Alice Duer Miller's story of a young fullback who inherited his aunt's stylish dressmaking establishment. But when Tamara (not to be confused with the dancer Tamara Geva) sang "Smoke Gets in Your Eyes" and joined with William Hain in "The Touch of Your Hand," the audience felt, and rightly, that it was hearing some of the most enchanting music of make-believe since *Show Boat*. Some of the drama critics thought the music not up to Kern's standard, but time has proved them wrong, since the passing years have awarded its songs an undebatable second place in the long Kern list. In the first scene, the veteran Fay Templeton, come out of retirement to play the brief role of the aunt, was called upon to sing "Yesterday," and quietly expire in her chair.

Only once more were Jerome Kern's melodies heard in a new Broadway musical comedy, in *Very Warm for May* (1939), a quietly charming piece, with book and lyrics by Oscar Hammerstein 2d, which never quite caught the public fancy. *Show Boat* was appropriately honored in 1946 by a revival produced without thought of cost by Hammerstein. With Carol Bruce in the Helen Morgan role of Julie and Kenneth Spencer taking over "Old Man River," sung originally by Jules Bledsoe and later by Paul Robeson, the revival ran a full year. In future seasons it is reasonable to imagine that other Kern musical comedies may be restored to the stage, for his tunefulness was true and sweet, and his sentiment still speaks to the present generation.

Richard Rodgers and Lorenz Hart renewed their association in 1935 with *Jumbo*—"a sane and exciting compound of opera, animal show, folk drama, harlequinade, carnival, circus, extravaganza and spectacle," Percy Hammond called it—devised by Billy Rose for the Hippodrome. In the following year Rodgers and Hart turned out, with George Abbott as author of the book, a less gaudy but historically more significant work, *On Your Toes*. As he returned to the producing field, Dwight Deere Wiman felt that the American musical theatre had reached a point of maturity that permitted the introduction of more serious dancing than it had known in the past. Within a plot of backstage ballet life, in itself a new subject on the American stage, he incorporated two major ballets, in addition to the expected incidental dances. From the Ballet Russe he engaged George (then Georges) Balanchine to create his first musical-comedy dances. Balanchine's "Scheherazade" ballet was perhaps an inevitable concession to a public not yet used to extensive dance compositions in a light entertainment. But with "Slaughter on Tenth Avenue," in which Ray Bolger and Tamara Geva gave a sardonic, vivid portrayal of an unmistakably American subject, Balanchine achieved a serious, tautly organized, forcefully projected work of art. For the first time, the dance department of a musical comedy took the center of the stage with claims to attention at least as irresistible as those of such superior Rodgers and Hart songs as "It's Got to Be Love" and "There's a Small Hotel."

Rodgers and Hart turned to a celebration of youth in *Babes in Arms* (1937), whose cast was composed largely of performers in their teens and early twenties. With two sixteen-year-olds, Wynn Murray and Mitzi Green, as his leading ladies, Robert Sinclair, who directed, sought to suffuse with un-Broadway innocence a cheerful tale about the children of touring vaudeville performers, spending the summer in a camp at Seaport, Long Island. George Balanchine exploited the talent of Duke McHale in "Peter's Dream," one of the earliest musical-comedy dream ballets, and Rodgers and Hart were at the top of their bent in the uninhibited song called "Johnny One-Note." The settings of Raymond Sovey and the costumes of Helene Pons caught the fancy of John Anderson, who wrote in the *Journal* of the dream ballet: "There were cardboard skyscrapers, swirling seas of blue-cloth ocean and the tropical enchantment of paper palm trees and cellophantasy mermaids."

The Boys from Syracuse (1938), for which George Abbott was producer as well as author of the book and stage director, was the lineal antecedent of *Kiss Me, Kate*. It was based on Shakespeare's *A Comedy of Errors*, but Abbott had the good sense to employ Shakespeare's web of double-identity situations without appropriating his lines.

Ronald Graham and Eddie Albert appeared as the two
Antipholuses, of Ephesus and Syracuse, and Teddy Hart
(the brother of Lorenz) and Jimmy Savo as the two Dro-
mios. The score and lyrics were fabulously brilliant in their
unfailing wit and their variety of texture and expression.

Until now, Rodgers and Hart had been too busy trying to
cure the aches and pains of the depression with merriment
and romance to give much thought to the soberer expression
of satire. With *I'd Rather Be Right* (1937), written in collaboration with George S. Kaufman and Moss Hart, they
made a bold gesture in the direction of political protest. In
As Thousands Cheer, the audience had peeked inside the
White House and seen the departure of the Hoovers. Now
Franklin Delano Roosevelt was put on the stage—a tap-
dancing Roosevelt, played to the life by George M. Cohan,
equipped with the requisite pince-nez and Hyde Park-
Groton inflection of speech. Only Cohan, or an actor of his
standing and his delicately adjusted control of his effects,
could have portrayed the popular President without giving
offense. One reporter remarked that Cohan's performance,
and the piece as a whole, resembled an entertainment given
by the Washington newspaper men of the Gridiron Club,
except that it was not given in private. The book poked
ridicule at the innumerable alphabetical agencies of the
New Deal; dealt summarily with Roosevelt's recent attempt
to pack the Supreme Court, and sent the bearded judges
into a lively jig; represented the defeated Republican candidate, Alf Landon, as a White House butler; worried over the
budget, which could never be brought under control; and
put into the President's mouth the confession, "The trouble with the country is that I don't know what the trouble
with the country is." At the finish, a White House Jamboree
was arranged to persuade the nation of the need for a third
term. *Of Thee I Sing* and *As Thousands Cheer* were round-

about by comparison; *I'd Rather Be Right* not only named names, but pursued its controversial themes to the bitter end.

Though their score and lyrics were admirably keyed to the tone of the Kaufman and Hart play, the participation of Rodgers and Hart in *I'd Rather Be Right* was in a measure an act of self-abnegation. The fine points of their work tended to be lost in the shuffle, and the piece was more Kaufman and Hart than Rodgers and Hart.

Their virtue was rewarded the following spring, however, for Dwight Deere Wiman's production of *I Married an Angel* (1938) inspired them to one of their most notable accomplishments. As perfect in every detail of conception and execution as *The Band Wagon* a few seasons back, *I Married an Angel* still remains one of Broadway's high memories. As a permanent fixture of its scenery, Jo Mielziner worked out a combination of curtains and panels providing a stage within a stage, and Joshua Logan's direction—his first musical assignment—took advantage of the possibility of presenting the action on a variety of interesting planes. As in *Stars in Your Eyes* the following year, the furnishings were whisked on and off by means of a treadmill, which also played a novel part in Balanchine's choreography.

The plot, derived from a Hungarian play by Janos Vaszary, told, in a vein half fantastic and half farcical, of Dennis King's infatuation for a genuine angel, in the form of Vera Zorina, who flew into his study after he had sworn that he would never marry a woman unless he could be certain that she was an angel. A former member of the Ballet Russe de Monte Carlo, Miss Zorina captured utterly the essence of her part, and danced enchantingly. A geographical sequence of dances representing the honeymoon reached an illusory and beautiful climax in a blizzard in the Eskimo country. The sophisticated worldliness of Vivienne Segal and the brisk energy of Audrey Christie were excellent foils for Miss Zorina's fragility. In their songs for *I Married an Angel*, perhaps even more than at any time before, Rodgers and Hart achieved the complete identity of purpose that was the hallmark of their mature output. Without thwarting his melodic feeling or his knack for a subtle harmonic twist, Rodgers was able completely to respect Hart's words. He never distorted their accent or inflection, and he manipulated his musical ideas in a way that kept the lyrics uppermost in the attention of the audience.

In *Too Many Girls* (1939), Rodgers and Hart dealt with college life, as put onto the stage by the ebullient George Abbott. Such engaging youngsters as Desi Arnaz, Eddie Bracken, Hal Le Roy, Marcy Wescott, and Mary Jane Walsh kept matters in a pleasant ferment, and the songs—notably "Love Never Went to College" and "I'd Like to Recognize the Tune"—were among the most delectable the pair ever turned out. From this they turned to Wiman's unsuccessful but handsome *Higher and Higher* (1940), in which a group of jitterbug dancers trained by Robert Alton and a highly cultivated seal named Sharkey managed to steal rather too much of the show from Jack Haley and Marta Eggert.

The summit of the Rodgers and Hart partnership was reached with *Pal Joey* on December 25, 1940. *Pal Joey* was an enlargement by the author himself of a series of sharp, slangy sketches contributed by John O'Hara to *The New Yorker*. O'Hara managed not only to write one of the most continuously witty books any musical comedy ever had, but also to create unwontedly lifelike characters. He recounted a gusty tale of a young heel who made and unmade himself by capturing and losing the fancy of a bored society woman.

A low-grade Chicago night club, said to be on Cottage Grove Avenue, was the chief locale. Robert Alton seized upon the opportunity afforded by a floor show to devise a superb variety of dances satirizing everything that was wrong and out-of-date in that field of entertainment. A song and dance depicted "The Flower Garden of My Heart," and another employed lights of changing colors corresponding to a series of colors specified in the lyrics. The girls were overdressed in feathers and frills and engaged in shockingly bromidic dance routines. As Joey, Gene Kelly, fresh from *One for the Money*, managed to present a character as lovable as it was despicable, and he danced with superb ease and bravado. Vivienne Segal, as the infatuated society woman, delivered "Bewitched, Bothered and Bewildered" and "In Our Little Den of Iniquity" with a cool literalness calculated to make the most of their rhyming innuendoes, and June Havoc, as Gladys Bumps, wrung the last drop of amusement from her portrait of an entertainer whose intellectual ceiling was appallingly low. One of her songs ended with these lines:

> "I'm a red hot mamma, but you're white and cold;
> Don't you know your mamma has a heart of gold;
> Though we're in those gray clouds, some day you'll spy
> That terrific rainbow over you and I."

But of all the satiric verses of *Pal Joey*, perhaps the most imperishable are those of the horticultural ballet:

> "In the flower garden of my heart,
> I've got violets blue as your eyes;
> I've got dainty narcissus
> As sweet as my missus,
> And lilies pure as the skies.
> In the flower garden of my heart,
> I've got roses as red as your mouth;
> Just to keep our love holy
> I've got gladioli,
> And sunflowers fresh from the south.

> *But you are the artist,*
> *And love is the art,*
> *In the flower garden of my heart."*

Only one more musical comedy, *By Jupiter* (1942), appeared before the partners were separated by a personal disagreement. Hart based the book and lyrics on *The Warrior's Husband*, by Julian F. Thompson, a play revealing the rule of the Amazons. Inversion of secondary sexual characteristics was the running gag of *By Jupiter*, and Ray Bolger acted and danced his way through the role of the pantywaist hero with consummate taste. Though it was an amusing *jeu d'esprit*, *By Jupiter* by no means repeated the achievement of *Pal Joey*, which was one of the great escapades of the American musical-comedy stage.

Rodgers and Hart were essentially an unaffected tunesmith and a quick-trigger versifier, who developed only gradually the sophisticated artifices and the taste for a drop of vitriol manifested by *I'd Rather Be Right* and *Pal Joey*. At heart they were rather simple, often even sentimental, artisans, ready to take at face value any workable book that came their way, and to do their best to add a special touch to it. Cole Porter, on the other hand, appears never to have been simple, never artless. Even in his early contributions to *Paris* and his first complete score, *Fifty Million Frenchmen*, he took a detached, wry, and often incredulous attitude toward the characters and contexts that were supplied him. A *mot* or a turn of phrase always meant more to him than anything else about his work; give him a choice between sacrificing the integrity of a character and sacrificing a rhyme, and he would unhesitatingly sacrifice the character. He always was, and still is, primarily a littérateur and genteel pornographer. Some of his songs have not had much heart to them, but none has ever lacked a glittering surface. By combing the functions of lyricist and composer, he has been able to keep a remarkable uniformity of texture in his verse-and-song conceits; but lacking a spontaneous sympathy for the homely traits of people, he has tended to become categorical—to supply each new show with songs of several standardized types. Yet his inexhaustible urbanity and his easy flow of stylized language and equally stylized music have made him the most reliable performer among American musical-comedy composers. No composer or lyricist has achieved a larger proportion of hits, and not even Rodgers and Hart have written a larger number of brilliant songs. Nor does he have only one string to his bow; he functions with equal felicity in a topical patter song like "You're the Top," an outright gag song like "Friendship," a pert exchange of amatory amenities like "I Get a Kick Out of You," and a broodingly erotic ballad like "Night and Day."

It was in *Gay Divorce* (1932) that the world first became acquainted with "Night and Day," which many consider if not the best, at least the archetypal, example of Porter's gift for extending a long-lined, dusky melody far beyond the usual confines of the standard thirty-two-bar structure. Porter showed the expertness and individuality of his musical style in its bitter-sweet harmonies and well prepared climax, and his impatience with convention in such lines of the text as "I've an O such a hungry feeling under the hide of me." Apart from "Night and Day" and one or two other songs, however, *Gay Divorce* was all exterior and "bedroom fiddle-faddle," and is not one of the noteworthy entries in the chronicle of its composer's career.

For several years in the middle 1930s, Porter maintained an extraordinary momentum. After *Gay Divorce*, each new piece was freshly triumphant. *Anything Goes* (1934) revealed an acuteness of perception and calculation he has never surpassed. A shipboard piece, *Anything Goes* presented Victor Moore as an unseemly character for the first time; carrying a machine gun and wearing the habiliments of a parson, he was in reality a gangster pigeonholed as Public Enemy No. 1. This whimpering menace was aided and abetted by William Gaxton, a man-about-town whose main business was to capture the affections of the strident, trumpet-voiced Ethel Merman. Between these two passed the compliments of "You're the Top," and Miss Merman was enabled to pull out all the stops in "Blow, Gabriel, Blow." The handsome settings introduced a new and important designer to musical comedy in Donald Oenslager. In its outlines, *Anything Goes* was actually a conventional affair, but, as John Mason Brown said, "if it stays for the most part within the time-honored limits of these conventions, it does so only to make clear why it is that time has honored them."

Experiments in dramaturgy never interested Porter, then or later. The usual shape and ordering of musical comedy, as these were handed down from the 1920s, have always been adequate to his purposes, since he needs no more than a reasonable excuse for songs and for the presence of capable performers to give the songs their due. His conception of the relation of music to a play has always been marked rather by a consummate mastery of the usual practices than by any search for strikingly new devices.

On a trip around the world, Porter and Moss Hart wrote *Jubilee* (1935), a merry dig at the British royal family that managed to find room for the insinuating "Begin the Beguine," a song that was not nearly as popular when *Jubilee* was at the Imperial Theatre as it became five or ten years later. *Red, Hot and Blue* (1936), a loud piece about a lost girl who could be readily identified because she once sat down on a red-hot waffle iron, pitted Miss Merman's lungs (in "Ridin' High") against Jimmy Durante's nose, and for good measure threw in the slapstick ballroom dancing of

ZICKA-SOUTH, INC.

911 Northridge   Greensboro, N. C. 27420

Instructions by: Phone No.:   Date Sent to Binder

Carl A. Rudisill Library
Lenoir-Rhyne College

ALL INSTRUCTIONS ON BINDING TICKET WILL BE FOLLOWED EXPLICITLY

LETTER SPINE EXACTLY AS FOLLOWS:	INSTRUCTIONS TO BINDER

Title:

Musical Comedy in
America

Smith   44777 64

Vol.:

Year

Call No.:

none

INSTRUCTIONS TO BINDER

___ Bind as is (with covers & ads)
___ Remove front covers
___ Remove back covers
___ Remove ads (front & back)
___ Remove all ads (extra charge)
___ Bind title page/contents in front
___ Bind index in front
___ Bind index in back
___ Hand sew if necessary (extra charge)
_____ Cover Color
Letter in: ___gold; ___black;
    ___white

LIBRARY BOOKS:

___Decorated covers; ___plain covers;
___picture covers (extra charge)

SUPER-FLEX (economy binding) Uniform height, white lettering. Covers & ads bound in. Cover color for **periodicals only** _____.
Books & Paperbacks — cloth colors random selected by binder; binder's choice of black or white lettering.
Paperbacks: ___Mount front cover; ___Bind in covers; **X** Discard covers.

Special Instructions:

Send two copies of binding slip with volume; retain one copy for your files.
If item returned for correction because of binder's error, original binding slip **must be** returned with volume.

BINDERY COPY

Paul and Grace Hartman and the life-of-the-party personality of Bob Hope, with whom Miss Merman shared the lyrics of "It's De-Lovely." In a sage comment to the press, Vinton Freedley, the producer, pointed to a change of fashion in chorus girls, a change that has persisted to our own day: "The hard type is out, and so is the languid show girl of a few years ago, the stately peacock who strutted downstage and flashed one little smile—at the orchestra conductor. Men nowadays like fresh, sweet girls—peppy and talented, yes, but untheatrical."

In *Leave It to Me* (1938), Victor Moore, as the gift of Topeka, Kan., to the diplomatic service, grappled piteously with foreign policy in the capacity of American ambassador to Russia. He shared top billing with Sophie Tucker, as a dominating ambassador's wife, and William Gaxton, as an omnipresent nuisance of a newspaper man. Moore was a loveable, henpecked simpleton, dreaming of the day he would be allowed to go back home, to order a double banana split at the corner drug store and wash it down with sarsaparilla. In a scene in the Siberian vastnesses, an unknown singer, Mary Martin, performed a discreet striptease as she sang "My Heart Belongs to Daddy." After the opening night she was unknown no more.

Mistaken judgment caused Porter, in 1938, to ally himself with a small-scale musical comedy, *You Never Know*, derived from the play *Candlelight*, by Siegfried Geyer. Libby Holman made her last musical comedy appearance in a role that gave her next to nothing to do, and Clifton Webb, Lupe Velez, and Rex O'Malley were among the other unhappy ones present. The following year (1939) Porter redeemed himself with *Du Barry Was a Lady*, in which Bert Lahr, as a washroom attendant, dreamed that he was Louis XV and that Ethel Merman was the lady of the title. Lahr gave one of the most remarkable performances of his career, a two-strata characterization in which words issued from the lips of the mincing, dandified king that he could only have heard in the washroom of the opening scene. The production, by Raoul Pène du Bois, was French and beautiful; Betty Grable acquainted the Broadway public with her legs; the chorus girls were lovely and animated. But under its veneer, B. G. de Sylva, its producer, intended *Du Barry Was a Lady* as a high-class modern low-brow smut show.

Panama Hattie (1940), with which De Sylva induced Porter to follow *Du Barry Was a Lady*, flung its dirt with a somewhat smaller pitchfork, but it again indicated that De Sylva was intent on recapturing the sub-intellectual audience for which he and Brown and Henderson had written in their days as musical-comedy authors. The sketches, blackouts, and dialogue of *Panama Hattie* ran to corn decidedly less green than that with which Ethel Barrymore was concerned that year; burlesque blue and the black of common dirt were the prevailing colors of the book— counterbalanced by the harmonious and gay pastel palette of Du Bois, again De Sylva's scenic designer. But smoking-room humor was balanced by sentimentality of purest ray serene when Miss Merman, as a Panamanian siren of dubious virtue, was called upon to lavish affection upon a small girl who strayed defenselessly into her life. Porter revealed an unwonted vein of bathos in her song, "What Say, Let's Be Buddies," but elsewhere spiked the score with many a piquant harmonic surprise and many a neat twist of sophisticated verse.

While these metropolitan revels thrived (though in infinitely smaller numbers than in the pre-depression years), operetta showed its customary unwillingness to perish. The opening of the Center Theatre at Rockefeller Center, in 1932, posed a problem to the owners: With the big Radio

City Music Hall a block up the street, there was no call for a second motion-picture house in the new development. After two unsatisfying years of devotion to the cinema, the Center Theatre was turned into a legitimate playhouse on September 22, 1934. The first attraction was *The Great Waltz*, Max Gordon's potpourri of waltzes by Johann Strauss, father and son, strung on a libretto alleged to have something to do with the facts of Strauss' life. Moss Hart made what passed for a book out of German sources, Marion Claire and Guy Robertson sang in it, Albertina Rasch worked out the sinuous group dances, Albert Johnson designed the settings, and Hassard Short directed. Good names, all of them; and everyone did all he could. As a result, *The Great Waltz*, in the inviting setting of the new theatre, prospered well, though nobody ever called it a work of art. The Center Theatre continued, after *The Great Waltz*, with similar items, such as *White Horse Inn* (1936) and *Virginia* (1937). But in time even the management tired of trying to find suitable spectacular operettas. In 1940, the house was turned over to an ice show, *It Happens on Ice*, and for a decade, until the habit was broken in 1950, almost nothing but skating was ever seen there.

Huge spectacles were for the most part impractical in the 1930s, since no money was available to finance them. The magic name of Max Reinhardt, however, was enough to obtain the $600,000 necessary to stage *The Eternal Road*, a pageant of Jewish history, at the Manhattan Opera House, with music by Kurt Weill and a book translated from the German of Franz Werfel. It was bigger, but not better, than *The Miracle*, with which, in 1924, Reinhardt's staging was shown to an American audience for the first time since *Sumurun*. The entire proscenium arch of the opera house was removed, and massive constructions of concrete were installed. As a result, the auditorium, made famous by

Oscar Hammerstein's Manhattan Opera Company, has never been of any use theatrically since then, for its out-of-the-way location on West Thirty-fourth Street has made its restoration a questionable investment. Despite its 1,772 costumes, or perhaps because of them, *The Eternal Road* was as crushing a bore as New York theatre patrons ever saw.

Throughout the 1930s, old-fashioned girl-studded revues put in their appearance only at widely spaced intervals. George White sought to make a comeback in hard times by reducing his conception, in 1932, to the modest size implied by the title *George White's Music Hall Varieties*. He ventured a full-sized *Scandals*, with Bert Lahr, Rudy Vallee, and Willie and Eugene Howard, in 1935, and another, still with the Howard brothers, in 1939. Earl Carroll's activities were even more vestigial; he presented an economical *Sketch Book* in 1935, and made a final, wholly unsuccessful stab at the *Vanities* in 1940. The old names and the old ideas were quite played out.

After the death of Ziegfeld, the *Ziegfeld Follies* disappeared from the scene until 1934, when a new edition was offered under the nominal patronage of Mrs. Florenz Ziegfeld (Billie Burke), with Shubert backing. Fannie Brice was back, in her old form, with a revivalist sketch, "Soul-Saving Sadie," a travesty on a fan dance at Minsky's, and the first of her fruitful Baby Snooks playlets. The production, however, lacked the intangible Ziegfeld touch. While it was competently put together, and undeniably furnished a good money's worth, it had more the scattered character of a Shubert *Passing Show* than the homogeneous texture of the old-time *Follies*. In 1936, the Shuberts produced another *Follies*, this time under their own name, retaining Fannie Brice, making an ill-starred attempt to win an American audience for Paris' admired Josephine

Baker, and prettying things up with Minnelli settings that were the *dernier cri*—and, incidentally, Minnelli's last work for Broadway before he left to continue his meteoric career in Hollywood. After a seven-year lapse, the *Ziegfeld Follies* were once more revived, in 1943, under the three-way sponsorship of Alfred Bloomingdale, Lou Walters, and the Shuberts. Though the show was handsome in a conventional way, with Watson Barratt décors, not even Robert Alton's exciting dances could counterbalance the fact that Milton Berle, Arthur Treacher, Ilona Massey, and Sue Ryan were all too far removed from the classic days of the *Follies* to know what it meant to be in them.

A more appropriate Shubert revue, because it geared present-day performers to present-day humors, was *The Streets of Paris* (1939). The last revue produced by the Shuberts, except for the *Ziegfeld Follies of 1943*, *The Streets of Paris* was so heavily loaded with talent that bargain-counter settings and a helter-skelter mode of presentation did not reduce its merriment. Bobby Clark sang "I'm Robert the Roué, of Reading P-a." Bud Abbott and Lou Costello emerged from limbo to become first-line comics overnight. Carmen Miranda came from South America, and, flanked by six suave Brazilians, wore headdresses of flowers and fruit, and cackled apparently sly little songs in Portuguese. Jean Sablon purred his café song, "Le Fiacre," with appropriate hoofbeats in the orchestra. Ramón Vinay, later a leading tenor at the Metropolitan Opera, had an inconspicuous assignment. Ben Dova performed his immortal drunk act, performing feats bordering on levitation as he hung perilously from a bending lamppost.

Even cheaper in outlay than *The Streets of Paris* was *Hellzapoppin*, a frank compendium of vaudeville acts over which the slapstick comedians Ole Olson and Chic Johnson presided, and to which they gave countless foot-pounds of personal energy. No attraction for thinking people, *Hellzapoppin* drew a huge popular audience, and kept its originators in work for three years, after which it was easy enough for them to assemble *Sons o' Fun* (1941) and *Laffing Room Only* (1944) without changing the formula an iota. The quick money that came rolling in for *Hellzapoppin* at the Forty-sixth Street Theatre box office led other producers to hope that a vaudeville bill disguised by a revue title would bring similar riches to them. Ed Wynn did well with *Boys and Girls Together* (1940), and so did the sponsors of other mixed bills called *Priorities of 1942* (with Lou Holtz, Willie Howard, Phil Baker, Paul Draper, and Hazel Scott), *Top-Notchers* (1942) (with Argentinita, Federico Rey, Pilar Lopez, Walter O'Keefe, Gracie Fields, and A. Robbins), *Show Time* (1942) (with George Jessel, Jack Haley, Ella Logan, and the De Marcos), and *Laugh Time* (1943) (with Ethel Waters, Frank Fay, Bert Wheeler, Buck and Bubbles, and the incredible dog act known as The Bricklayers). The public soon found, however, that these tiresome titles were attached to equally tiresome exhumations of ancient acts and songs, and the vaudeville revival ceased as abruptly as it had begun.

War and Post-War Years

THE SECOND World War gave Broadway fresh impetus. Prosperity, or something that passed for it, was back again, and a big new audience, composed partly of service men, had discovered the legitimate theatre. At the Stage Door Canteen and in their tours of army camps here and abroad, theatre folk had discovered that their gifts as entertainers were valuable to morale. A fresh ardor pervaded Broadway, and each new musical show seemed to be more exciting than it actually was.

Cole Porter was one of the first to react to the mood of the times, with *Let's Face It* (1941), a musical version of *Cradle Snatchers,* a farce written in 1927 by Russell Medcraft and Norma Mitchell. Herbert and Dorothy Fields brought the book up to the minute by involving three ladies at a rest camp in complications with Danny Kaye and Benny Baker, who appeared as inductees in the Army. A scene detailing the tribulations of the soldiers drafted under the new universal conscription law was inserted for topical laughs, and Kaye was a tireless, rapid-fire corporal. The wittiest song, however, had nothing to do with military affairs; it was a diatribe against rural life entitled "Farming."

Let's Face It barely scratched the surface of wartime subject matter, for the United States did not enter the war until more than a month after it opened. Porter's Something for the Boys (1943), genuinely a wartime diversion, was placed in and near an Army camp, with Ethel Merman as a girl who could receive radio messages through the fillings in her teeth. Jack Cole's dances were a stroke of genius. Without being mere drills, they were built out of military formations, except for a big party scene, which maintained a similar regularity of design by employing square-dance figures. Toward the end of the evening, with little or no excuse for it in the plot, Ethel Merman amazed her audience by abandoning her characteristic ramrod stance, donning moccasins and a long, black, stringy Indian wig, and intoning duet-wise with Paula Laurence one of Porter's most convulsing trick-rhyme songs, "By the Mis-sis-si-ni-wa"—or, as the music actually went, "By the Mis-sis-sis-sis-sis-sis-sis-sis-sin-i-wa," which rhymed terminally with "since you've been awa'."

After getting a decidedly second-class inspiration, Mexican Hayride, out of the way as a piece for Bobby Clark, Porter turned his thoughts to Billy Rose's new brain-child, the revue Seven Lively Arts, which opened at the Ziegfeld Theatre on December 7, 1944. Seven Lively Arts was devised by Billy Rose as a costly token of his proprietorship of the handsome Joseph Urban-designed theatre, into the possession of which he had only recently, and very proudly, come. As though the musical contributions of Porter were not sufficient ornament for so monumental a landmark in Broadway history, Rose engaged Igor Stravinsky to compose a score for a *ballet blanc* choreographed by Anton Dolin, in which Dolin and Alicia Markova were the leading dancers. This piece, known subsequently as *Scènes de Ballet*, and now a feature of the Sadler's Wells repertory, was less to the liking of a majority of the customers than Porter's songs and Jack Donahue's typical musical-comedy dance routines.

Rose spent a fair share of the $350,000 production money of *Seven Lively Arts* upon the hire of a stable of big names, but unhappily he was not able to require his authors to supply top-drawer ideas, nor could he receive full value from performers supplied with second-class material. Beatrice Lillie carried much of the show on her shoulders, with Bert Lahr helping out as effectively as circumstances would allow. Ben Hecht wrote comments for Doctor Rockwell to deliver. Moss Hart, George S. Kaufman, and several other schooled practitioners wrote sketches, which were directed by Philip Loeb. Norman Bel Geddes devised the settings and Mary Shaw and Valentina the costumes. Robert Shaw trained the chorus, and Maurice Abravanel conducted the orchestra. Hassard Short took care of the lighting, and staged the ensemble numbers. Opening-night customers paid $24 for orchestra seats, and were served champagne in the intermission. Perhaps there were too many expensive chefs. At any rate, *Seven Lively Arts* failed to jell, and it is still spoken of nostalgically as something that might have been wonderful, but wasn't.

In his next assignment, *Around the World* (1946), Porter's songs were again obliterated by too elaborate a superstructure. In attempting to return the Jules Verne romance to the Broadway musical stage, Orson Welles—who was author, director, and one of the principal actors—simply had too many ideas. The production, wrote Howard Barnes in the *Herald Tribune*, "combines silent movies, Hoboken melodramatic satire, a magic show and Olsen and Johnson japes in a singular potpourri." Robert Davison provided a resourceful stage setting equipped with panels at right and left, in which miniature scenes were enacted while the bigger ones among the thirty-two different settings were prepared on the main stage—which, in turn, was so planned that the front and back halves could be used either separately or together. *Around the World* had everything from an elaborate circus at Yokohama (with acrobats and tight-rope walkers) to a breathtaking pint-size reproduction of a western railroad train falling through a trestle. Welles himself overacted in classic fashion as the Copper's Knark, and Arthur Margetson gave a drily self-contained, and very British, performance as Phileas Fogg. But there was too much staging; the script was laborious and weak, despite Welles' efforts to gag and trick it up; and Nelson Barclift's choreography was as feeble as Porter's songs, which were about the poorest he ever wrote.

These two disasters—*Seven Lively Arts* and *Around the World*—cast a long and depressing shadow over Porter's reputation in the theatrical world. He was finished, people said; never would we hear more of the inventive rhymes and the well-pointed tunes that brought him his fame. *Kiss Me Kate* (1948) routed the prophets of gloom, and proved, if anything, that Porter was at the peak of his powers, and needed only the help of a good book to bring forward a spate of songs as exhilarating as any he had supplied since *Anything Goes*.

For their libretto, Bella and Samuel Spewack used the play-within-a-play device, striking a parallel between the real-life conduct of an acting couple—divorced but still in love—and the behavior of Katharine and Petruchio in a road-company performance of Shakespeare's *The Taming of the Shrew* in Baltimore. *Kiss Me Kate* was one of those well-favored musical comedies that got off on the right foot, apparently, from the first planning stages, and never got off it. It was superlatively handled in every department, and each contribution was perfectly geared to the others. Hanya Holm's choreography, wider in range than the work of most of her more celebrated contemporaries, covered a gamut, as *Variety* put it, "from ballet to hot hoofing," and always seemed to come up with the proper ideas at the proper time. Lemuel Ayers' designs for the scenes and the costumes and John C. Wilson's perceptive and expressive stage direction added the final polish to the performances of a personable cast headed by Alfred Drake as Petruchio and Patricia Morison as Katharine. And what a brilliant and diversified set of seventeen songs the rejuvenated Cole Porter turned out! *Kiss Me Kate* was perhaps the only Porter score in which not a single song was weak or careless. The musical literature of Broadway was perceptibly enriched by such deft pieces as "I Hate Men," "Wunderbar" (with its vicious parody of Viennese operetta music), "So in Love Am I," and the extroverted "I've Come to Wive It Wealthily in Padua," in which the name of the city rhymed with "what a cad you are" and "how mad you are." Obviously Cole Porter belongs to the future of the musical stage as well as to the past.

No sooner had Pearl Harbor been attacked than Irving Berlin began to talk about reviving and expanding *Yip, Yip, Yaphank*, the revue he wrote and appeared in during the first World War. Until this war began, however, he remained faithful to escapist materials. Returning from Hollywood, he contributed the music and lyrics of *Louisiana Purchase* (1940), a piece vaguely satirizing the Huey Long régime, which was less engaging for its materials than for the knowing performances of Victor Moore, William Gaxton, Irene Bordoni, and Vera Zorina, and for the fresh impression given by Carol Bruce's youthful singing.

Berlin then contracted to provide some of the songs for Michael Todd's revue, *Star and Garter* (1942), along with Harold Rome and Harold Arlen. Todd's revue was based on the assumption that since the Minsky burlesque houses had been closed by legal action, it was a logical move to bring burlesque into the big time at a $4.80 top. He spared no cost with Harry Horner's tasteful settings and Irene Sharaff's equally attractive costumes, and he entrusted the direction to a wise showman, Hassard Short. As a result, even Gypsy Rose Lee's lyric and classical stripping and Carrie Finnell's flamboyant exhibition of mammalian control did not keep *Star and Garter* from seeming much like any other well-mounted revue lucky enough to boast Bobby Clark as its star. In *Peep Show* (1950) Todd again sought to dress up burlesque for the carriage trade, this time with Bobby Clark as stage director.

Only ten days after the opening of *Star and Garter*, Berlin took part in the première of *This Is the Army*, at the Broadway Theatre, on the carefully chosen date of July 4. *This Is the Army* was the show Berlin had in mind when he talked of reviving *Yip, Yip, Yaphank*. In the course of preparation it took on a wholly different character, and about the only resemblance it bore to its predecessor lay in its all-soldier cast, and the reminiscent voice of Berlin singing "Oh, How I Hate to Get Up in the Morning."

Under the stress of patriotic wartime emotion, *This Is the Army* provided an incomparable experience. The three hundred military participants had been drilled and rehearsed to the last degree of precision. More important, they had been given good material to work with, and Sergeant Ezra Stone's direction was on the same high level as Berlin's vivacious score. A scene representing the Stage Door Canteen, with soldier impersonators of such luminaries as Jane Cowl, Lynn Fontanne, and Gypsy Rose Lee, attained instant fame, though other more masculine features of the show were equally worthy of praise for their entirely professional pace and presentation. In the last analysis, the most stirring moments were the massed scenes in which purely military formations and drills were turned into genuine choreography, under the direction of Private Robert Sidney and Corporal Nelson Barclift. The effectiveness of the spectacle was enhanced in September by the addition of a new finale, in which the entire stage was triumphantly filled by uniformed men with upraised and crossed bayonets, ready to go to war.

Returning to civilian considerations at the end of the war, Berlin turned out, with the expert literary coöperation of Herbert and Dorothy Fields, the biggest popular success of his Broadway career in *Annie Get Your Gun* (1946). Ethel Merman spanned two New York seasons in the title role of Annie Oakley, the Ohio girl who could outshoot the best shots in Buffalo Bill's Wild West show. Mary Martin headed a "national company" in 1947. Duplications were presented, with immense éclat, in London and in Australia, and a Parisian version, with Lily Fayol as a gunwoman of Montmartre stripe, triumphed under the title *Annie du Far-West*.

Annie Get Your Gun was completely devoid of novelty or aesthetic risks. It was a thoroughly standardized product, produced by Richard Rodgers and Oscar Hammerstein 2d with unerring comprehension of all the ingredients and proportions of the recipe for success, handsomely designed by Jo Mielziner, and staged by Joshua Logan with rare common sense. The Fields duo had learned by now, perhaps better than anyone else in the book-writing business, how to tell a story without wasting a word; and Berlin, on a high wave of inventiveness, dotted the score with such superlatively efficacious songs as "Doin' What Comes Naturally," "Show Business," "You Can't Get a Man with a Gun," and "They Say It's Wonderful." Helen Tamiris reverted to high, wide, and handsome devices of traditional musical-comedy choreography in a ballet depicting the induction of Annie Oakley into the Sioux tribe, and offered a counter-argument to those who had been led by some of Agnes de Mille's ballets to believe that musical-comedy dancing should wear its art on its sleeve. Neither Miss Merman nor Ray Middleton, as her heart interest Frank Butler, let the authors or the composer down for a minute. As Robert Garland observed in the *Journal-American:* "She's no longer Miss Merman acting like Ethel Merman. She's Miss Merman acting like Annie Oakley."

In the summer of 1941, George Abbott, contemplating plans for autumn production, gave thought to the probable effects of universal army conscription upon male actors of draft age. Why go to the expense of putting together a potential hit show, he reasoned, only to see its cast and chorus progressively depleted by the inexorable action of the selective service boards? Why not produce a show with a cast well below the minimum draft age, and thus guarantee the permanence of its personnel? The cast and book of *Best Foot Forward* (1941) were the result of this consideration. John Cecil Holm, author of *Three Men on a Horse,* a farce Abbott had directed with conspicuous success (transformed in 1941 into a musical comedy, *Banjo Eyes,* for Eddie Cantor), put together a serviceable libretto about a Hollywood siren who put in her disruptive appearance at an innocent prep-school prom. Abbott held countrywide auditions for new talent, and discovered, among others, the rough-and-ready Nancy Walker and an appealing little colleen named Maureen Cannon. Rosemary Lane—later supplanted by Joy Hodges—was the visiting motion-picture queen. Ralph Martin, who had supplied vocal arrangements for *Pal Joey*, *Louisiana Purchase*, and several other prominent musical comedies, composed a first score so copious that *Best Foot Forward* sometimes tended to turn into a cantata. But the piece was quite winning, for the youngsters carried out their tasks in a candid and unassuming way, and raised the roof with their rousing football song, "Buckle Down, Winsocki, Buckle Down."

In *Beat the Band* (1942), his next musical production, Abbott turned to the glorification of jive, jitterbugging, and hepcat interests. A fierce and noisy post-adolescent revel composed by Johnny Green, who had once supplied Libby Holman with "Body and Soul," *Beat the Band* relied chiefly upon its two orchestras, on the stage and in the pit, reaching its climax midway in the second act with the hot trumpet licks of Leonard Sues in "Steam Is on the Beam." Some of the songs sounded to Brooks Atkinson "less like music than the clearing of a throat," and often seemed to have "no notes at all." But there were stunning sets by Samuel Leve and costumes by Freddy Wittop (known as Federico Rey when he engages in Spanish dancing), energetic dancing by Doris York and Marc Platt (Marc Platoff of the Ballet Russe de Monte Carlo, who dropped the Russian suffix and restored his original Seattle patronymic when he went into show business), and passable choreography by David Lichine, in his Broadway bow. The run of *Beat the Band* was constricted, however, by its specialized appeal, and by a threadbare book detailing the romance of Jack Whiting, as a band leader, and Susan Miller, as a Caribbean actress.

In contrast to *Beat the Band*, whose stridency only a confirmed jive addict could love, *On the Town* (1944) was a youthful fancy nearly everyone loved. Produced by the new team of Oliver Smith and Paul Feigay, themselves not yet out of their twenties, *On the Town* was an extension and amplification of a ballet, *Fancy Free,* which Leonard Bernstein, as composer, and Jerome Robbins, as choreographer, had conceived for Ballet Theatre. Since a full-length musical comedy, unlike a ballet, needed a book, one was provided by Betty Comden and Adolph Green, fresh and unspoiled humorists who had climbed to attention through their informal performances in a Greenwich Village basement café.

Though its central characters were three sailors and the girls they met on shore leave, *On the Town* was in every way one of the most literate works Broadway had yet produced. While the audience was not aware of it (so spontaneous were the antics of the youngsters), the carefree story was firmly controlled by an exceptional amount of strictly formal planning of the music and the choreography. Bernstein was eager to demonstrate that all manner of structural subtleties could be concealed under the happy-go-lucky rhythmic exterior of the Broadway tunes, and when the extended ballet episodes came along he was ready to cope with them with a musical command such as only Kurt Weill had hitherto been able to call upon. Robbins' dance designs were equally seriously conceived, and the dances and the music were born together, through painstaking daily colloquy between composer and choreographer. At its best *On the Town* was supremely imaginative, with Oliver Smith's settings and Alvin Colt's costumes conspiring with the music, the dances, the earthy comedy of Nancy Walker, and the fleet grace of Sono Osato to give a lively yet poetic panorama of "New York, New York." Manhattan has not been so buoyantly treated by its own theatre people since that time.

In *Billion Dollar Baby* (1945), their second and last joint production, Feigay and Smith undertook a satire of the

1920s, a decade now become—to the bewilderment of those who felt they had quite recently lived through it—an object of derision to the younger generation. Betty Comden and Adolph Green upheld their standard of *On the Town* in the lyrics and book, George Abbott's direction was blunt and funny, and Oliver Smith's settings were broadly to the point. But Jerome Robbins, though he had investigated the Charleston and other manifestations of the era in question, lacked a first-hand feeling for the requirements of the dancing, and only those who could not actually remember the 1920s felt that he had quite equaled his accomplishment in *On the Town.* For *High Button Shoes* (1947), on the other hand, Robbins dreamed up a parody of Mack Sennett's Keystone Cops and bathing beauties which was a convulsing interlude in an otherwise bromidic musical-comedy flashback to the year 1913.

The cessation of hostilities quickly returned a great many actors to civilian life. To celebrate their demobilization, and also to earn a little money, a group of veterans got together for a revue, *Call Me Mister* (1946), containing mementoes of military life and impressions of the non-military existence seen from the ex-fighting-man's perspective. Harold Rome wrote songs and lyrics more innocuous and less tinged with social protest than those of *Pins and Needles*, setting the tone for a show that was pleasant enough, but devoid of distinction. The timeliness of *Call Me Mister* earned it a profitable run.

The first revue since the *Ziegfeld Follies of 1943*, *Call Me Mister* encouraged new faith in non-book shows, especially when prepared in terms of a restricted budget. Several subsequent revues were launched, of which *Lend an Ear* (1948), and *Small Wonder* (1948) were much the cleverest. Dating back several years to an informal revue first given at Carnegie Institute of Technology in Pittsburgh, and later in a summer theatre at Cohasset, Massachusetts, *Lend an Ear* brought back from Hollywood a former Carnegie Tech student, William Eythe, who had been seen by film scouts for the first time at Cohasset. It also focussed attention upon Carol Channing, who in 1949 triumphantly appeared as Lorelei Lee in the musical version of Anita Loos' *Gentlemen Prefer Blondes*. *Small Wonder* employed nineteen performers, one of whom was Tom Ewell as the Normal Neurotic, to present its skeptical and critically oriented sketches and its slick dancing, choreographed by Gower Champion. The adroit lyrics, if anything too sophisticated, were by Phyllis McGinley and Billings Brown, another name for Burt Shevelove, who was also director and co-producer.

One of the indirect effects of the war was a renewed enthusiasm for that perennial escapist form of entertainment, the operetta. The best-considered efforts in this field were those of Yolanda Merö-Irion's New Opera Company. Along with more serious endeavors along the lines of grand opera, the company, with Lodewick Vroom, produced *Rosalinda* (1942), the brilliant Max Reinhardt version of Strauss' *Die Fledermaus*. The gracious Jarmila Novotna of the Metropolitan Opera sang the title role in *Helen Goes to Troy* (1944), a rather ruthlessly modernized variant of Offenbach's *La Belle Hélène*. The production was superbly mounted, with settings and lighting by Robert Edmond Jones, in one of his rare concessions to light entertainment; with choreography by Léonide Massine, stage direction by Herbert Graf of the Metropolitan, and gleaming costumes by Ladislas Czettel; and with Erich Wolfgang Korngold, himself a composer of reputation, as conductor. In the same year, Felix Brentano directed for the New Opera Company a handsome revival of *The Merry Widow*, with the delectable Marta Eggert as the Widow, and her husband, Jan Kiepura, every inch an operatic tenor in the part of Prince

Danilo. George Balanchine choreographed the waltz and the attendant divertissements with charm and taste; Howard Bay designed the settings, and Walter Florell the costumes. A luxuriant opéra-bouffe revival of Offenbach's *La Vie Parisienne*, was also accomplished, in 1945, before the New Opera Company fell short of funds. Massine again supplied the choreography and Czettel the costumes. Ralph Herbert directed, and Richard Rychtarik created the settings. All these New Opera Company productions, like its concomitant staging of Verdi's *Macbeth*, were enormously admired, but only *Rosalinda* prospered.

Balanchine was responsible for much of the success of *Song of Norway* (1944), a pastiche of rearranged Grieg music and bogus biography brought from the Pacific Coast by Edwin Lester. Because the plot, fortunately, was too spare to fill the whole evening, Balanchine tacked on at the end a long, elaborate, and cleanly composed ballet, also entitled "Song of Norway," in which, for three weeks at the start, Alexandra Danilova and Frederic Franklin of the Ballet Russe de Monte Carlo participated. A full year of prosperity for *Song of Norway* induced Lester to bring *Gypsy Love* eastward in 1946. A crude coalition of Victor Herbert's *The Fortune Teller* and *The Serenade*, it was a hopeless botch from the first.

Meanwhile Kiepura and Miss Eggert, finished with touring in *The Merry Widow*, dedicated themselves to *Polonaise* (1945), a wallow of sentiment and Polish nationalism in which a great deal of Chopin music was mired. The Ballet Russe suffered one more depredation in the engagement of Tatiana Riabouchinska as *prima ballerina*.

Richard Tauber, another celebrated tenor, followed Kiepura's example, making his first, last, and only Broadway appearance—subject to constant absences caused by the illness that led to his death the next year—in Lehár's *Yours*

Is My Heart (1946). In 1947, Bobby Clark did his best to reanimate Herbert's *Sweethearts* by injecting into it his special prescription of horseplay. In the same year, Oskar Straus' *The Chocolate Soldier* failed to make much headway, despite fashionable settings by Jo Mielziner and extensive choreography by Balanchine. A still more disastrous box-office calamity was *Music in My Heart* (1947), an attempt to prove, by means of snippets of Tchaikovsky music and half a dozen really handsome ballets choreographed by Ruth Page, that the true secret of the Russian composer's melancholia was his unrequited love for a French singer named Desirée Artot. *Magdalena,* staged on the West Coast by Homer Curran in the summer of 1948 and brought to New York that fall, misrepresented life in South America, to a musical score of loudly orchestrated rag-bag leavings by Heitor Villa-Lobos. Since that time it cannot be said that traditional operetta has enjoyed a favorable standing on Broadway, though one of its perennial resuscitations may always occur on a moment's notice.

Bordering on operetta were two period musical comedies offered to the wartime escapist audience. *Bloomer Girl* (1944) evoked the militant feminism of Dolly Bloomer, with artful costumes by Miles White, lilting music by Harold Arlen, and an Agnes de Mille ballet that viewed the Civil War in gloomy terms. *Up in Central Park* (1945) returned Sigmund Romberg to the theatre as the composer for Herbert and Dorothy Fields' quiet and agreeable memento of Tammany's heyday. An ice-skating ballet, devised by Helen Tamiris in the manner of Frederick Ashton's *Les Patineurs,* was especially felicitous.

The Theatre Guild contributed to the prevailing mood of nostalgia by asking Elie Siegmeister to arrange a "salute to American folk and popular music," *Sing Out, Sweet Land* (1944). A rather bloodless compendium of Americana, its best features were the ballad singing of the jovial Burl Ives and the neatly patterned dances devised by Doris Humphrey and Charles Weidman, for whom this was the last joint undertaking. Events of still less moment in the early 1940s were Hoagy Carmichael's debut as a musical-comedy song writer in an abortive nonsense starring Kitty Carlisle, *Walk with Music* (1940), and Al Jolson's momentary return to the stage, with Martha Raye, in *Hold On to Your Hats*, an attractively produced show with music by Burton Lane and lyrics by E. Y. Harburg—the pair who later cooperated in *Finian's Rainbow*.

Fantasy had returned to the musical theatre with *I Married an Angel*. The trend was carried further by *Cabin in the Sky* (1940), an imaginative exposition of the Negro folk outlook upon life, death, and immortality. While *Cabin in the Sky* awakened overtones of the classic Negro fantasy *The Green Pastures*, its presentation was more sophisticated, at the same time that its plot and characterization retained no less connection with the realities of everyday life. The action presented the struggle between Lucifer, Jr., and the Lawd's General for the soul of Little Joe, who had a hard time remembering to be good. Petunia, with her deep faith in prayer, assisted the Lawd's General, while the worldly Georgia Brown did her best to add force to the devil's overtures. Ethel Waters, as Petunia, and Katherine Dunham, as Georgia Brown, were perfectly cast and ideally contrasted in style. Todd Duncan, the Porgy of *Porgy and Bess*, sang admirably as the Lawd's General, and Dooley Wilson portrayed the pathetic Little Joe with an instinct that was infallible. George Balanchine and Miss Dunham both had a hand in the choreography, which was as wide in range and as brilliant in execution as any the Broadway stage has seen to this day. Vernon Duke (whose alter ego is Vladimir Dukelsky, the symphonic composer) composed his one genuinely distinguished light score, and John La Touche made his first reputation with the happily turned lyrics.

After *Cabin in the Sky*, Miss Dunham and her company struck out on their own, returning intermittently to Broadway in fast-paced revues compounded of Caribbean folk and American jazz evocations. Her most elaborate production, *Carib Song* (1945), bogged down under the weight of Baldwin Bergerson's music and William Archibald's book; and Mary Hunter's direction was not able to save it. Miss Dunham and her company have always, since *Cabin in the Sky*, succeeded best in their most informal endeavors.

Miss Dunham once undertook the choreography for a musical play in which she and her company did not appear. *Windy City* (1946), which opened at the Shubert Great Northern Theatre in Chicago and never came to New York, brushed within an inch of success, but somehow its picture of life on the South Side of Chicago, decorated by some of Jo Mielziner's most striking settings, never quite jelled. Perhaps the chief trouble was Walter Jurman's watery imitation-Rachmaninoff music; for Philip Yordan's book was cogently put together. Miss Dunham has never created a more breathtaking dance than one that was performed up, down, and around the steel pillars of an elevated railroad structure.

Windy City was potentially a better conceived venture than *Beggar's Holiday* (1946), which borrowed from it the opening scene of the blank wall of a building, with a high catwalk upon which various people scurried about. John La Touche planned his book as a modern interpretation of John Gay's *The Beggar's Opera*, and in a measure it was successful. But his love of verbiage got the better of him in the lyrics, and Duke Ellington, drafted into the musical-comedy field for the first time, revealed an almost complete inability to relate his musical compositions to dramatic situations. Oliver Smith and Walter Florell accomplished spectacular results with the settings and costumes; and Valerie Bettis revealed glimmerings of her powerful talent despite the amorphousness of her first choreographic contributions to Broadway. As an object lesson in democracy, a mixed cast of Negro and white performers—headed by Alfred Drake, Zero Mostel, Avon Long, Bernice Parks, and Mildred Smith—was employed, and for the first time Broadway saw a white man make love to a Negro girl in simple, natural terms. Everyone wanted *Beggar's Holiday* to succeed, but it could not, for it was too chaotic.

Far happier as a demonstration of the gifts of Negro artists had been Billy Rose's production of *Carmen Jones* (1943). In the hope of giving immediacy to the Carmen story, Rose engaged Oscar Hammerstein 2d to rewrite the libretto. Hammerstein changed the locale to North Carolina, where a tobacco factory is quite as normal a phenomenon as the original cigarette-manufacturing establishment in Seville. Retaining the main features of the Meilhac and Halévy libretto, Hammerstein performed the seemingly impossible feat of transferring its people and incidents into entirely different ethnic surroundings. Since a large part of Bizet's music was retained, somewhat caponized at times by Robert Russell Bennett's editing and reorchestration, Hammerstein applied his phenomenal skill to the task of writing lyrics that were appropriate and believable in diction, faithful to the meaning of the original, and equipped with satisfactory vowel sounds.

With Muriel Smith and Muriel Rahn alternating in the title role, *Carmen Jones* aroused 231 audiences to enthusiasm by the directness and force with which the dramatic action made its points. Charles Friedman, who staged the book, taught his actors economy and well-pointed ensemble playing. Eugene Loring, abandoning his dancing functions with Ballet Theatre, was alive with choreographic ideas, and the dancing of his severely trained group proved to be perhaps the most telling single feature of the staging, upon which Hassard Short kept a supervisory eye. Howard Bay's settings—so elaborate that they occupied more than their fair share of the floor space—employed a unique device of color. Each scene was a monochrome. Both scenes of the first act (outside the factory, and by a roadside) were yellow. The scene in the café "run by my friend Billy Pastor" was purple. The country club which replaced Bizet's smugglers' scene in the mountains was blue. The final scene, not technically a monochrome, was done in red, black, and white. Raoul Pène du Bois designed the costumes for each scene either in obedience to the ruling color or in subtle counterpoints to it.

Less persuasive as a spectacle, because it was overelaborate, was Robert Edmond Jones' treatment of the settings and costumes for Michael Myerberg's well-intended production of *Lute Song* (1946), an adaptation by Sidney Howard and Will Irwin of a Chinese classic, *Pi-Pa-Ki*. Nearly everything was misconceived about *Lute Song*. The story, concerned with two women in love with the same man, was thrown out of focus when Mary Martin was engaged for the cast. An established star since *One Touch of Venus*, Miss Martin dominated the stage to a degree that was not warranted, and apparently nobody was able to persuade her that a touch of Broadway song-plugging was out of place in the hollow songs Raymond Scott wrote for her. When Dolly Haas replaced Miss Martin as partner to Yul Brynner on the tour, a better balance was established, but it was too late.

In a mixed vein of fantasy and realism, *The Day Before Spring* (1945) investigated—not without overtones of *Lady in the Dark*—the psychic life of a married woman who, at a college reunion, met the man she did not marry, and came within an inch of running off with him—an act which would have spoiled everything for her, since she really loved her husband all the time. This tale, supplied with ineffectual dream ballets choreographed by Antony Tudor (in his introduction to Broadway) and danced by Mary Ellen Moylan and Hugh Laing, was woven into a musical comedy of smooth texture, in which the songs and dances grew naturally out of the contexts of the action. The piece enjoyed no more than a *succès d'estime*, for it was rather pale, and became uncomfortable in a scene in which Irene Manning, as the wife, listened to advice from Plato, Freud, and Voltaire. To the composer, Frederick Loewe, and the author of the book and lyrics, Alan Jay Lerner (previously represented only by *What's Up* in 1943), it provided an opportunity to sharpen the talents they were soon to call upon in *Brigadoon*.

Fantasy took full possession of the affections of the New York public in *Finian's Rainbow* (1947), which added the Irish town of Glocca Morra to the map of Broadway's never-never-land. Finian McLonergan, accompanied by his irresistible daughter Sharon, had come from Ireland to the United States in order to bury in the Rainbow Valley in Missitucky a pot of gold Finian had stolen from the leprechauns. Og, a lithe and indefatigable leprechaun, had followed them in the hope of getting it back. The conventional features of the plot hinged upon the pot-of-gold situation; but much of the energy of the librettist was devoted to the task of giving Senator Billboard Rawlings of Missitucky, an ardent advocate of white supremacy, a satisfactory dressing-down. With remarkable adroitness, *Finian's Rainbow* slid back and forth between the imaginary realm of the leprechauns and the uncomfortably real world of race prejudice. Michael Kidd's flexible choreography, in which it was difficult to tell when action was ending and dance was beginning, served as the chief emollient in a play whose opposing elements ought normally to have engendered a great deal of friction. Equal credit for the believable realization of the conceit was due to Bretaigne Windust, who left the non-musical field of *Life with Father* and other plays to apply his directional skill to *Finian's Rainbow*.

The main parts of the two McLonergans, the leprechaun, and the girl who made him renounce leprechaunship in favor of a human existence, were all characterized and presented with unusual felicity. Albert Sharpe, imported from Ireland, was pricelessly right as Finian. Ella Logan, as Sharon, knew how to make the audience lose its heart both to her and to Glocca Morra with the first phrase of her singing. David Wayne accomplished the unlikely trick of imbuing a leprechaun with manly proclivities. Anita Alvarez, whose role compelled her to remain mute through most of the evening, conversed fluently with her dancing. In every regard *Finian's Rainbow* bordered upon first-class lyric drama, except that most of it, when one took it home and thought it over, was not as distinctive in artistic substance as it had seemed to be in the theatre.

Fantasy without social preachment was the métier of *Brigadoon* (1947). The plot, a variant on the *Connecticut Yankee* device, told of the encounter of two disillusioned Americans with the inhabitants of a mysterious Scots village which appeared from nowhere once every hundred years, and where the archaic folkways never changed. A piece that might easily have turned into a commonplace, milk-and-water operetta was made captivating by the perceptive direction of Robert Lewis, who knows better how to make a fantasy credible than most of our régisseurs, and by the strong dances choreographed by Agnes de Mille.

In several earlier musical comedies—*Oklahoma!, Carou-*

sel, and *Bloomer Girl* among them—Miss de Mille had demonstrated that the choreography of a Broadway show could be a reasonable extension and amplification of the plot. *Brigadoon,* however, was her chef d'oeuvre, and she has not had occasion to equal her work in it since. Not only did the dances originate spontaneously in the plot, but Miss de Mille explored an artistic dimension beyond that of the materials she had used before. The impressive funeral ceremonial, accompanied only by the snarling wail of bagpipes, would not have seemed out of place in the most serious ballet, nor would the traditional sword dance which James Mitchell performed with superb élan during the wedding ceremony.

The score by Frederick Loewe amounted to less than the dancing. He was too ready to abandon the vein of Scotch folk music, which brought him his most attractive results toward the beginning, in favor of desultory love songs, whose routine aspect was enhanced by some of Alan Jay Lerner's lyrics.

The death of Kurt Weill in April, 1950, removed from the American musical theatre its most accomplished craftsman. In Germany, before the Hitler régime forced him out, Weill attained an immense reputation for a series of stage pieces that reflected the confusion and moral unrest of the post-war period. The most famous of these, his paraphrase of Gay's *The Beggar's Opera* entitled *Die Dreigroschen-Oper,* was presented in New York in 1933, with a cast unable to handle either its pithy style or its intellectual outlook, under the title *The Three-Penny Opera.* Its innuendo and sardonic manner were beyond the grasp of an American audience that felt no need for that particular form of expression, and one of the most remarkable satiric efforts of the twentieth century withered after twelve performances.

Later on, those who attended French motion pictures were given a second chance to admire the work, in René Clair's *L'Opéra de Quat' Sous.*

Weill came to the United States to live soon afterward, and in 1936 wrote the pungent incidental music for the Group Theatre's memorable production of Paul Green's play *Johnny Johnson.* His second American assignment, in 1937, was *The Eternal Road.* In 1938 he formed what looked at first glance like an unlikely partnership with Maxwell Anderson, to write *Knickerbocker Holiday,* a musical comedy about New York in the days of Dutch rule in the seventeenth century. Peter Stuyvesant, with his historic silver peg-leg, was impersonated by Walter Huston. The list of characters was studded with such well-known names as Vanderbilt, Van Rensselaer, De Puyster, and Roosevelt. Since the idea of writing *Knickerbocker Holiday* was suggested to Maxwell Anderson by Washington Irving's *Father Knickerbocker's History of New York,* Irving appeared anachronistically in the show, in the shape of Ray Middleton. In one of his happiest achievements, Anderson suffused the lines and lyrics with the glow of life and beauty, and at the same time presented an eloquent argument for the democratic conception of government. Weill's music was mixed in quality. At its worst it was both more sophisticated and more banal, in the continental jazz manner, than the run-of-the-mill products of Broadway. On the other hand, Weill was a full partner with Anderson and Walter Huston in the triumph of the moment when Huston, in a voice hardly more than a confidential whisper, posed the problems of advancing age in the "September Song."

Weill's best gift to the American stage, beyond all debate, was the refined and sensitive score for *Lady in the Dark,* which opened, with Gertrude Lawrence in the central role, on January 23, 1941. In *Knickerbocker Holiday,* Weill had worked with an author who was, in effect, a gifted amateur in the musical branch of the theatre. In *Lady in the Dark* he was associated with two of the most assured artisans of the trade—Moss Hart, who wrote the book, and Ira Gershwin, who wrote the lyrics.

By no stretch of the imagination could *Lady in the Dark* be described as a simon-pure musical comedy. It was a serious drama, with dream interludes of song and dance expertly integrated in the basic structure. The chronicle of a successful but troubled magazine editor who found her true self through the aid of psychoanalysis, *Lady in the Dark* derived its format from the contrast between the actual world and the world of fantasy brought to consciousness by the device of the psychoanalytic couch. The action moved back and forth between Liza Elliott's office and the doctor's consulting room, which evaporated in the imaginings and recollections of Liza's subconscious—fortunately an exceedingly vivid and colorful one. The contrast of the tailored modernity of the office and the clipped dialogue that took place in it with the riotous decorations and unpredictable free associations of the dream scenes made these musical episodes doubly effective. Like the pieces of a jigsaw puzzle, the dream passages fitted into the surrounding narrative with constantly increasing intelligibility; at the end, but only then, it was possible to see the dexterity with which action, spectacle, lines, lyrics, and music had been put together with uncommon lucidity of purpose.

Miss Lawrence's performance—for which she is said to have received $3,500 a week, a percentage of the gross receipts, and the guarantee of a three-month summer holiday —was one of the supreme virtuoso feats of the modern theatre. From her everyday character she moved, within a split second, and with no possibility of the external aid of changed makeup, into a variety of startlingly different phases. She became the schoolgirl selected at graduation time as the most popular member of her class, not, as she privately wished, the most beautiful. In the gaily colorful circus scene, over which Danny Kaye cracked the whip as ringmaster, she sang of Jenny, who always made up her mind (Kurt Weill's contribution to sultry music of the "Eadie Was a Lady" school). As the central figure of the New York Chapter of Liza Elliott Admirers, she lived up to the terms of the admirers' apostrophe:

> "Oh, Fabulous One in your ivory tower—
> Your radiance I fain would see!
> What Mélisande was to Pelléas
> Are you to me."

Mary Garden's Mélisande sang no more affectingly than this Liza Elliott, in such simple and melodious lyrics as "My Ship" and "The Princess of Pure Delight." It was a many-sided performance, in which each new facet was as arresting as the last.

Although Miss Lawrence quite properly dominated the evening, the men in her life were able to hold their own— Danny Kaye, as an effeminate photographer; Victor Mature, as a "hunk of man"; and Macdonald Carey, as the explosive, solid, straightforward managing editor Liza finally found she loved. Harry Horner's settings, derived largely from German functionalist techniques of the 1930s, made use of two revolving stages in a manner that expedited the shifting of scenes without calling attention to the machinery for its own sake. Irene Sharaff designed the costumes for the fantasies and Hattie Carnegie those for the office; Albertina Rasch contributed her last significant choreography; and at the conductor's stand Maurice Abravanel, formerly of the Paris Opéra and the Metropolitan, brought out the fresh and interesting timbres of Weill's masterly instrumentation without overbalancing Miss Lawrence's slender voice.

Such opportunities as those afforded by *Lady in the Dark* come seldom, and Weill's later Broadway pieces were not its equal. *One Touch of Venus* (1943), in which Mary Martin brilliantly impersonated a statue of Venus which came to life, was bright and entertaining in lighter vein, and contained one particularly expressive song, to Ogden Nash's text, "Speak Low." *The Firebrand of Florence* (1945), with Earl Wrightson as Benvenuto Cellini, failed to create a stir. *Street Scene* (1947), was more an opera than a light entertainment. *A Flag Is Born* (1946) and *Love Life* (1948) are better forgotten. *Lost in the Stars* (1949), a musical version of Alan Paton's South African novel, *Cry the Beloved Country*, reunited Weill and Anderson, but the product of their labors was maladroit in its failure to contain the music naturally within the story; and—unhappily, since this was Weill's last work—the score was at no point worthy of comparison with his best earlier music for Broadway.

Weill's operatic experiment with his setting of Elmer Rice's *Street Scene* added a page to the chapter contributed by serious opera to the history of the Broadway theatre. Though some wishful thinkers have professed to discover a steady progress on the part of the bored public toward the acceptance of opera as an amusing evening's diversion, the facts do not wholly bear them out. Serious musical endeavors have never been unwelcome on Broadway, if someone wanted to pay their costs. *Cavalleria Rusticana* has been presented on Broadway, and so have Verdi's *Macbeth* and Douglas Moore's *The Devil and Daniel Webster*. *Everywoman* had a musical score by George Whitfield Chadwick, who was anything but a light composer, and Engelbert Humperdinck, who wrote *Hansel and Gretel* and *Königskinder*, composed the incidental music for *The Miracle*. None of these belong within the scope of a book intentionally limited to the lighter phases of the New York stage, for they pose problems of value judgment requiring the entirely different, and perhaps more unrelenting, aesthetic standards that are customarily applied to works conceived unequivocally as art objects, and only secondarily as entertainments. For the same reason, Virgil Thomson's *Four Saints in Three Acts*, Benjamin Britten's *The Rape of Lucretia*, Marc Blitzstein's *Regina*, and Gian-Carlo Menotti's *The Telephone*, *The Medium*, and *The Consul*, along with Weill's *Street Scene*, require treatment not here but in some other book whose critical assumptions are appropriate to the discussion of opera. Perhaps the operatic repertory of Broadway will grow rapidly from this point forward, thanks to the relative success of *The Consul*; but even if it does, *Kiss Me, Kate* will still be separated from operas like those of Menotti (for all their command of contemporary trick stagecraft) by a gulf as wide as that between *The Merry Widow* and *Der Rosenkavalier*. And up to now, the Menotti operas have been the only ones to make a dent at the box-office.

The two greatest popular successes of the 1940s, *Oklahoma!* and *South Pacific*, resulted from the coalition of Richard Rodgers' talents with those of Oscar Hammerstein 2d. Rodgers had scarcely terminated his association with Lorenz Hart before word circulated that he and Hammerstein had agreed to work together, under the auspices of the Theatre Guild, on a musical adaptation of Lynn Riggs' folk play, *Green Grow the Lilacs*, in which Franchot Tone and June Walker had appeared for the Guild in 1931. In March, 1943, a tryout audience in New Haven saw the new piece, which then bore the non-committal title, *Away We Go.* Midway in the Boston engagement the name was changed to *Oklahoma!*, and *Oklahoma!* it remained when what was to be the longest run of any musical piece in Broadway's history began, amid tumult and cheering, at the St. James Theatre in New York on March 31, 1943.

Any first-year dramatic student can readily prove that *Green Grow the Lilacs* was more tightly constructed than *Oklahoma!* The Rodgers and Hammerstein musical comedy was sprawling in outline, ready to stop on a moment's notice for a song or a dance, and less authentic musically than the cowboy songs of Riggs's play. But its gangling good nature proved to be its best asset. Though its pace was really swift, under Rouben Mamoulian's direction, it always seemed easygoing and possessed of plenty of time and space.

Rodgers and Hammerstein were ideally suited to each other, to so phenomenal a degree that there almost seemed in retrospect to have been a disparity—unnoticed at the time—between Rodgers' flowing lyricism and Hart's brittle, caustic wit. In any event, the sunny homeliness of Hammerstein's book and lyrics—which concealed, as in *Carmen Jones*, consummate craftsmanship—inspired in Rodgers an upwelling of friendly melodies whose inflections often suggested a folk feeling, even though they were not literally based upon folk idioms. Without quite knowing what had happened to him, perhaps, Rodgers took a long step away from Broadway toward a more universal and less insular type of light music. Without losing touch with his audience and their predilections, he made of *Oklahoma!* more of an operetta and less of an out-and-out musical comedy than any of his earlier works.

The union of two sympathetic temperaments created the first all-American, non-Broadway musical comedy (or operetta; call it what you will) independent of the manners or traditions of Viennese comic opera or French opéra-bouffe on the one hand, and Forty-fourth Street clichés and specifications on the other. *Oklahoma!* turned out to be a people's opera, unpretentious and perfectly modern, but of interest equally to audiences in New York and in Des Moines. Its longevity and sustained popular appeal are explained by the fact that it transcends the outlook of Broadway musical comedy without disturbingly violating the canons of presentation to which the musical-comedy public is conditioned.

The performance of the first cast—nearly everyone has appeared in *Oklahoma!* sooner or later—was admirably calculated to strengthen the good features and disguise the defects. Alfred Drake developed an appealing drawl as Curly, and sang "O What a Beautiful Mornin'" with artless ease. Celeste Holm, a newcomer from Chicago with less than a year's stage experience in *Papa Is All*, revealed scintillant comic gifts as the girl who couldn't say No; and everyone else was ebullient and natural.

Agnes de Mille's dances, numerous and elaborate, combined square dances and cowboy movements with balletic devices, to the unbounded delight of the audience. At the end of the first act she set a fashion, which quickly became a rubber-stamp in later shows, by introducing a dream ballet purporting to act out the difficulty that Laurey, the heroine, had in making up her mind. (Between *Oklahoma!* and *Lady in the Dark* there was grave disagreement over the advantages of making up, or not making up, one's mind.) Miss de Mille's personal touch in the choreography consisted in the combining of pure dancing with pantomime in a way that related the dances clearly to the story. Though she has tended to repeat her tricks in subsequent musical comedies, she helped a great deal toward solving the problem of bringing ballets into the line of action.

The stage decorations of *Oklahoma!* were refreshing and entirely appropriate. Lemuel Ayers employed a poster style for the exterior scenes, in which unessential details were eliminated without sacrifice of color and virility. Miles

White made a 1900 Sears-Roebuck catalogue his bible, and designed costumes that were fabulously gay without forcing themselves out of context.

In the same year (1943), Rodgers himself produced a revival of the Rodgers and Hart classic, *A Connecticut Yankee*. Time had not dimmed the best of the Hart lyrics:

> *"Thou swell! Thou witty! Thou sweet! Thou grand!*
> *Wouldst kiss me pretty? Wouldst hold my hand?"*

For Vivienne Segal, as Morgan Le Fay, there was a new song, in the double-entendre vein of *Pal Joey*, "To Keep My Love Alive."

Two years after *Oklahoma!*, the next Rodgers and Hammerstein collaboration, *Carousel* (1945), came along. The book was based on Ferenc Molnár's *Liliom*, shifted to a New England locale and equipped with a clambake. The evening started out marvelously, with a scene on a merry-go-round as giddy and beautiful as the one in *The Band Wagon*. In the course of events Rodgers proffered many winning tunes, especially the infectious "June Is Bustin' Out All Over." But as the drama developed tension and mystical implications near the end, Rodgers displayed, as he had once before in his ballet score for *Ghost Town*, an inability to deal with musical problems that lie off the beaten track of show music. His attempt to write dramatic recitative was merely trashy, and *Carousel* ended in an abrupt downward plunge. For a time, however, it challenged the popularity of the older *Oklahoma!*

In *Allegro* (1947), ushered in by the longest and most persistent barrage of advance publicity any musical attraction had ever received, Rodgers and Hammerstein went arty. The enterprise brought expensive elaborations of music, dance, and stagecraft to a trivial life-chronicle of a young doctor who, at thirty-five, was forced to choose between a rich but empty practice in Chicago and a poor but honorable career of humanitarian service as his aging father's associate in the town in which he was born. That he chose the nobler course amounted to the final affront in a story that all evening piled cliché upon bromide and stock character upon contrived situation.

The staging of *Allegro* consisted largely of gadgetry raised to the *n*th power. Recollecting some of the devices he used in *I Married an Angel* and *Stars in Your Eyes,* Jo Mielziner again equipped the stage with a treadmill upon which bits of setting, furniture, properties, and actors rode on and off stage, with tormentor curtains at each end which rose unobtrusively as they passed through. At the back of the stage the usual backdrop was supplanted by a large screen upon which singularly uninventive images (nothing more exciting than the balloons at a college dance) were now and again projected. Many interesting visual effects were achieved by exploiting the whole gamut between transparency and opacity upon the curtains that separated the front half from the back, as well as by various colors, angles, and intensities of lighting. The stage was frequently monopolized by a verbose speaking chorus, reënforced by a singing chorus ready to commit itself on any subject. These imperious groups served as a combined Super-ego and Id for the young doctor, leaving remarkably little for John Battles, who played the role, to do in his own behalf except respond in a chain of reflexes.

Allegro had been described in advance as an adventure into the domain of serious lyric theatre. Actually its heavy superstructure of external production rested upon an excessively weak substructure of ideas. After the first flurry, the public saw through its pretenses, and its patronage lasted less than a full season.

With *South Pacific* (1949) Rodgers and Hammerstein returned to a more normal field of operation. *South Pacific* actually made some of the advance in the direction of seriousness which *Allegro* claimed to be making. Excerpts from James Michener's *Tales of the South Pacific* provided Hammerstein with suitable materials for an attractive and believable romance between an island planter (Ezio Pinza) and a fresh and spirited nurse from Little Rock, Arkansas (Mary Martin). Both Hammerstein's book and Joshua Logan's clarifying direction made *South Pacific* more nearly a wholly satisfactory drama than any musical piece since *Lady in the Dark,* and Miss Martin and Pinza gave thoughtful, well-characterized, technically mature performances on a far higher level than that of most musical-comedy acting.

Though it has not the choreographic elaborations of the Moss Hart play, *South Pacific* resembles it in the exceptional extent to which the songs and ensembles develop spontaneously within the action, instead of being thrust upon it. The abandonment of formal choreography in favor of Logan's resourceful and beautifully fluid handling of the group scenes enabled the stage director to control the dramatic values at every point, and to see that even the minor actors never slipped out of character. Rodgers' score, filled with his most inviting outlay of tunes since *Oklahoma!,* was also expertly calculated, for even the set pieces and obvious hit tunes belong to the play and do not disturb its progress.

Though it was not an example of wingèd inspiration, *South Pacific* must be accounted the most useful and instructive musical entertainment of the immediate post-war period. The integrity of the writing and of the production as a whole will make it more difficult for dramatically implausible musical pieces to win acceptance in the future. Musical comedy and the allied forms of entertainment are still, in the last analysis, more dependent on craft than on art, and the craft displayed in *South Pacific* will stand as a model for a long time to come.

The Past, the Present,
and the Future

MUSICAL COMEDY has often been called the only unique
American contribution to the theatre. This claim is not
merely oversimplified; it is false, or partly false, in two opposite directions. That musical comedy is not the only unique
American contribution can be seen by a moment's contem-
plation of the "living newspaper" technique of the 1930s,
which may have originated in German expressionist devices,
but possessed its own special manner of presentation; or the
prose style and the whole conception of tempo and dy-
namics of such playwrights as Clifford Odets and Lillian
Hellman, who capture a wholly American idiom and rhythm
of expression; or the prose-poetry of Tennessee Williams,

who has a completely American notion of what poetic values are and how they should function in the theatre; or the machinery of farce as revised by George S. Kaufman and Moss Hart, who devised for that métier an idiom as distinctly American as that of Odets and Miss Hellman in the serious drama.

That musical comedy, on the other hand, is something other than an all-American victory over European lethargy and conventionality has, I should hope, been sufficiently demonstrated by the findings of the preceding chapters. In its basic form, musical comedy is not specifically American even now. The theatrical form in which speaking and action are alternated with musical set-pieces and usually with dances, with some sort of plot as the chief unifying factor, is the form of Singspiel, comic opera, operetta, opéra-bouffe, burlesque (in its historic aspect), and pantomime as well as of modern American musical comedy. It is, in short, the form of all musical works for the stage except revue, ballet, and through-composed opera.

American contributions to theatre-music form have taken the shape of surface improvements or alterations in the conventions of presentation. In such musical comedies as *Finian's Rainbow* and *South Pacific*, the machinery was better oiled than it had been before. The interpolated numbers emerged from plot and characterization more smoothly and spontaneously, and in one way or another created some illusion of helping to move the plot forward. But it all boils down to a matter of greater technical acumen in concealing the joints, rather than a revision of the single basic form that applies to all light pieces for the musical stage—except the revue, which is substantially a glorification of the variety show.

Perhaps the most noticeable job of concealing the joints was accomplished in *Lady in the Dark*, in which the psy-

chiatrist's couch provided a flamboyantly effective instru-
mentality for breaking over from realistic action into song
and dance. The very flamboyance of the device, however,
made it a one-time affair, useless in general practice since it
was just one more way of tempering the artificiality of the
traditional alternating structure of musical comedy. *Allegro*,
it is true, did reach after something new in the way of form
by trying to graft the use of a narrator, radio-fashion, onto
the usual procedures of musical comedy. The experiment
turned out to be pure hokum, for there was no need for a
narrator when all the visual facilities for action were present;
and the speaking choirs, projections, and tricks of staging
were so crudely used that they amounted to no more than
window-dressing.

The plot materials of the Broadway musical stage today
are American in varying degrees. Certainly the subject matter and viewpoint of contemporary musical pieces are drawn
more largely from the American scene and from American
experience than they were before the first World War. Since
about 1915, when American subjects came to be the rule
rather than the exception, there has been no fundamental
change in this regard; and European materials have by no
means been completely eliminated even yet. The plot of
Brigadoon was a German Romantic fantasy given American
and Scotch trimmings. *Carousel* was a Hungarian play,
moved uneasily to New England and given a clambake. *On
the Town*, on the other hand, was pure urban-American;
and *Oklahoma!* was pure rural-American. But the Harrigan
and Hart farce-comedies in the 1870s and 1880s, and
Charles Hoyt's *A Trip to Chinatown* in the 1890s, were
pure urban-American, too; and if there was no counterpart
to *Oklahoma!* in those earlier days, it was because the west,
having been only recently discovered, was not yet in need of
rediscovery. *Kiss Me, Kate*, which collates a literary classic

with a modern American plot, has its antecedents not only in *The Boys from Syracuse* but in such early burlesques as *Evangeline* and *Hiawatha*.

In general, the type characters of contemporary musical comedy continue to follow immemorial formulas of the light musical stage, though their outward attributes have been changed to conform with the times and with our national predilections. The routine love-match between people of discrepant social stations and backgrounds is repeated in *South Pacific*, in which the amatory interest between the planter and the nurse attains its end despite obstacles no less formidable than those separating a nobleman from a peasant girl. The heavy villain in *Oklahoma!* speaks with a drawl and surrounds himself with dirty pictures in a smokehouse, but he is the same miscreant more naïve audiences used to hiss in the 1890s. The soubrette, with or without a heart of gold, and the regulation comics, both low and effete, are still with us a good deal of the time, though it is now unfashionable for the very best musical comedies to employ them without a great many refinements.

There is no denying, however, that the whole tone of American musical comedy over the past thirty years has reflected in striking fashion our national moods, attitudes, and interests. The cynicism of the 1920s was mirrored in the shows whose main concerns were raucous jazz, naked girls, and jibes at prohibition. The saddened 1930s, the years of the depression, produced sharp social protests, expressions of nostalgia for better days, and idealistic hopes for the future. The late 1940s and early 1950s have plumped for Romantic escapism, whether into Scotland, the islands of the Pacific, or the United States in the mid-1920s.

The lyrics, choreography, and music of Broadway musical entertainments have made steady progress—particularly in the last thirty-five years—toward an unmistakably American character, and toward general artistic excellence as well. The lyric writers, perhaps, have done the best work of anybody. In the later decades of the nineteenth century, punning, pat rhymes, stereotyped imagery, doggerel structure, and high-sounding *thees* and *thous* were slowly nudged out of the way. Slang crept in the back door, through the burlesques and farce-comedies, and in the 1880s and 1890s became, rather self-consciously, an important feature of the best musical-comedy lyrics. In the era of Lorenz Hart, Ira Gershwin, B. G. de Sylva, and early Cole Porter, lyrics came to be written wholly in the American language, with no hangovers except satiric ones from the artful verse of comic opera. When talking pictures and the depression forced Broadway to cater to a class instead of a mass audience, words of more than two syllables and increasingly erudite references became permissible in the lyrics of all but the most low-brow shows, and rhyme and rhythm schemes that were inventive rather than conventional became a requirement of the trade. An interesting example of the indigenous nature of present-day lyrics is the text of "There's No Business Like Show Business," which had to be equipped with new ideas for the Paris version of *Annie Get Your Gun*, since there are no French equivalents for its concepts.

Nationalism is a harder thing to define in the realm of music than in that of words. Perhaps the lumbering waltzes of the 1890s were American, since they certainly did not sound like Strauss or Offenbach. But it was ragtime, and later jazz, which first gave an indisputable national color to American musical-comedy music. Though Europe, and particularly Germany, tried to appropriate American jazz, it never sounded like the same thing. Even today, with the crest of the jazz wave many years in the past, the rhythm of Broadway musical comedies is suffused with syncopations and figures which became rooted in our national musical consciousness in the 1920s, and the melodies are constantly influenced by tin-pan-alley and folk elements, and by a prosody that faithfully represents characteristic American verbal inflections and speech habits. At the same time, musical-comedy music has displayed a constantly increasing urbanity and internationalism over the last two decades, as its composers have become better-educated musicians. Present-day scores have a wider vocabulary and expressive range than earlier ones, because the American elements which still give the music its special idiom have been absorbed into cosmopolitan techniques.

Choreography, as opposed to the dance routines of soloists and chorus girls, has scarcely more than a twenty-year history in musical comedy. The stylized convolutions of the Albertina Rasch girls and the pioneering efforts of Charles Weidman made way for the triumphal entry of George Balanchine onto Broadway; and the success of "Slaughter on Tenth Avenue" in *On Your Toes* admitted the ballet to a new partnership with the musical and literary elements in the productions of the later 1930s and the 1940s. Agnes de Mille's ability to integrate her ballets with action and characterization enhanced the reasonableness of extended dances in the eyes of the general public. Today, only a *South Pacific*, which has an equally cogent substitute to offer in Joshua Logan's handling of the concerted scenes, can afford to overlook the important function of the choreographer. Nor was progress confined to the field of ballet, for Robert Alton showed, before his departure for Hollywood, the extent to which popular materials could be given a comparable choreographic integrity.

If I have leaned over backward, in summarizing the status of musical comedy today, in the direction of minimizing its qualities of uniqueness or the magnitude of its development, I have done so for one main reason. There is a widespread belief today that musical comedy is becoming more and more serious in its artistic accomplishments, and that in a few more years it will grow right into American opera. This strikes me as a misinterpretation of the facts in the first place, and as an undesirable hope in the second. The American audience has become more experienced and more sophisticated over the years, and its entertainment naturally has moved onto an increasingly high plane of craftsmanship and literacy. But musical comedies and revues are still entertainments; if they are art at all, they are only incidentally so. A musical comedy does not exist for the same purpose as an opera, nor, essentially, does it employ comparable musical or plot materials.

It is not likely that opera can ever appeal to the wide musical-comedy public unless it makes as many popular concessions as *The Consul* did, in which case it becomes questionable as opera. I should hate to discover that I am wrong, and that *Finian's Rainbow* and *South Pacific* will one day be regarded as the prototypes of American opera. For if I am wrong, there will be no more chapters to add to this book.

Index

355